Virginia Blackburn was brought up in the USA, Germany and Great Britain. She studied English at Cambridge University and went o to become a highly successful journalist. She has written for a host of newspapers, including the *Express*, *The Daily Mail*, *The Telegraphy*, *The Sunday Times* and the *Evening Standard*. She is the author of *Victoria's Secrets*, *Robbie's Secrets* and *Geri's Secrets*, plus *Being Kylie* and *Chris Tarrant: The Biography*. She has also written two novels.

Virginia Blackburn

ANT & DEC

THE BIOGRAPHY

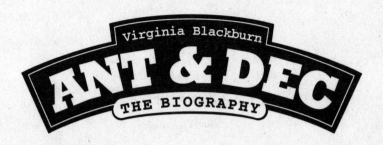

Virginia Blackburn

ANT & DEC

THE BIOGRAPHY

JB

JOHN BLAKE

Published by John Blake Publishing Ltd,
3, Bramber Court, 2 Bramber Road,
London W14 9PB, England

www.blake.co.uk

First published in paperback in 2005

ISBN 1 84454 133 9

British Library Cataloguing-in-Publication Data:

A catalogue record for this book is available from the British Library.

Design by www.envydesign.co.uk

Printed in Great Britain by Bookmarque

1 3 5 7 9 10 8 6 4 2

Papers used by John Blake Publishing are natural, recyclable products
made from wood grown in sustainable forests. The manufacturing
processes conform to the environmental regulations of the country of
origin.

Every attempt has been made to contact the relevant copyright-holders,
but some were unobtainable. We would be grateful if the appropriate
people could contact us.

Contents

Acknowledgements

With very many thanks to
Peter Hill, Simon McWhirter, without whom
I could not possibly have written the book,
and Jane Sherwood.

1

Byker Boys

DECLAN DONNELLY WAS excited. Aged just 12 and already a seasoned performer, the young Dec had heard that something was happening in his native Newcastle, something that might just change his life. A television programme was going to be made in his home town, a programme for children, and Dec felt there might be a part for him. And so, not yet in his teens, he made a phone call.

'I took the phone call from Dec in 1989 round about March, when we were beginning to look for cast for the new show *Byker Grove*,' says Matthew Robinson, the show's producer and director, and now Executive Producer of TV Drama for the BBC World Service Trust. 'He had heard that we were looking for people and he had that sort of outgoing, confident personality, even at that age. He just rang and said, "I hear you are looking for people, would you see me?"' It was quite something for any child, particularly one as young as 12, to do.

And it wasn't as if Dec came from a particularly privileged background. Declan Joseph Oliver Donnelly was born on 25 September 1975 to Anne, a housewife and devout Catholic, who helped clean the local Catholic church, and Alphonsus, known as 'the Fonz', a plumber. Very much the baby of the family, Dec was the youngest of seven, with his eldest sister Patricia heading the sibling line-up at 12 years older than him.

Then there came Eamon, 11 years Dec's senior, Martin, ten years older, Dermott, seven years older, Moira, six years older, and Camelia, just two years older than her little brother. 'I grew up on a council estate, the smallest boy in my Catholic school and certainly not the best-looking,' Dec recalled many years later. 'All I really wanted was to be a footballer. Of course, I didn't make it.'

Dec's parents, who were originally from Northern Ireland but moved to Newcastle after they got married, bought a house on the Cruddas estate in 1988 for the princely sum of £10,000 – a house that they live in to this day, having declined Dec's offers to buy them a new one. It was a rough area to grow up in. The area was rife with drug users and dealers, so there was the occasional police raid and sporadic outbreaks of violence. The young Dec, however, managed to get through it relatively unscathed. The worst thing he ever did was to steal a packet of balloons – and then feel so guilty he returned them to the shop.

The Donnelly family was religious, and the infant Dec

joined St Michael's Roman Catholic Primary School. His childhood was fairly uneventful: he fell off his bike at the age of six and bit his tongue; he deliberately wet himself because he didn't like the yellow trousers his mother had forced him to wear – all standard stuff for a boy. Academically Dec was middle of the road; he was certainly no dunce, but neither was he particularly interested in school work. One school report read, 'Must try harder.'

Right from the start, though, he was an entertainer. Dec's parents ran the Tyneside Irish Club and in no time at all the youngest of their brood, having already started entertaining his relations, was taking to the stage. Dec was just five when he made his debut. He was soon accustomed to performing with a band in the background and a microphone in his hand. To this day he is an accomplished Irish dancer. And right from the start he had charm.

Dec's very first thoughts about his future career couldn't have been further removed from what would actually happen. The role that religion plays in Dec's life should not be underestimated: he was and is a regular churchgoer, and as a child he seriously contemplated joining the priesthood. He was very close to his brother Dermott, who did end up as a priest, and both gave the matter serious thought before Dec saw it wasn't for him. 'It was something I thought I could do and maybe I should do,' he said. 'But I went through the process and realised I couldn't do it.'

But Dec certainly liked acting, becoming involved in amateur theatricals and developing a love of comedy that was to become a significant influence as he grew up. He would watch the small-screen giants of the day, and was able to reel off his favourites many years later. '*Morecambe and Wise, The Two Ronnies, Terry and June, Auf Wiedersehen, Pet, Russ Abbot's Madhouse,*' he recalled. 'I loved Kenny Everett. A punk called Sid Snot when you are eight is absolutely hilarious.'

He wasn't interested, though, in what are considered to be mainstream children's programmes. 'I didn't watch *Blue Peter* when I was a kid, that wasn't how my life was,' he says. 'I could never relate to telly like that, and there are loads of kids who can't. Growing up on a council estate in Newcastle, I never made models of things out of cornflake packets. I was climbing trees and playing football.'

Unsurprisingly, Dec was a very popular little boy and, as the youngest of his family, received an enormous amount of attention, all of which helped to bolster his personality and especially his self-confidence. That assuredness led Dec to take the initiative in a way that is almost unheard of in 12-year-olds. Having learned that auditions were taking place for a new children's series, Dec rang the show's producers and asked for a try-out on the new programme. Impressed, they said yes.

Dec remembers that it was his father who initially suggested he audition. 'I went, "Nah,"' he says. 'Then I sneaked the phone in the other room and rang the BBC in Newcastle. They said, "Oh, just write to the producer." So I found out his name, wrote him a letter and I got an audition.'

Given that the programme makers were looking for bright and sparkling children from the North-East to star in the show, the timing couldn't have been better. 'That is quite something to do at the age of 12,' says Matthew Robinson. 'Dec had been involved in a local pantomime but there's no fully fledged youth movement for children who are interested in acting in Newcastle and it's difficult for kids to find an outlet, which is why he called us.

'From the moment he walked in, I knew he would get the part. He had a combination of confidence and charm that was irresistible – and he knew it. He already had the tricks of the trade – he knew how to ingratiate himself with people. But he didn't come across as being obnoxious. In fact, he was adorable, like a puppy or a kitten.'

And so television history, in the form of a ground-breaking children's TV show, and a spectacularly successful showbusiness career, in the form of Declan Joseph Oliver Donnelly, began.

There was no indication quite what was to come, back in March 1989, when the sensation that was that brand-new type of children's television show initially took off. Matthew Robinson already had various television successes under his belt, including *Coronation Street* and *Dr Who*, and was now about to start work on a new children's programme, one that would highlight real-life issues while assembling a star cast. It was to be called *Byker Grove*. He had never before even visited Newcastle, where the series was to be set and filmed, but vividly remembers how it all began.

'I was called in by the production company, Zenith North, to make a pilot six episodes for a brand-new teenage soap,' he says. 'I was asked to be producer/director from the very start, which meant actually setting the show up, casting it and finding a place in Newcastle to shoot it, basically setting the style, tone and pace of it. There weren't any drama schools for children up there, or any real proper ones. So the only way to do it was to go round the schools. We went out to countless schools and kept our eyes out for young people who had talent and potential.'

The decision to film the show in Newcastle was deliberate and extremely fortuitous. The BBC, like so much of the rest of the country's media, was dominated by shows made in the South-East, and so it was felt that setting the show in the North would fulfil the Corporation's remit to reflect the whole of the country rather than one small, albeit influential, area around London.

'Politics at the BBC was very different in those days,' says Matthew. 'There was a genuine attempt to move production away from London to the regions and Newcastle hadn't had a big network show for a long time. So a decision was made back in 1987 by the Controller of BBC1, the head of children's television and a big production company up there. They got together and said, Wouldn't it be good if we did something up in Newcastle?'

They were clearly right. The show is still running after 16 years and it is the longest-running independent show in the country now.

And certainly Matthew was taken with Newcastle right from the very start, crediting it with contributing hugely to the lasting success of the show. 'There's no doubt about it,' he said, recalling his first view of the city. 'I'm not trying to flatter the people here, but there is something just wonderful about Newcastle people. I felt it the moment I arrived. It just feels open, friendly and welcoming. There's a warmth and humour and somehow we managed to capture that and put it in the show.

'The very first high spot of my time on the show was my first trip to Newcastle in 1989, when, coming up for the first time and coming over the railway bridge on a very clear, beautiful, sharp March morning, I saw the fantastic view. I suddenly realised I had this exciting new programme to mould and to bring to the screen and I thought, I'm going to make this work and I'm going to find a group of young people who, at the moment, don't know I'm coming for them. I'm going to make it really work for the BBC, for the city and for me as well.'

And so casting began. Dec got the part of Duncan in the show, but he had yet to meet the man – or rather, boy – who was to become his best friend and professional partner: it was to be a year before Anthony David McPartlin came on the scene. Nor was it immediately apparent that he and Ant were going to end up as the show's two stars.

'Declan began on *Byker Grove* in the original cast back in 1989,' says Dee Wood, who was head chaperone on the show and became very friendly with the boys during the years they were on it. 'He was a lovely lad but quite quiet and didn't stand out particularly in those early days. His mate Ant joined in the second series and although there wasn't that strange kind of magnetic bond at first between them it wouldn't be long before they began to emerge as a force to be reckoned with.'

Meanwhile the series launched. From the start, *Byker Grove* was meant to be a children's television series with a difference: it set out to tackle the difficult issues facing children today. Nor did it involve the kind of *Blue Peter* children Dec spoke about: instead it centred round a youth club in the suburbs of Newcastle and went on to deal with, among much else, child abuse, the death of a joyrider, teenage pregnancy and being gay.

Cast, crew, indeed everyone involved, was determined to make the show a success. 'Because *Byker Grove* was a new venture and Matthew Robinson was passionate about the show and the kids, everyone who was involved with the production, cast and crew were extremely enthusiastic,' says Dee. 'Everyone gave the show everything they had and the whole phenomenon that is *Byker Grove* became one great big happy family. The dedication and professionalism of the cast was quite astounding for such a young, inexperienced bunch. Ant and Dec were no exception and, as the years went by and they grew as artistes, they achieved huge respect from all the crew and directors as being two extremely good and easy actors to work with.'

The first episode went out on 8 November 1989. 'My idea at the start, apart from following the storylines given at the time, was to make it very lively, relevant, sharp, edgy and different from *Grange Hill*,' says Matthew. 'I think we succeeded because, within two or three weeks of the head of children's drama seeing the rushes, she had commissioned two more series of 20 episodes. It hadn't even gone out, but she was so taken with what she was seeing coming through that she committed herself to two years of production.'

The preparation that had gone into making the show such a success had been painstaking. One of the earliest and most important decisions revolved around the setting of the youth club that gave its name to the series, a decision that almost came about by accident, because the building involved was originally destined to act the part of a pub. Byker Grove itself actually was an old Victorian pub called the Mitre, in Benwell, Newcastle, where it is set in huge grounds.

'I was with our production manager, Andy Snelgrove, on the very first day of the location hunt and we thought we'd set out to find a pub, and Andy said he knew this strange pub in a place called Benwell,' says Matthew. 'He drove me there on the first morning, the first location we looked at. I got out of the car and within ten seconds – I remember it incredibly well – I turned to Andy and said, "It's absolutely great, not for the pub, but for *Byker Grove*."

'It had such fantastic atmosphere and space. I'm not saying a building or a location is the most important part in a drama series – what's important are the storylines, the writing and the characters and the actors. But it was a fifth major element, securing that place. It has a magical quality about it. Kids just love seeing it, set up on a bit of high ground. It's a mixture of a fairy palace and a devil's hideout. It's got this wonderful double-edged sword feel to it.'

The building has quite a history, extending further back than the Victorian era. Originally called Benwell Towers, it dates from 1221, although most of the current building went up in 1831. Built close to Hadrian's Wall, it was home to the Shafto family, made famous by the traditional song 'Bobby Shafto', until Bobby's son Robert sold it in the 1770s. The Shafto family are still buried in the grounds.

In 1831 the house was developed by John Dobson into the building it is now, after which it had an interesting history: it was used as a fire station in World War II, and after the war as a training centre for the National Coal Board. Next it became a playground, a restaurant and then a pub, before playing the role of Byker Grove itself, a role it retains to this day. It also has its own resident ghost.

The show proved an instant hit, so much so that the makers of the show immediately realised they were going to have to expand the format. '*Byker Grove* started in 1989 in a series of six, like a pilot series,' says Andy Snelgrove, the show's production manager from 1989 to 1996 and now an independent producer of educational and training programmes. 'At that time the cast was only nine characters. We started in May in that year at the office and there was obviously a lot of press speculation about this show. We got a very good audience when it went out and it was recommissioned for 20 episodes for the next year, so we needed a lot more cast and more storylines.'

And then along came Ant. But initially it was not plain sailing, as it had been for Dec, for Ant showed none of Dec's puppyish qualities and his appeal wasn't immediately transparent: as he himself said, 'I was Joe Ordinary. When you read interviews with rock stars and comedians, they say, "I was different at school." Well, I wasn't. I was quite good at my school work, quite good at sports, but I never really excelled until I got on the telly.'

Anthony David McPartlin was born two months after Dec: on 18 November 1975. His family lived in a council house on the Fenham estate, very close to Dec's home. Ant's mother, Christine, a beautician, brought the family up single-handedly, while his father Raymond ran a pub. His parents separated after having another baby girl, Sarah. Raymond went on to remarry, to Maxine Laugher, a catering assistant, who in 1992 gave birth to Ant's half-sister, Emma. At the age of ten, Ant had to become very much the man of the house: he soon became accustomed to looking out for his younger sister while his mother was out at work. All of this background emerged when the boys were adults: Ant is much the more domesticated of the two, perfectly capable of running his own household, while Dec famously once had to ask one of his sisters how to open a tin of baked beans – and then had to consult Ant for advice on how to heat it up.

The young Ant coped with it all remarkably well. He later revealed that he didn't see his father that much – 'Just now and again' – but is adamant that the experience didn't scar him. 'I was fine, to be honest,' he said. 'There was no issue with it. It was normal where I grew up. I suppose I became quite domesticated. I used to cook for my sister when we got home from school and Mum was at work.'

Ant's first school was Wingrove Junior School, his most overriding memory of which is having to do an entire gym session in pink M&S Y-fronts as his mother had forgotten to pack his gym kit. Like Dec, Ant was heavily influenced by the television of the day: 'We grew up watching [*Noel's*] *House Party* and *Russ Abbot's Madhouse*,' he later recalled. 'That stuff fascinated us as kids. The sheer excitement to be had over a tea-time fry-up!'

Not, of course, that he dreamed that he, too, might one day be one of those Saturday night entertainers. But he was interested in performing from an early age, and managed a bit part in an advertisement and on the children's television show *Why Don't You?*, for which he had to audition by pretending to be an old man driving a bus. He didn't enjoy the experience. 'I got the mick taken out of me so much by other classmates,' he recalled, 'I thought, Nah, I can't be dealing with this.'

Fortunately, however, Andy Snelgrove, now scouring the area for new children to join the class, knew nothing of this reluctance. A drama teacher at Ant's school had seen he had some potential and arranged for him to go for an audition for *Byker Grove*. Ant remained unconvinced. 'I didn't want the recognition, the hassle, the jealousy,' he said. But his mother was also determined that Ant would attend the audition and, when she learned from one of Ant's friends that he was planning to skip it, took him there herself. 'That mate grassed me up to my mum, who frogmarched me to the audition,' Ant recalled. 'So I have him to thank for where I am today.'

'One of the things I did was going round schools and youth groups looking for talent,' says Andy Snelgrove. 'We looked at around a hundred institutions, one of which was Rutherford School in Newcastle. I auditioned a bunch of teenagers including Ant, who of course didn't actually know Declan at the time. Ant was just one of the guys. He was charming. He was outgoing. He was good. I think he had been in a quiz show as a youngster, when he was seven or eight. I seem to recollect he said at the time he came along for a laugh and to meet a bunch of people. He obviously had the basic sort of personal qualities that you needed and the camera really liked him, which does help.'

It took a while for these qualities to shine through, though, for the young Ant was very different from the young Dec. 'He was quite gauche and awkward,' says Matthew Robinson. 'He was like a puppet whose strings had got muddled up. But that was because he was 13 and was in the phase between child and adult, which can make people very awkward indeed. We saw something, though, and hired him for the part.'

The part in question wasn't the one that was to make Ant famous: it was a paraplegic in a wheelchair. 'Ant came in a year later, in 1990,' says Matthew. 'They [Ant and Dec] weren't paired up as a couple at the start, as a sort of buddy pair. That didn't strike us at first; in fact, Ant was brought in for a different part initially. It's extraordinary the way things work out, as, if he had played the part we offered him, had I not changed my mind at the last moment, I don't think Ant and Dec would have happened.

'He came in to play the part of a young, budding footballer whose back had been broken in a footballing accident. That character was only going to last for about one and a half series, or that is what we planned. Well, Ant came in to do that and when I looked at the audition tapes it was almost the day before we started shooting his first scene in the wheelchair, and I thought, No, we've got it wrong. He would actually be much better as the character we just brought in who was a sort of very cool, hip-hop-type, PJ the DJ-type character, so we swapped him at the last moment. There was a guy who was going to play PJ the DJ, so we made him the footballer.'

Even then, it took a little while before Ant relaxed into the role. He was a little bumbling, and nothing like as relaxed as his future best friend. 'I don't think Ant would mind me saying that quite a few people thought he was a little wooden to start with,' says Matthew. 'I remember someone saying to me after a couple of episodes, "I don't know who that plank of wood is; he's not up to your normal standards." Ant was going through a gawky, young teenager period, but we stuck with him, and it wasn't very long before his character developed into someone who was always joking and playing pranks.'

Something else was becoming clear, too. Ant was beginning to get on exceptionally well with one of his co-stars, and that chemistry was coming through in the programme. Ant and Dec were becoming friends, not just any old friends, but seriously good friends. The two formed a bond straight away. 'We just clicked,' said Ant. 'We've been mates ever since. I remember my first day on *Byker Grove*. It was my first big job in telly, I was only 13 and very shy. Dec was the little guy at the back.'

And Dec says, 'I first remember Ant looking really miserable, sitting all on his own in *Byker Grove*. I first saw him at the launch of the second series and I thought, Who's that miserable old bugger? He was sitting in the corner with his head in his hands. I only spoke to him when we started acting scenes and, from the Newcastle United shirt I was wearing, Ant deduced I was a Magpies fan like him.

'People still come up to me and say, "Is Ant all right? He looks really unhappy." He's just got that sort of face. The characters we played were best mates and every day we were hanging round on the set together. It turned out we liked the same things and we became best mates in real life, too. I remember the first Christmas I got a card from Ant and inside it said, "PS: Do you fancy coming to the Sunderland game on Saturday?"'

The producers of the show noticed the growing friendship, too. 'After a few episodes, we realised that PJ the DJ and Duncan made a great buddy pair,' says Matthew. 'So, when we made series three, we went out of the way with the writers to write them as a pair of best friends. I know when they met on location in 1990 that they did get on very well together, right from the word go. So they were obviously friends off screen, and then we made them friends on screen the following year. They used to go to the football together whenever they could.

'I think there are a number of very interesting elements

here that set them above the rest. I think, to start with, their own personalities made a difference. They are both of them like the boy next door, no question of it, in differing ways but there are similarities. They have got a lot of natural charm. Mothers wouldn't worry about their daughters going out with them and yet at the same time they are individually sexy as well. But not in a particularly threatening way, in a boy-next-door way, so that they can appeal not only to the girls themselves but also to their parents, and I think that is very unusual and gives them an enormous audience of peers in their range. You would want your daughter to marry one, you know.'

Dec took it all with a pinch of salt. 'The boy I play is very gullible,' he said at the time. 'I'm more cynical and determined. *Byker Grove* does tend to run my life and I do get fan mail, but the girls who write are in love with the character, not me.'

Anyway, it was the chemistry between the duo that made them stand out from the crowd. 'When they left the show in 1993, I said to them, "Always stick together. Do not have a row. Do not go your separate ways,"' says Matthew. 'Individually, they'd have done well, but together they could take over the world.'

As the show became established, so the boys' fan base began to build. Apart they were appealing young actors, but together they were far greater than the sum of their parts. And as the chemistry on screen and off continued to grow between the two, so the show's viewers also began to respond to that special something the pair had.

'They were hugely popular; the office was inundated with fan mail,' says Simon Heath, who had been a script editor for the show. 'They were in a show where they were pretty much playing themselves. It was clear they had winning personalities and a naturalness in front of the camera.'

The boys were fast becoming celebrities, and it is to their enormous credit that, despite becoming successful so young, they never, even at the earliest stages, let the adulation go to their heads. 'The thing that amazed me was that they had an immensely loyal fan support,' says Andy Snelgrove. 'I remember rolling up to studios in Chelsea for an interview. We didn't know where it was and were trying to find it when we saw half a dozen loyal fans hanging around. I don't know how they knew where we were going because we didn't even know. It was just an act of faith by them.

'Another time, I remember going down when they had a personal appearance on TyneTees, on a Saturday morning youth sequence for the TV. I went down to pick Declan up for it at about seven in the morning and there they were. Declan's loyal fan base was camped out round the side of the house.

'But both those guys were very good. They understood who these people were, for some reason, why they did what they did, and they were always very kind to them. And it's one of the qualities that really has sustained them through success, and sometimes less success. They have a natural kind of instinct for the people they are talking to and also they knew who they were. People would sometimes turn up at the recording studio in Newcastle and, although they couldn't kind of let them hang out there, Ant and Dec would always find time to say, "Hello, how are you?" and things like that. So they kind of kept that article of faith with their fans and supporters.'

It helped that the show wasn't based in London. Had they grown up witnessing celebrity aloofness, they might not always have remained so grounded, but in a place like Newcastle, with family and friends to knock any growing pretensions out of them, the two kept their feet on the ground. 'One of the things that made them that way was that they weren't in a metropolis,' says Andy. 'They were in an outer spiral arm of the TV world in Newcastle, which is fine, but you are not so far removed from reality. Sometimes kids go to these great stage schools and life is a bit unreal at times, whereas if you are in Newcastle you can't believe in your own bullshit too much, you know.'

The programme makers were also careful to make sure the duo knew what was expected of them. Some child stars have all but been thrown to the wolves, but Ant and Dec were fortunate, in that they had people teaching them how to behave. 'We tried to get them to meet the journalists and tell them what they do,' says Andy. 'The people who were new to it [showbusiness] could see what the others did and knew the business of moderating what you did because you would have to justify it to your mates afterwards. It all meant that they learned how that world of glamour and public presence can do you good or can equally take revenge on you if you are not loyal to what you are perceived to be.'

And so, always the consummate professionals, the two boys learned right from the start how to act. 'They both came in determined to be as professional as they could be, and there weren't too many shenanigans as I was quite strict with them up there,' says Matthew. 'I kept the kids under control and made them realise it was a professional job, albeit that they were young teenagers.

'So they learned to be disciplined. I've heard from people in the business now, whether they are in light entertainment or format shows, they are always on time, they know their lines and they don't fall out with the crews. And they don't put on airs and graces. I like to think that all goes back to the training they had at *Byker* – but I think they had it in them anyway.'

2

Today Newcastle ...

OFF THE set, Dec was attending a real-life youth club, too, run by the Reverend George Curry, of St Stephen's Church in the Elswick district of Newcastle, and his impeccable behaviour was obvious here, too. 'He was on *Byker Grove* at the time [he came to the club] and some of the girls were interested in that fact,' says the Rev Curry. 'The thing that struck me was that he was a quiet lad, a truthful lad and an extremely pleasant chap. Obviously people were interested in him because he was on *Byker Grove* but he didn't have girls after him.

'He was just such a very friendly, pleasant, lovable lad who people warmed to. I felt he had good relationships with people. There were about 20 lads and lassies at the club and their ages varied from senior-school age through to 18, but there weren't many very young kids. We did a whole host of things ... football, table tennis and pool. Declan was a very good pool player. He knocked spots off me. I remember him most for the pool.

'What I noticed about him when he came was his quite forceful personality and his pleasant demeanour. The West End of Newcastle had the worst reputation for crime, drugs and violence. A lot of lads at the club were very bad. Some people were quite capable of vandalism and violence. Those were things that were everyday experiences. These people were "workie-tickets", that is, chancers. Declan was so different. He was quiet, he was thoughtful, he was warm-hearted and he wanted to just enjoy being with people and enjoy a game of pool and the like.

'I can't talk about his success, about his TV world, but I remember him talking once or twice about where things would go next. He was self-effacing and I think that is one of the reasons why they have been such a success. They can fool around and stuff and they have a twinkle in their eyes, but there was never anything malicious in it. Declan was always on an even keel, never chasing, in the way some people would, after sex, drugs and drink. He just wasn't interested in that.

'We had a club for young boys and lassies and we wanted to get them off the streets and we wanted children to have somewhere to go to keep out of trouble. Not that he needed to keep out of trouble. And he was different from the ordinary lads you came across in Newcastle. He had obviously been taught the difference between right and wrong. I can't speak highly enough of him.'

Professionally, everything was also going well. *Byker*

Grove was everything its creators had hoped for: a resounding success. And, as the show developed, cast and crew made real friendships, as well as socialising with one another away from the set. Ant and Dec, already very popular among their fellow actors, took part with gusto, standing out from the crowd in the real world, just as they were beginning to do on the show.

There were group outings, some of them riotous occasions, according to chaperone Dee Wood, who was there to keep an eye on the children. 'Every year for quite a number of years, a few of us staff who were good friends took all the young cast on a weekend away at Clennell Hall in Northumberland, which is unfortunately closed now, and we all stayed in five log cabins,' she recalls. 'These weekends turned into something of a legend. We had huge fun. Actually, watching the antics in camp on *I'm a Celebrity, Get Me out of Here!* reminded me of a lot of the discomforts of those weekends.

'Every time we went, we held a talent contest in the entrance hall of the big house. One particular contest was very memorable, when Ant and Dec and their good friend Rory Gibson, who played Lee in *Byker*, did their rendition of a Doors number, with Ant as lead singer. It was one of the funniest moments, as bare-chested they cavorted about the room playing air guitars, trying to be extremely provocative. I think all of the cast that were there that year will remember that performance.'

The boys were close to Rory, but teased him incessantly. 'Although the three of them were the best of mates, poor

Rory used to get the mickey taken out of him constantly,' says Dee. 'One night I remember in particular the three lads were sharing a room inside the main hall. We had been camping in the grounds but torrential rain washed all our belongings away and I think the owners took pity on us and gave us all disused rooms in the building. Anyway, Ant and Dec locked Rory out of the room and he spent the night sleeping, or not, as the case may be, under the extremely loud, chiming grandfather clock on the landing.

'It was Easter time and the lads had won some large Easter eggs in the talent contest the night before. So when Ant and Dec were at breakfast the next morning with everyone else, Rory came down late with his face covered in chocolate, licking his lips and proclaiming to Ant and Dec that he'd eaten their eggs. You should have seen their faces.'

The participants on the show would hold other, regular entertainments as well. 'Another memorable and stunning Ant and Dec performance was at one of the regular *Byker Grove* karaoke nights,' recalls Dee. 'They sang 'Me and Mrs Jones' – a fab song, and they really did it justice. I think that was the turning point as the girls in the cast certainly saw them as the new sexy lads that night. Ant was always the biggest wind-up merchant and prankster of the two, always getting up to mischief with various members of the cast. Dec was the more serious and moody of the two, but was always in big demand with the girls.'

The frolics were mainly for fun, but they had a more serious impact as well. The boys weren't just larking around: in some cases they were actually learning their trade. 'I was stage-managing a few shows for the amateurs at the Tyne Theatre in those days,' says Dee, 'and eventually talked the lads and another good mate of theirs, Steven Bradley, who played Speedy, into getting involved with the shows to give them a little bit of a variety of experience.

'They did several shows, usually backstage. But I have a much better secret. *The Wizard of Oz* was just too much of a temptation for them as performers and they ended up fabulous, fat little Munchkins. And not just any ordinary Munchkins, either. They played the Mayor of Munchkin City, the coroner and the leader of the lollipop league, no less. In fact, there's a video of the show floating around somewhere. I'd love to see it again.'

As the boys grew up, they were beginning to earn good money. The temptation would have been to splurge but, apart from one incident involving Ant, the two displayed a wisdom beyond their years, neither flashing their cash around nor frittering it away. In any case, that episode involving Ant seems to have taught him a lesson. 'I blew all my *Byker Grove* money on CDs, clothes and holidays,' he admitted. 'When you're 15 and you've got money, you're going to spend it. My mum killed me when she saw my bank statement. All I had left was £50. I was grounded for ages.'

It was a one-off: the boys have been financially sensible ever since.

The two boys weren't merely popular on television: they were well thought of at school, too. Ant attended Rutherford School, a comprehensive and, as he put it, 'one with girls and a lot less testosterone flying about', while Dec went to

St Cuthbert's High School, an ex-grammar school, whose old boys also include Sting and Neil Tennant, of the Pet Shop Boys.

David Stapylton, the deputy headmaster of St Cuthbert's, remembers the young Dec with fondness. 'He was well behaved and popular, with a good sense of humour,' he says. 'He was enthusiastic and academically above average. After he left school I bumped into him at Wembley when Newcastle United were playing Chelsea. His brother Dermott is a priest and works with the Youth Mission team at the school. Once he did a spoof where he did a video link-up with Declan to talk about the school – it was actually a pre-recorded video – and right at the end Declan said, "And I've got a message for Mr Stapylton ...", at which point the screen went dead.'

Despite their growing celebrity, the boys never let their newfound status give them an inflated idea of themselves. It's always the beginning of the end for a showbusiness personality when they start to believe their own publicity, and perhaps the secret to Ant and Dec's longevity is that they have simply never allowed this to happen. Even now, the two eschew much of the nonsense that constitutes a 'celebrity lifestyle' and, more remarkably still, back then, when they were two small boys from working-class backgrounds well on their way to becoming television stars, they remained firmly grounded.

'I clearly remember Dec coming to the youth club [at St Stephen's Church] when he was 14 or 15,' says the Rev Curry. 'He was already in *Byker Grove*, but he was very down-to-earth. There was never any doubt in my mind that he would do well because he wasn't the type to let an opportunity pass him by. Declan is a fine young man and I am delighted he has done so well. I never doubted he would.'

It was a solid background that served the boys well, for they soon discovered that, just as its founders had intended, *Byker Grove* wasn't just any old children's programme. In fact, some of the subject matter got so close to the bone that it provoked debate as to what is actually acceptable on a prime-time children's television show, and nowhere was this more the case than in 1994, when one boy, 15-year-old Noddy, was seen kissing another, Gary, in a darkened cinema. There was immediate uproar.

First up was Tory MP Harry Greenway, who called the programme 'disgraceful'. He was followed by Stephen Green, of the lobby group Christian Voice, who called the BBC 'thoroughly irresponsible'. Tory MP Nicholas Winterton wasn't too happy, either. 'As adults, we know it goes on, but that doesn't mean the BBC has to screen it,' he said. 'It's like violence – we know it's there, but that doesn't mean we necessarily want to see it.' And the late Mary Whitehouse was more disgusted still. 'The BBC should not touch the issue of homosexuality on a children's programme like that. I totally support the objections of people who complained. The pressure to normalise homosexuality is very ill chosen.'

The BBC was unmoved. '*Byker Grove* has a long tradition of responsibly tackling issues facing teenagers,' it replied. Matthew Robinson, who, incidentally, is the brother of the erstwhile gay rights campaigner Tom Robinson, was even less apologetic. 'This shows a teenager's confusion and discovery as he grows up,' he said at the time of the furore.

'It wasn't a snog. It was a peck on the cheek. Viewers have seen Noddy with a girlfriend, but he never really liked their physical relationship. When Gary came on the scene, Noddy misinterpreted the situation. They went to the cinema and he kissed Gary, who is heterosexual. Gary thinks it is sick and we will see how Noddy suffers prejudice and bullying. We aim the show at 12- to 16-year-olds and there are a lot of sticky, tricky situations at that stage. I know there were a lot of complaints, but I don't think they were justified.'

Another subject the series tackled was drugs. Again it was inundated with letters of complaint when it screened scenes of children indulging in drug-taking, but this time round Ant and Dec themselves spoke up for the show. 'Hopefully, airing the topic on *Byker Grove* has highlighted the problem,' said Dec, adding that he was tired of parents refusing to acknowledge what was really going on among the nation's children. 'It's shocking that kids are using drugs. But the show has been quite weirdly attacked for being too realistic.

'The programme has dealt with joyriding and, more recently, drugs – but why shouldn't it? These are all things kids come into contact with. After the drug storyline, we had masses of complaints because you saw the drugs and people acting under the influence of them. But how many teenagers haven't seen drugs being used? Kids at school talk openly about being stoned. We hope we can make parents aware of what is really going on. Drugs are a real problem and hopefully our dealing with the subject will help save some people from the dangers.'

Dec knew what he was talking about: growing up on a council estate meant he saw the ravages caused by drug use at close quarters. But it was a brave comment to make – especially as he was himself still only in his mid-teens.

And, of course, relationships featured on the show – just as they were beginning to in real life. Girls were starting to take an interest in Ant and Dec, an interest that was enthusiastically reciprocated. Both of them were making tentative efforts to establish relationships, with varying degrees of success. 'The boys got on so well with everyone,' says Dee. 'Jill Halfpenny, who plays Kate in *EastEnders*, had a soft spot for Ant and the feeling was definitely mutual. However, when they had their first real date without the rest of the cast in tow, he took her to the pictures. I know they won't mind this because they've both talked and laughed about it numerous times since. But they both relayed that it had been very weird: it was like necking with their brother or sister in the back row. Not nice really. Needless to say, there was never a repeat date. But they're great friends still.'

Of course, the two were also the subject of a great deal of attention from *Byker Grove* fans. Again, they both behaved well: despite undoubted opportunities, neither got himself – or indeed anyone else – in trouble. 'I think they were kind of straightforward guys,' says Andy Snelgrove.

'I'm trying to find the right words because they were very conscious of it all, because they were very proper. They obviously loved the attention and loved the company of the girls, but they always behaved very well towards them. There were lots of opportunities but they didn't take advantage of them because they had deep roots in their community and they had the respect of their colleagues. They were great company.

'The word "gentlemen" sounds pompous, but that is what they were. They had a sense of being part of a community, and it was like a job, although they were going to school at the time. I think it's because there was always the reality of being part of this community – both where they lived and from their role as part of the show. There were 15 principals and a supporting cast involved. Tyneside is a comparatively small city and it's not a huge media industry here. There are very few secrets in a city this size.'

It wasn't long before the two found girlfriends. Ant had started going out with his co-star Nicola Bell, who played Debbie in the series; not to be outdone, Dec got together with Clare Buckfield, of *2 Point Four Children* fame. 'I was there when they met in Harlow at a charity do with Frank Bruno, and the cast of *Grange Hill* was there,' recalls Matthew. 'I was there when their eyes first met.' The boys – Newcastle's finest – were growing up.

The news about the new relationships eventually got out, and the boys addressed the subject with their customary tact. 'At the moment my love life is OK,' said a rather coy Ant when he was finally persuaded to talk about it. 'We've been seeing each other on and off for 18 months. We haven't seen a lot of each other recently because I've been away. If I went out with her every day the relationship probably wouldn't have lasted as long as it has.'

Dec was equally settled. 'If I hadn't been in *Byker Grove* I probably wouldn't have met Clare,' he confided. 'We've been going out for more than a year now. We talk a lot on the phone, especially when I'm away, so I suppose it can be a very expensive relationship. Before I was acting, I wasn't very popular with girls and I was shy as well. Work has really helped me to make a success of my love life.'

It was typical Dec, and the kind of comment that, as a later interviewer once remarked, made you want to start cutting up the boys' vegetables for them. But, beneath the cute exteriors, solid professionals were emerging. The duo were now earning £300 an episode – Dec, in a rare display of extravagance, bought himself a sky-blue MG Metro turbo for £950 – but they were also growing up. One of the problems with appearing as a child on children's television is that you will one day outgrow your role: actors might be able to appear for decades in a soap like *Coronation Street*, but that option is not available when the focus of a programme is a youth club.

And the work was beginning to take its toll. The duo were having to juggle school work and a professional life, on top of which they were beginning to experience what every successful person encounters – jealousy. 'Our lifestyles have changed quite a lot because of the show,' said Ant at the beginning of 1994, shortly after they had left *Byker Grove*.

'When we get time off, we just want to sit at home, because we're too tired to go out. And, even if we want to go out, there are now places we can't go because we seem to get a lot of abuse.'

Dec took over. 'There are times when I want to go into town to shop, but you know you can't because you know you'll either get abuse from lads or girls being all funny,' he said. 'In Newcastle we get a lot of aggro. But it's different when we go to somewhere like London, where we get a great reception. There seems to be a lot of jealousy in Newcastle.' There certainly must have been at the time – Ant and Dec almost never criticise their beloved home town.

Stories also began to circulate about other work they were doing, including one bizarre episode in which the two had to withdraw from doing an advertisement for Biactol because they couldn't agree on which one would be the spotty one. Talk of a split between the pair, however, would seem to be a little premature.

'They do joke about how much fan mail they get and mock if one gets more than the other,' said a spokesman for the company. 'But trying to decide which one would have to be spotty and play the sad before-the-spot-cream victim was crazy. They couldn't decide who it should be and we didn't want to favour one over the other, so in the end they pulled out. They wouldn't have minded the money but they had a good laugh about it.'

They had a good laugh about most things. By now the friendship was rock solid both on and off screen and, whatever the future held, the two were best to stay together.

But that future was increasingly becoming an issue to be dealt with: by the end of 1993 they were both 18 and clearly growing too old to continue on *Byker Grove*. But no one seemed to be exactly sure what they would or should do. Further academic study didn't look very likely: Ant and Dec both got mediocre GCSE grades, and both quit their A-levels after two months. So what to do now?

The duo themselves, when told that their time on the show was drawing to a close, were devastated. 'We didn't want to leave, no way,' Dec said in an interview years later. 'We were gutted. *Byker Grove* was great. I was 18 when I left. The only prospects either Ant or I had was getting a proper job or going back to college. We were both supposed to be studying performing arts, but we never went much anyway.'

Ant was equally dismayed at what was to come. 'We were pensioned off at 18, it was horrible,' he recalled. 'I didn't want to leave.'

But leave they had to, in one of the weirder farewells to television characters: PJ was to be blinded in a freak paintballing accident and 'sent off to blind school' (Ant's words) and Duncan, his faithful friend, was to exit soon after, having snogged PJ's ex-girlfriend. But, in one of those massive strokes of luck that can do so much to boost a career, just before the final drama began, Matthew Robinson decided that the characters of PJ and Duncan make record a record. 'I was listening to Radio 4 and there was a news item about techno-music, saying that any youngster could buy £100 worth of equipment and put a record together, so I thought it would be a great story for the show.'

And so a storyline was hatched. PJ and Duncan sang a song called 'Tonight I'm Free' in a nightclub. The club's unscrupulous owner made a bootleg copy of the record and released it: poor PJ and Duncan, however, made not a penny from it and stormed off, vowing never to have anything to do with the music industry ever again. In reality, of course, the song was a boon, a lifesaver and a career saver, and the chance to launch a brief, but for a time highly successful, pop career.

'I thought it was an ideal storyline for these two characters, and I went to London and got a record company interested in releasing their song at the same time,' says Matthew. 'I remember the record producer saying, "Oh, *Byker Grove*'s just a children's programme." I said, "Look, you are missing out if you don't take this record. The post for these two is just unbelievable." I faxed through some of the fan letters, 20 or 30, just a fraction of what we had, and he said, "I see what you mean."'

Dec remembers the period with a certain amount of wonderment. 'On one of our last days on set, the producer came running out just as we were leaving,' he recalled. 'He said, "Guys, there's a record company on the phone. They want to offer you a contract." We said, "Yeah, right, of course there is," and kept walking. A couple of days later our agent called. It turned out there really was a record company and they were waving a big chequebook. We couldn't believe our luck.'

In actual fact, it wasn't quite as smooth as that: the transition from child star to pop star was not without hiccups. The record deal didn't kick in straight away and, after leaving the show, the two were temporarily without direction. For the one and only time in their career, the duo didn't work together: Ant signed up for a BTEC in performing arts, hoping to go on to drama school in London.

'I knew I loved acting and performing, but there weren't many outlets for actors in Newcastle,' he recalled. '*Spender*, *Byker Grove* and the occasional Catherine Cookson drama. I signed to an agent and did a lot of waiting around. I did a Brecht play as part of the BTEC, *Circle of...* something or other. I played the lawyer to the king, which is supposedly a good comedy part.'

Yet Ant didn't really feel he was going anywhere. It was a miserable time for the boys, but then Telstar finally signed them and released the record. Even though the song only reached number 62, the label clearly realised it was on to a good thing and made preparations for Ant and Dec to launch their pop careers proper. It was a massive stroke of luck and both were well aware what they owed their alma mater. 'I haven't a clue where we'd be without *Byker Grove*,' Dec said a few years after leaving the show.

'*Byker* was our break. We had five good years there and built up a following with the audience of *Byker*. It was the fans and viewers of *Byker* who got us our record deal. They were the ones who rang the record companies to get our song released. We owe a heck of a lot to *Byker*. I would hope I would always have made it into the business somehow, but I don't know how I would have got a break or what would have made me any more different to the lots of other talented people out there who want to do it.'

As the two began to establish themselves as pop stars under the names of PJ and Duncan, there were more upheavals in their lives: both split up from their girlfriends. Both were genuinely upset but, to be brutally honest, the timing of the splits wasn't bad for their careers. They were on the verge of releasing a second single, 'Why Me?', which went on to get to number 27 in the charts, their newly unattached status was no discouragement to their growing legion of fans, although both were cautious about beginning any new romances. They were, however, prepared to play it up for all it was worth.

'I'm not ready to date seriously again, but we have had quite a few offers from girls,' said Ant, aka PJ. 'I am a bit surprised that girls think of us as sex symbols. But it is very flattering. We both love girls and we've been getting lots of sexy suggestions, and a few photos, too. Neither of us has an ideal woman in mind, so we might fall for anyone.'

There was one bonus, at least – he still had his best friend to cheer him up. 'It was terrible at first, but we agreed it was best if we split up,' said a glum Ant. 'We just didn't really see that much of each other, so it was a bit pointless still going out. Luckily, Declan was around to help me get over it. I miss her, but it seemed like the best option. I'm just about getting over Nicola. Work has consumed me and taken most of the heartbreak away and Declan becoming single at around the same time has been an added help.'

In Dec and Clare's case, however, the separation was not to prove permanent. 'Breaking up with her was very tough,' Dec admitted. 'We'd been going out for over a year, but then decided we just had to call it a day. It is really difficult getting over your first love. I know I'll never ever be able to forget about it. But it was time for it to come to an end. I'm pretty sensitive and when it ended I did cry. It was just better to get it out of my system and try to start again. PJ was a great help and the fact that we went through similar feelings together helped. In fact, we were like agony aunts to each other.'

As their fans, weeping in sympathy, rushed out to buy the new release, Dec went on to reveal a surprising insecurity about his appearance. 'Even though I feel I will be able to meet someone else, I do have a self-confidence problem because of my lack of height,' he said. 'I'm short and I worry that I won't be able to find a date smaller than me. When I was at school, I was the victim of abusive nicknames – some people still call me titch. I have to admit to cheating about my height sometimes. I stood on two beer crates when we did a signing in a record shop – and we use a few tricks for photo sessions, too. With the music side of things, I am very much someone else's pawn but I can trust them to choose what's best for the band. I just need a girlfriend who can accept this.'

There weren't exactly any shortage of offers, but by mid-1994 the boys were having a lot of fun playing on that singleton status. As they got ready to launch their third and most successful single, 'Let's Get Ready to Rhumble', which made it into the Top Ten, there was yet more on the subject of the search for love. 'I'd just love it if girls would ring us and ask us out on dates,' said Ant as the two, professional to the core, got ready to man a special phone line run by the *Daily Star*, in which the fans were invited to ring in for a chat. 'We don't have any love life to speak of any more and I really miss it. If any girls think they're the type for us, hopefully they can muster up the courage to give us a call on the *Daily Star* hotline.'

Ever obliging, Dec explained what that right type might be. 'People tell us we're heartthrobs, but it doesn't seem to get us anywhere,' he mused. 'I'd really like girls to call me, but they'll have to accept that I'm a very old-fashioned type. It's a bit weird in this day and age, but I really like to wine and dine girls. I love to make a fuss and I go very slowly in my relationships. My ideal date is the girl in the Wonderbra ad [Eva Herzigova.] If anyone can measure up to her, just give me a call!'

3

Let's Get Ready to What?

ANT AND DEC had by now built a massive fan base. One fan who remembers them fondly from those early days is Natalie Cambrook, now 23 and living in Tokyo, where she teaches English. 'I met them a couple of times,' she recalls. 'The first time was after they had been on *The Word* on Channel 4 and they were going to be on Saturday morning telly the next day. Me and my friend went and camped out at the studios at the BBC overnight. There was no one else there because they weren't that massive yet but at about 2am a big van pulled up and some blokes started to get out. It was PJ and Duncan and they had driven past on their way to their hotel and had seen us in our sleeping bags. They came and asked us what we were doing and they couldn't believe it because it was the first time anyone had camped out for them.'

It turned out that the boys were quite as thrilled as the

girls. 'They said to us, "This is amazing, we've never had anyone actually kip outside to see us before – are you mad?! We have made it! People are sleeping out for us,"' Natalie continued. 'They were so excited. We had photos taken with them and got signatures and the lot. I was only about 13 or 14 at the time. It was so exciting. They were really, really nice and really genuine people and they were really surprised that we were sleeping out there for them.'

It wasn't to be the last time they met. Some years later, when Ant and Dec had really hit the big time, the girls encountered their idols again. It emerged that the boys hadn't forgotten that early encounter, and were keen to thank their young fans for their support. 'The next time we met them was in 1995, when they were Ant and Dec and they had a gig at the Albert Hall, which was their first big sold-out show,' says Natalie. 'We were waiting outside the backstage door for them and a guy came out and said, "I've got two backstage passes if you want them." He took us inside to the VIP area and we were just trembling. It was the first night of their tour in 1995, so they had an after-show party – Boyzone, Peter Andre, the Backstreet Boys, Sean Maguire and Deuce [with whom Ant's girlfriend Lisa Armstrong was a singer] were all there. I remember being very surprised about how highly regarded they are by the other pop stars, some of whom were a lot more successful than they were. They really respected them.'

The boys' behaviour towards their two young fans is a testament to quite what decent men they really are. 'I then met them at the very end of that tour,' says Natalie. 'It was

23 December and we went down to see them play in Cornwall. We were booked into the same hotel as them and we were the only fans that had got into that hotel. And they remembered us from that first night [outside the studio]. We were so chuffed. We were still only very young girls and they were about 20 at the time. But they were always absolute gentlemen with us. They are simply very special.'

The two were now turning out to be quite as professional as singers as they had been actors. That summer they went out on a roadshow with the likes of Bananas In Pyjamas, Let Loose and Luciana, while putting in appearances on all the requisite television shows and at all the HMV shops they could find. And the subject matter of the day continued to be girls, girls, girls. It is expected of pop stars who appeal to the, shall we say, slightly less grown-up girl, that they give every appearance of being girl-mad without stepping over the line, and Ant and Dec, aka PJ and Duncan, were proving complete pros. The following is an interview they gave on how to appeal to the opposite sex in early 1995 and if anything sums up the Ant and Dec of that year this does:

Ant: Now I don't know about all the other fellas, but I like a girl to look natural. So Lycra skirts and shorts and lots of make-up don't really do it for me. Cut down on them.

Dec: This one's for the boys. Remember to keep well stocked up on hair gel, especially if you use as much as I do.

Ant: Love bites – don't do them, mate. I never have love

bites, basically because my mum would kill me if she saw any on me.

Dec: Don't waste time thinking, Why me? Make the most of your good points and just forget about the bad ones.

Ant: A hint about hats – and I know quite a bit about them. They look cool, but always have a brush handy for when somebody unexpectedly whips it off your head.

Dec: Trainers are tops. But remember not to let them turn out like Ant's and get all whiffy.

Ant: Now not all men like those tight muscly bums. I'm a man who likes a nice voluptuous bottom, OK.

Dec: Remember to eat a decent meal every day – none of this junk rubbish.

Ant: It's all right to spoil yourself now and again. A nice, long bath or a massage does wonders for anybody.

Quite how many of the boys' 12-year-old fans were in a position to treat themselves to a massage is a moot point, but the boys – and their careers – were on a roll. They had discovered there was life after *Byker Grove* – and it was a life they were now intent on living to the full.

It wasn't just the boys who were growing up: their fans were, too. And the older fans were a lot more aggressive than the youngsters, to the extent that the clean-living duo now even found themselves the target of groupies. And for them it was a shock to the system. They had been on the receiving end of adulation for some years now, but these girls were something different. They were adopting the age-old tricks of the groupie to get near to their heroes – booking into the same hotels, sneaking into hotel suites, posting condoms decorated with their phone numbers – moves that astonished the boys.

At the time, it was all dismissed as mere high jinks. 'It can be quite frightening when you get surrounded by a big gang trying to snog you at once,' said Dec brightly. 'But we're having great fun with it.' Dec also was clearly getting over his break-up with Clare. 'We haven't exactly behaved like monks,' he announced cheerily. 'We like girls too much for that. But neither of us has a steady girl at the moment. It's a case of young, free and single – but too busy to do much about it. Our schedule is so frantic that we never get much of a chance to get to know anyone really well and, despite all the offers we get, it would have to be a very, very patient girl who'd be willing to put up with all the mayhem that surrounds us at the moment. I guess you could say that we are just enjoying window-shopping for girls at the moment.' In reality, he had been alarmed and shocked by the fans' behaviour. Dec wasn't just a gentleman, he was a good Catholic boy, too.

And there were other downsides to their fame. The boys were now targets for jealous young men who resented their fame, money and growing popularity, and, after Ant was beaten up in a nasty incident in his home town, they were forced to hire minders. 'I attended a film première and later, on my way with three girls to a club, I went into a phone box to make a call,' he recalled. 'When I came out the lassies were being hassled by three blokes. I asked the girls if they were OK and the next thing I was punched in the face. Then the yobs got me on the ground and really laid into my face and body with their fists and boots. I got a terrible hiding and suffered lots of cuts and bruises before they cleared off. There was nothing I could do to defend myself.'

It was a nasty shock, but, by way of consolation, there had been quite a turnaround in Ant and Dec's careers. Just over a year earlier the two had been in serious danger of fading into obscurity: now they were, if anything, better known as pop stars than they had been as actors. And, ironically, it was their popularity as the singing duo PJ and Duncan that actually led them back to television and their presenting careers.

In February 1995 the two were asked to do a slot as announcers on the Children's Channel during half-term. It was a challenge. Presenting is actually far more difficult than acting, as there is no script to stick to, on top of which it is essential to be able to defuse any potential crises. As it happens, Ant and Dec were to prove very good indeed at this kind of work, but a first attempt at anything is always nerve-racking, and so it was to prove for the pair. 'We were a bit nervous at the thought of presenting for a whole week, but we've been given some good tips,' said Dec. In fact, the show went well, and was followed shortly afterwards by the first series of *The Ant and Dec Show* on BBC1, an anarchic children's show which started winning the boys a whole new set of devotees.

The show, which first went out in April 1995, was

intended to be knockabout stuff. The duo publicly talked about the pranks they aimed to play on their guests, including spying on them in their dressing rooms, plaguing them with nuisance phone calls and drenching them with gunge. 'We didn't want normal kids' TV stars to appear on our show,' said Dec. 'We wanted wacky celebs who were guaranteed to go totally mental. But, because people think of us as wind-up merchants, they are really terrified about appearing on the programme. Some have cancelled at the very last minute.'

It was all grist to the mill, and, of course, some celebrities managed not to be too terrified to appear on the show. 'Rolf Harris is one of our first guests,' said Dec. 'He's a real eccentric. We're also planning to get Ken Morley, who plays Reg Holdsworth in *Coronation Street*, to appear. He is a Northern hero. We'd much rather have him on the show than some stuck-up Jessie. Once people have seen the show, they'll realise we are not out to take the mickey all the time. However, we can't resist giving guests a bit of stick just for the fun of it.'

The show was an immediate hit, not least because of Ant and Dec's willingness to laugh at themselves. In one sketch they donned gladiator-style costumes for the sole purpose of showing up their lack of muscle, while climbing on tea crates and bashing each other with giant toothbrushes; in another they stood on upturned wire in-trays dressed in cricket pads and duelled with giant cotton buds.

And it was not only children who loved it: the critics did, too. One wrote: 'A new children's entertainment, *The*

Ant and Dec Show, started yesterday on BBC1, starring junior heartthrobs Ant McPartlin and Declan Donnolly, formerly unknown to me, but apparently already involved in the popular music industry (so I believe, m'lud). But if they are famous, they clearly deserve to be. The show, staged in front of an enthusiastic studio audience, was casual, funny and surreal (the Vic Reeves influence was evident) and I particularly enjoyed Donnelly's repeated non sequitur: "A holiday on the Isle of Wight is cheaper than you might think."'

However, there were ructions from some quarters. Right from the start, the boys were determined to push the boundaries, and they succeeded all too well. In what was to become an ongoing row about the programme, a boy had his head shaved after losing a quiz show in a weekly slot called 'Beat the Barber', provoking widespread condemnation, while the boys were also accused of using bad language. The BBC responded cautiously. 'Cheeky language was used in a joke about singers Robson and Jerome, but this reflects traditional playground cheeky humour,' said a spokesman. 'It is the sort of language which children find amusing, but which is not particularly offensive. We are sorry, however, if anyone was offended by their good-natured brand of humour.' Ant and Dec shrugged the off criticism, as well they might. Their television careers appeared to be on the up once more.

And in fact the controversy had been created quite deliberately. 'The BBC asked us to double the audience and having analysed the figures we realised that the missing element were boys aged nine and over,' says Conor McAnally, the producer of *Ant and Dec Unzipped*, who went on to work on *The Ant and Dec Show*, *SM:tv*, *Slap Bang* and various other Ant and Dec-related projects. 'We knew that we could hold the boys if they sampled the show but no amount of advertising or promotion would make them tune in, so we created a few stunt television items which would result in big playground gossip.

'In the first show there was a fight between Ant and Dec, there was an unseen rude photo of Katy Hill and the show was "taken off the air" by BBC bosses – and there was "Beat the Barber". The gossip happened, the audience tuned in and the show became the number-one children's show at the time. The thinking behind "Beat the Barber" was this – the BBC is too nice to kids in kid shows. Television, especially BBC kids' television, was treating kids in a very patronising manner and one of the manifestations of that was the whole concept of the consolation prize. You don't get consolation prizes in the playground or in life, so we wanted to create something that had real jeopardy, but was safe and that had a real consequence if you gambled.

'The original thought was to shave off an eyebrow but we discovered that in some cases they don't grow back, so we went for the hair instead. I don't accept that the item was cruel. Each kid knew the full story before taking part. It was about consequences, not cruelty. Interestingly, we never had any complaints from kids – they loved it – the complaints were all from adults. It was the BBC show which drew the most complaints in the children's department up to that moment, but it was also number one. So we were doing something right!'

Musically, Ant and Dec were doing well, too, winning the Best New Act gong at the Smash Hits Awards. By mid-1995 they'd had five hit singles and an album, *Psyche*, that had gone platinum, selling half a million copies and getting to number five in the album charts, as well as sell-out dates when they went on the Psyche Tour.

Touring was to prove a slightly unnerving experience for Ant and Dec, given that live entertaining is very different from filming a children's series in a studio. It was one that the boys took some getting used to. 'There was so much screaming, I had ringing in my ears,' said a slightly shell-shocked Ant. 'It was really nerve-racking. I thought I was going to faint. Declan used to have Cadbury's Buttons thrown at him, while I used to have loads of Smarties, and it's not a nice experience having a tube of them bouncing off your head.'

But they still managed to find time to enjoy themselves. As utterly devoted to Newcastle United as they always had been, they were delighted when they were invited to help launch the team's new strip. The two joined Kevin Keegan and the team and paraded around St James' Park, the Magpies' home, in the new look, which consisted of black and white stripes teamed with a granddad collar. 'It's great to be here,' crowed Dec/Duncan as the waiting teenage girls screamed their approval.

This appearance established an enduring friendship with Newcastle United player Peter Beardsley, who has remained in touch with them ever since. 'Probably the first thing I did with them, they came to one of our kit launches,' he says. 'And since then we have kept in touch all the time now. Top lads. Absolutely fantastic. They are diamonds. We have been playing together in the Soccer Sixes for years up here [the North-East] and down in West Ham, but the problem they have now is that they are too busy. To be fair to them they often turn up last minute, but you always keep a place open for them, you know.

'Ant is a very good goalkeeper, fantastic goalkeeper. And Dec, you can tell, although he doesn't play as much as he would like to play, you can tell by his football abilities he is a player. They both know the game very well. In a football sense they live it and they are desperate to succeed and be on the winning team. They love it.'

As their careers developed, Ant and Dec began to travel more: not just within the UK, but worldwide. And given that they were by now so famous and successful in the UK, big-budget video shoots were in order, which meant more trips abroad. This also provided some merciful respite from the fans, as the boys discovered when they shot the video for their song 'Stuck On You' in Miami. 'Miami has been our most exotic location,' said Ant. 'Nobody batted an eyelid when we were filming. If we had been in Newcastle, we would have been surrounded by a large crowd.'

And there was some interest in the boys in other parts of the world, such as South-East Asia, which has long offered a warm welcome to fresh-faced British pop stars. In Japan, too, Ant and Dec went down a treat, even if they did succumb to food poisoning during the tour. They also toured in Europe, where the antics of some of their fans seem to have been an eye-opener, although by now the duo were getting a little bit more used to such things.

'Germany was the best,' said Dec. 'We were at this after-show party in a hotel, having a few drinks. When we left the party, there was a line of girls sitting outside. We said goodnight to them and got into the lift. The next day somebody explained to us that all those girls are there for the taking, and you just point to them and take them back to your room. We said, "You can't just do that. You've got to buy a drink and make conversation." I didn't think all that stuff actually happened.'

Ant felt much the same. 'I never got too bothered by that kind of stuff, probably because most of our fans were very, very, very young.'

That was certainly true. The boys themselves recalled one witticism from their days on the road: 'It's like that joke,' said Dec, '"What's got 40 legs and no pubic hair? The front row of a PJ and Duncan concert."' But the older groupies also persevered. Photographs taken at the time show the duo mobbed by girls bearing highly suggestive placards: '"Point your Erection in my Direction" – that was one,' recalled Dec.

'"Put your Nobs in our Gobs" … if we'd said, "Go on, then", we would have got arrested,' said Ant.

And, very wisely, the boys never made the mistake of believing their own publicity. They both knew all along that this was not to be the career path they would follow to their dotage. Rather, it was an enormous piece of luck that they were kept busy as they decided what they wanted to do next. Perhaps the most important aspect of their music career was that it kept them in the public eye, while broadening their fan base. And they knew it. Asked much later if the songs were bad, Ant replied, 'Some of the early ones were pretty poor. But there's some stuff I'm proud of. Not that I'd necessarily put it on at home. I did always think, How long can we possibly get away with this?'

It was almost inevitable by this stage that the two would have to leave Newcastle. Like it or not, the centre of the entertainment industry in Britain is London, and Ant himself had admitted there was little in the way of television work in the North-East. The boys weren't merely professional, they were also pragmatic, and with one near miss on the career front behind them – the dry patch after the end of *Byker Grove* – they were determined to take matters into their own hands.

And so they moved down to London, to a rented £500,000 flat in Kensington, one of London's most fashionable areas. Home life was exactly what you would expect of two young men living on their own for the first time. Their answerphone message was typical: it consisted of the opening scene from *Pulp Fiction*, 'Freeze, you muthafuckers!' and the boys yelling in the background, 'We can't get to the phone! We're being robbed! Call the police!' Luckily, no one did.

Their housekeeping skills left something to be desired, too. 'Although their flat is mega-posh from the outside, it's a tip inside,' said an insider on their show. 'Dec leaves the cleaning to Ant, who manages to get round to it about once a month. The floor is littered with empty beer bottles, old pizza boxes and dirty ashtrays. There are Oasis posters and pictures from *Loaded* magazine peeling from the walls. I'm sure the neighbours wish they were quieter and I know the porter is not happy with them. But they're just living like any hot-blooded 20-year-old lads.'

The boys were unapologetic, and, now they were at the centre of the action, started hanging out with the likes of Robbie Williams – an increasingly tortured soul who would do very well to take Ant and Dec's straightforward approach to life – and, apparently, Liam Gallagher. It was quite a change from *Byker Grove*. 'They have put us straight on a few things,' said Dec. 'They told us to have a good time, go to parties and make the most of our success. We have told our record company that we are going to live the way we want – which is fast! Now we've got our new flat in London and started having a great time hitting the clubs, there's no stopping us. We love a drink and are getting used to this lifestyle. It's one long party.'

Indeed, the boys were on a roll. Their second tour, the Christmas Cracker Tour, was as successful as the first. A second album, *Top Katz*, also released under the name PJ and Duncan, came out. This time the two had actually written some of the music and, although it didn't do as well as *Psyche*, it was considered a respectable enough performer. There were shows in Australia and Japan, where they had managed to hang on to the number-one slot for five weeks, and a tribute to the 1960s boy band the Monkees, when they did a cover of 'I'm Not Your Stepping Stone'. For this they flew to Los Angeles and linked up with former Monkee Micky Dolenz, who gave them a car that featured in the original series, which they then used in the song's accompanying video.

The two were beside themselves with the thrill of it all. 'The Monkees are the best,' said Dec. 'I'd rather put on one of their records than anything by the Rolling Stones. They made great pop, but added that extra dimension with their humour. They just seemed to have so much fun. I used to sit there, glued to the box, and wish that I was around in the Sixties.'

Nor was that all. Although they were seasoned old pros by this point, having been performers since before their teens, the boys still managed to give an impression of wide-eyed wonder at everything they encountered. Not for Ant and Dec the presumption that they were megastars in their own right: as they strolled through LA they acted as thrilled as any tourists at the famous names they encountered. 'We love a drink and have been hitting the bars in downtown Los Angeles,' said a happy Ant.

'We have been basking in the craziness of it all. LA is wild! It's full of mad people who just want to hang out and have fun. Everyone you meet is an out-of-work actor who only last week went up for a role in the next Tarantino movie. You walk into bars over here and you see faces out of the movies. I was in Johnny Depp's Viper Room and I saw Brad Pitt and Courtney Love drinking at the bar. It blew me away to see them in the flesh. I thought, in my very best Beavis and Butt-head accent, "Ha, ha! Cool!"'

Back in England, though, the thrill of it all was beginning to wane. Ant and Dec were now preparing for their third tour, the Out on the Tiles Tour, but they were getting tired; they no longer wanted to be known as PJ and Duncan and, as 1996 wore on, their punishing schedule was beginning to take its toll.

Everyone involved, including the two singers, realised they had only a limited shelf life as pop stars, and so everyone involved wisely decided to take advantage of the opportunities while they were there. But it was exhausting. The two boys were no slouches, but, with renewed interest from television companies coming in on top of their pop career, they conceded something had to give and cut back slightly on their work commitments.

'We had a lot of trouble with our workload and were fed up with always being on the road,' Dec said in 1996. 'For three years, we were working solidly. It all became a strain and both of us thought last year that it was simply too much. We sat down and decided that we should have more time to ourselves. We told our record company that we were going to live the way we wanted.' And that meant a little bit more time for fun.

They were also making plans to get back on to television. *The Ant and Dec Show* was to return to our screens, which was excellent timing for the two, given that their recording career was beginning to peter out. And the boys – not that, at 21, they really were boys any more – were growing in other ways as well. It was around this time that Dec and his brother Dermott gave an interview to CAFOD (Catholic Agency for Overseas Development) in which they talked about their Catholic faith.

'Religion is still a major thing for me,' said Dec. 'Although I've moved to London and I share a flat with Ant now, I've still got two crucifixes in my room and a bottle of water from Lourdes beside my bed. It [joining the priesthood] was something I thought I could do and maybe I should do. I was discovering religion and reading through the Bible and thinking about things. But I went through the process and realised I couldn't do it. That's why I've got a lot of admiration and respect for our priests. It's a great skill to have, to be on call for all those people and bringing that message. But it wasn't the right thing for me to do – I had to go and be a pop star instead!'

Dermott, who had by now become a priest himself, also spoke. 'Declan was the youngest, so he got a lot of attention,' he said. 'That's where he got the idea of being a showman. He performed for us first. We would egg him on, doing breakdancing and that.'

That religious faith, alongside a certain level-headedness that Ant and Dec both possessed, was to keep the two grounded. They would give interviews not only about their careers but each other, too – and, given that they were now sharing a flat, the friendship had grown stronger still. 'The music side of things meant we saw even more of each other, so if we didn't get on, then it would never have lasted this long,' said Dec. 'It's pretty scary at times, especially when you're being smuggled in and out of hotels all over the world being treated like something special. You have to remember that we were still kids at the time, both aged 16 – and I don't know about Ant, but all that attention would have got to me if I hadn't had someone else to share the load.'

Ant was equally effusive about Dec. 'I love his sense of humour and I think he likes mine as well,' he said. 'A lot of the time we'll be sharing a private joke and people around us won't know what the hell we are going on about. If Dec wasn't around, I'd be talking to myself. Unfortunately, our sense of humour got us into trouble a few months ago when the BBC received loads of complaints about some stunts on our TV kids' show. We think the kids want to watch shows which reflect what goes on in the playground, but obviously it upset a few parents.'

Dec on Ant: 'Ant's a bit quieter than me. That's not to say I'm a loudmouth, although Ant probably would. He's a bit of a thinker, but it's best not to be fooled by that because he's a great laugh. If you want to have a silly conversation, then there's no one better to do it with. The best thing about Ant is that he's never full of himself. He's got a good nature. One thing that always sticks in my mind is the day we went to see the Newcastle players at their training ground. In the car, Ant was saying, "I'm gonna ask Beardsley this" and "I'm gonna tell Keegan that." When we got there, he was dumbstruck. We were introduced and he just had this amazed look on his face. Beardsley and Keegan never got to hear about "this and that".'

Ant on Dec: 'I like Dec so much that I agreed to share a

house in London with him. I wouldn't say Dec has many annoying habits, but there is one thing that winds me up. If we are having a heated discussion, Dec has this trick of covering up his ears and going, "Not listening, not listening," like a little kid would. Usually I can handle it when he acts like a child, but on one occasion in Spain I just lost it and we started brawling in the hotel lobby. We soon realised it was ridiculous and it turned into a play fight, but our agents and roadies were really worried that we'd fallen out big time. Their reaction was funnier than the fights.'

In reality there was no chance of the two falling out. Given that they lived together, worked together and spent their spare time socialising together, it is fairly obvious that theirs was, and is, a friendship that runs deep. In fact, it's because of this that the two have often had to put up with rumours that they're gay – rumours both find hilarious. Ant once explained the reaction he got when he returned to Newcastle, to be greeted on the street with 'Howay, PJ, ya daft little poofs!' He explained, 'Back in Newcastle, it's assumed we're gay. One day, I said, "Look, how am I a poof?" "'Cause yer on telly, aren't ya?" he says. "Oh, that's right, aye," I says. "There's me, John Major, Terry Wogan. He had his own show for ages – he's fuckin' raging, he is!"'

Their comedy also lent itself to misinterpretation, not least because it can be extremely camp. Their shows have featured a male dance troupe called the Gay Grahams, and other characters include a sleazy tabloid hack called Brian Lying, who can only talk in *Sun*-style headlines. But the boys continue to laugh it off. 'In Newcastle, we got stick just for being on the telly,' sighed Dec. 'But working in TV, we've come into contact with a lot of gay people and, because that's happened while we were so young, we haven't grown up with any prejudices.'

In fact, both boys had rediscovered romance: Ant had linked up with the singer Lisa Armstrong from pop band Deuce, while Dec had been reunited with Clare. 'We didn't spend enough time together and I was a bit manic,' he admitted. 'I was a prat but I have calmed down now.' He might have done, but Ant and Dec's lifestyles certainly hadn't. The two of them were now running two parallel careers: they were both still pop stars and television performers and for the moment, at least, that's the way they wanted it to continue. The boys have always recognised the fact that if an opportunity is not taken it might well disappear – and that was not a mistake either of them intended to make.

4

Serious Concerns

THE SECOND series of *The Ant and Dec Show* was now in full swing, with the two proving masters at what they did best: being themselves. Enormously affable, the boys would choose subjects that amused them and carry on a surreal, stream-of-consciousness conversation, like this one, where they are trying to work out why there is a bus company in Bristol called Badgerline:

'It must be the badger capital of Britain.'

'I reckon it's one of them ancient tales, like where the badger saved Bristol from drowning.'

'Actually, aye, that rings a bell ...'

It was in the making of this show that the boys met Dean Wilkinson, who was to become another long-term collaborator. Dean was a scriptwriter with Ant and Dec on *The Ant and Dec Show*, *Ant and Dec Unzipped*, *The Ant and Dec Christmas Special*, *Friends Like These* and *SM:tv* and now has his own sitcom on CBBC called *Bad Penny*, which he describes as a non-PC mix of *Monty Python* and *The Goodies* aimed at children. He is the best-selling author of the spoof-Camelot *Legends of Arthur King* series, the rights to which have now been bought by the BBC and for which Ant and Dec wrote a foreword.

'I met them when they were PJ and Duncan and they were singing, which wasn't so good,' Dean recalls. 'I had taken scripts to the BBC and they were going to do the second series of *The Ant and Dec Show*. I hadn't seen them perform on TV. I was a bit hesitant at first because all I knew was PJ and Duncan but when I met them I thought, We have a new Morecambe and Wise here. My first impression was that they are two gifted, but modest, down-to-earth lads. They are not big-headed in any way. There is a saying in showbusiness "The bigger the star, the nicer they are" and it is so right with these lads.'

But, despite the show's popularity, there were problems. The boys were trying to get away with what, for them, constituted bad behaviour: that slot, 'Beat the Barber', continued and, if the hapless youngster involved didn't manage to do just that, his head was shaven. This continued to raise eyebrows in a good many quarters, to which Ant and Dec's defiant response was that they'd shave those very eyebrows too, and presented a foretaste of problems ahead.

Not that they were too worried. Although they were now based in London, both frequently returned to Newcastle, despite the problems that are often inevitable with fame, to recharge their batteries and prepare to take on new goals. 'I can't understand it when people forget where they came from,' said Dec. 'I never want to lose my accent and I don't want to forget all my mates.'

But he had to be careful in his behaviour. 'If you don't buy a round and you're making lots of money, you're a tight git,' he said. 'But if you get all the rounds in, then you're a flash git. You have to be careful to take your turn like everyone else.' Even so, the duo's parents couldn't have been more proud of their increasingly illustrious sons. Ant once said of his mother, 'She'll hand out signed photos to people who've never heard of us, like the gas man.'

It is this normality, though, that has saved them from becoming monsters. 'They've coped well,' says Matthew Robinson. 'I've worked with a lot of actors who've achieved great fame and something happens to them: it's very difficult to stop your ego getting warped. Somehow Ant and Dec have done it. They think it's all a dream and it might be taken away from them tomorrow. They go back to Newcastle a lot; they're close to their families, who won't put up with any nonsense.'

But, in their professional lives, changes were afoot. The 'Beat the Barber' slot was upsetting parents – including Ant's mother – and so was the boys' language. They were being blamed for being smutty and using innuendo, despite the fact that it was the parents, not the children, who actually understood any double entendres used. Ant and Dec were called the bad boys of the BBC and its switchboard was flooded with calls from irate adults.

But, if the boys were upset, they certainly didn't show it. They were in Japan when they heard about the complaints. 'I just went, "Yesss!"' said Dec. 'We got a reaction. Normally, the BBC might get 13 calls about a children's show. We got over 50 for the first programme; for the second we got 100.'

Ant was equally unmoved. 'Aye, it's not as if people were saying it's crap – I'd have been upset at that,' he said. 'But people were complaining about things we've never said or done. They complained about Leslie Grantham being on the show because he was a convicted murderer! Aye, but didn't they notice he was on *EastEnders* for years as well?' 'And I never said "arse",' added Dec. 'I might have wanted to, but I know you can't on a children's show.'

Eventually the second half of the show was re-edited, something the boys weren't happy about. 'That was disheartening,' said Ant. 'We didn't bother going in for the re-edit. I'd rather a different version went out than none at all, but I'm sorry nobody got to see the show as we made it.' It signalled a change in direction for the two.

Despite the fuss, the BBC wanted to keep Ant and Dec on board – and its judgement was sound, because the show went on to win a BAFTA – but the boys had other ideas. There were still the remnants of the music career to get on with, but, much more importantly, the pair had by now set up their own production company, Ant and Dec Productions, and so had much greater control over their future than they'd had in the past.

'Famous people have a shelf life – unless they're like George Michael or Madonna and can keep on reinventing themselves,' said Ant, displaying a wisdom beyond his years. 'People grow tired of you and that could happen to us, too. At least having our own company means we can go on making programmes for other people, even if we aren't in front of the camera ourselves.'

But, while they may have been turning into canny businessmen, in public they treated the establishment of their own company in the usual *Boy's Own* way. 'We own the company with two partners,' Ant said brightly. 'It's really funny. We have board meetings and get really bored. We pass notes to one another and make paper airplanes. We're true executives.'

Not to be outdone, Dec explained their roles in the company. 'Chair board meetings, buy scripts, sign cheques,' he said. 'We're not like Chris Evans, though. We don't shout.'

And the duo did feel it was time for a change. The BBC had let them down, or so they felt, and so, with the second series of *The Ant and Dec Show* in the bag, the boys made the decision to move to Channel 4 with their next offering, *Ant and Dec Unzipped*. It seemed like a canny move. 'Channel 4 offered us more money to make the show, a later time slot, and much more support,' said Dec. 'It was a shame, but it has been better for our careers. The new show is what we wanted to do, but we had to wait through those two series to get here.' The future was bright. The future, with yet more merriment and mayhem, was here.

The move to Channel 4 certainly heralded a change in direction. For a start, Ant and Dec would be able to get away with much more than they could on the BBC, not least because the show was going out in the evening. Secondly, and more importantly, the duo were gradually inching away from children's shows into mainstream television.

Both were well aware that they had a far greater chance of maintaining a long-lasting career if they appealed to all ages, and now was the time to do something about it. Oh, and then there was the money. The deal was worth about £300,000 each, ranking Ant and Dec among the highest-paid performers in children's television and pushing them into the big league in the adult world, too.

The two continued to display that astute business sense that had been increasingly in evidence in recent years. They knew exactly what they were doing, and why. 'We've got fans who started following us when they were 15, and they'll come backstage after a concert now and tell us they've passed their driving test, or got engaged or whatever,' said Ant, explaining the rationale behind the show. 'That's one reason we moved to Channel 4: our fans are getting that bit older.'

The new, grown-up show – 'We were involved in the budgets and everything,' said Ant – opened with a dig at the Beeb. For poking fun at the public service broadcaster's high moral stance, Ant was found 'guilty of filth, obscenity and saying "buttocks" at tea-time'. He was promptly sent to jail, from which he emerged six months later as a voice intoned, 'Nelson Mandela, Arthur Fowler and Anthony David McPartlin – all victims of the BBC.'

'The joke is, I go to prison for broadcasting obscenities on the BBC last year, although Dec gets away with it,' said

Ant. 'I am filmed having to wash in the shower with the other prisoners. It was scary, because it was a prison and they were all real inmates. But the prisoners were really nice and asked for our autographs.'

Unsurprisingly, the two were excited about their new show, boasting about its all-star line-up. 'We've got Peter Beardsley,' said Ant. 'He's so modest, he plays a different "modest" character each week. Dannii Minogue plays Princess Hotty Totty in *Geordie Gordie*, a take-off of Flash Gordon. She ties me up to a bed – I hated that! Then there's Sean Maguire, *O-Zone* presenter Jayne Middlemiss, who's a Geordie slapper called Emma Dale, Robbie Williams, and Big Ron from *EastEnders* plays my prison guard, but without his sheepskin waistcoat. We'll always have a nice girl on the show so we can try to get off with her, but we always fail.' And, again cocking a snook at the BBC, there was a slot called 'Learn to Swear with Ant and Dec'. 'We'll probably get loads of letters from angry mums,' sighed Ant.

Behind the scenes, equally illustrious names were to be found. One of the contributors to the show was the great Eddie Braben, who had also been the scriptwriter for none other than Morecambe and Wise, although this, ironically, undermined the boys' confidence in their own abilities. 'The scripts he sent us were magical,' said Ant some years later. 'There was stuff that you could picture Eric and Ernie doing so well.

'It was slightly intimidating. I didn't think we could pull that off, especially not then. It was still the early days, we were still in a pop band doing these pop videos where the director would be going, "Right, be sultry, be pop band pin-ups." Then we'd go into the studio and they'd go, "Right, we want you to be a Chinese magician and his assistant." We were riddled with low self-confidence at the time. We weren't great songwriters, we weren't the best singers, the pop career was kind of a blind alley.' But they managed to put on a brave face to the rest of the world: no one, watching them back then, would have had any idea about the nerves the two suffered from.

One person who was less than thrilled about the duo's new show was one Chris Evans. He was at the time still presenting *TFI Friday*, which was aimed at exactly the same audience as *Ant and Dec Unzipped*. This didn't go down well. A notoriously competitive man and one who, unlike Ant and Dec, never shied away from making his feelings known as vigorously as possible, he promptly insisted the programme went out on a Tuesday and not on the same night as his own show. They were clearly touching a nerve – and one that was to win the day for them in the long term.

While Ant and Dec are almost universally liked, the same is not true of Chris Evans, and it told. After his long break from British TV screens, Evans initially found it difficult to find a new role in the industry, a situation which was greeted in some quarters with unalloyed delight. It is very difficult to imagine a similar reaction were the boys to find themselves going through a similarly tough patch. Their professionalism – the fact that, as they pointed out, 'We don't shout', their level-headedness and their ability, in an industry known more for ego than modesty, to have remained utterly grounded – has made them extremely popular among fans and colleagues alike.

Nor would they flaunt their wealth, claiming firmly that the excess associated with celebrity is simply not for them. 'We don't do the pop star tantrum bit,' said Dec. Both denied that their lifestyle was glamorous except 'compared to that of someone on the dole' and both eschewed ostentation – their biggest indulgence was the occasional chauffeur. In fact, according to them, they could scarcely be more normal. 'We go home, dump our bags and scripts in the hall, have a beer, play Striker on the PlayStation and watch *Only Fools and Horses*,' said Ant. The message was clear: they hadn't lost touch with their roots.

And, as their fan base continued to grow, so they encountered increasingly unusual behaviour. One adult fan changed her name by deed poll to Declan Donnelly, while others christened their babies after their heroes. 'We once stopped at a service station on the way to a gig,' Ant recalled. 'A bloke who was carrying a baby came up to us and said, "It's a shame my wife isn't here. She's just had another little boy and called him Declan." There he was, talking away, in spite of the fact that his wife had just named his son after another man – after one of us, in fact.'

At last *Ant and Dec Unzipped* began, but, despite its later time slot of 6.25pm, the two almost immediately ran into trouble. Dec read out on air a fictitious letter from a Mr P Enis, which had irate parents writing in to complain. The two shrugged it off. 'The good thing about having your own TV show is that you can get all your heroes on,' said Dec.

'We've had some brilliant-looking women in! Topless model Joanne Guest and the twins from *Sweet Valley High*. They were very beautiful and were up for everything ... well, within reason!'

Perhaps to make up for all this public drooling, they also had Dec's girlfriend Clare. Other larkish skits included setting up a dating agency, with Gaby Roslin no less, as a client, and a character called Mr Swaps, who traded whatever he had in his 'swapping pocket' for various weird and wonderful collectables. Another feature, in rather more dubious taste, showed a waitress dispensing milk from her breasts.

Meanwhile, owning their own production company was paying dividends in other ways, too. The duo bought the rights to a film about two Geordie rock singers battling to make it in the music industry, with a view to playing the lead roles themselves. It was a clear indicator that Ant and Dec's ambitions were growing.

By the time of the General Election in May 1997, the boys were riding high, and so to celebrate the ascendancy of New Labour – no Tories, they – the two held an election party at Chelsea Town Hall. Richard Branson, never one to miss out on an opportunity for self-promotion, donated an ocean of vodka, with the result that the party got out of hand. Local residents called the police to complain about noise levels, which nearly resulted in a nasty fracas: three policemen turned up, to be greeted by a clearly worse-for-wear Ant.

The supermodel Sophie Dahl stepped in as mediator. 'Things got heated – Ant was a bit merry by that time,' said one reveller who was present. 'But Sophie turned up and calmed things down.' She did indeed: so captivated were the policemen by her voluptuous charms that they stayed on as guests until the end of the evening – and even lent their helmets to Sophie and her new Geordie friends.

Other projects were afoot. The two did a trial week as presenters of *The Big Breakfast*: it went so well that there were rumours Channel 4 was trying to get them to present the show on a regular basis. They were also embarking on another musical tour, to coincide with the release of their third and final album, *The Cult of Ant and Dec*. Recorded under their own names rather than their PJ and Duncan monikers, this garnered surprisingly good reviews. The duo had written it all themselves, too.

Even the *Guardian*, always the first to disdain the cheesy, grudgingly admitted, 'They wrote most of the songs, including the almost Blur-esque "Better Watch Out" and didn't make a bad job of it. There's even an adults-only hidden track in which they pour scorn on other acts. Tolerably fun.' It was high praise indeed – not least as the paper followed it up with an excellent review of the duo's concert at the Royal Albert Hall. The *Independent* was equally impressed with the event: 'In years to come, those who saw Ant and Dec at the Royal Albert Hall that night in 1997 will be able to look back and say, "I was there."'

The boys had a singular way of amusing themselves on tour: they would play pranks on each other and whoever else happened to be around. 'We'd get each other's hotel keys from reception and ransack the room,' Dec recalled.

'Sometimes I'd turn his bed upside down or pack all his stuff in a bag and take it away.'

'I once put fruit in his pillowcase and he didn't notice till next morning when it was all squashed and a real mess,' said Ant. 'And we used to gang up on outsiders and be a complete nightmare. Once we got into our tour manager's room and totally trashed it. We emptied everything out of his suitcase, then hid in the wardrobe. It was at least a couple of hours before he came back. But when he saw the mess, all he did was shrug. We were so disappointed. We were always getting telephone calls from our manager telling us to grow up!'

The tour went on to cover much of Britain and some countries in South-East Asia, including Japan but, despite plenty of positive reviews, the two seemed to sense that, give or take the odd concert, their musical career was all but over. Acknowledging that they were lucky to have two careers, Ant remarked, 'The time will come when we have to make a choice, but I think it will probably happen quite naturally. I suppose everything is up in the air and we'll just have to wait and see what happens.'

As so often is the case in life, what actually happened proved a considerable shock: both careers began to falter. For a start, despite the positive reviews, the album didn't do well, notching up sales of just 60,000 copies. Telstar promptly dumped them in the middle of the tour, which led to bruised egos all round. 'We were in Japan when we had a call from a lawyer,' said Dec. 'It was a shock, that call. Till then, we'd wake up every day and we were pop stars. Suddenly, it was all off.'

But, if the boys had any regrets about the wisdom of giving up their pop career, those regrets should have been well and truly dispelled after an appearance on *The Mrs Merton Show*. The boys had been asked on to the programme, fronted by the comedienne Caroline Aherne, at the height of their singing career. Appearing on the show was not for the faint-hearted: Caroline, dressed up as the redoubtable pensioner Mrs Merton, would make a point of putting her guests on the spot. So it proved with Ant and Dec. Given that they were themselves fast emerging as masters of mischief, the two should perhaps have been expecting what was to come, but they didn't. And when it did come, the request seemed as innocent as it could get. Would they, enquired Mrs Merton, sing 'Happy Birthday' to a member of the audience?

It is one of the few times in their career that the boys have been totally wrongfooted. They declined to sing. They would not sing. They absolutely refused to sing … And all the while, expressions that can only be described as panic, fear and utter terror shot across their faces. Mrs Merton, needless to say, had a field day. Joke followed joke: was it possible, perhaps, that there was a very good reason the boys were refusing to sing? Were their voices not quite up to it? As singers, were they in reality merely very good actors? And so it went on, with the two bravely endeavouring to take it on the chin, while in reality desperate to get off the show.

'I really enjoy the singing side of things,' said a slightly defensive Ant, questioned about the whole debacle some time later. 'There are a lot of people buying the records for whatever reason. I think we are now becoming ironic heroes. We've got a bit of a student fan base who think we're kind of ironically cool. *NME* are writing about us now and a few of the Indie mags have jumped on the bandwagon. It's quite funny, we've become pop heroes. We always knew it wasn't going to last forever.'

But it had been a respectable innings: in total, they sold 600,000 albums and the boys were happy to go back to their roots on television; Telstar, meanwhile, had done well with Ant and Dec, but realised the relationship had run its course. This wasn't altogether the end of the duo's musical associations: there were still World Cup anthems to come, not to mention hosting *Pop Idol* and the Brit Awards, but, for now, it was back to a future on their first love, TV.

'They learned very quickly – how to play instruments, how to write their own songs,' says Phil Seidl of Telstar. 'They knew their limitations and strengths. Maybe if the TV show hadn't come along at some stage, we could have made them cheesy, in the style of Steps and Wham! – you're so cheesy and naff, you're cool.'

But it was not to be. Fundamentally the boys wanted to be television stars, not pop stars, and they soon learned to enjoy their musical career for what it was. 'When we started out,' said Ant, as their reign as songsters wound to a close, 'we looked at Take That's career and we thought we'd like to be as big as them. And then we realised that there was no way we was gonna get that big, that soon. We were quite upset, but then we just resided in the fact. And now, I'm pure happier, me.'

And it certainly hadn't been an entirely smooth run. Groupies, Mrs Merton and falling sales figures aside, the duo had seen the nastier side of the business and it involved the behaviour of some of their fans. Ant and Dec, it goes without saying, were charm and responsibility personified when it came to their followers, but the same cannot be said for the followers themselves.

For some time the twosome included a moment in the act in which they chose a girl from the audience, called her on to the stage and sang 'Girlfriend' to her: the unfortunate youngster who was chosen in Glasgow, and who was only just into her teens, had her arms broken by jealous rivals after the show. The boys stopped beckoning girls on to the stage when they heard about that.

The end to Ant and Dec's music career might have been a shock, but it wasn't entirely unexpected – the two had always said they knew it couldn't last. What was of rather more concern was what was happening with their television career, for, despite all the high hopes surrounding *Ant and Dec Unzipped*, and despite the fact that it, too, went on to win a BAFTA, the show was not a success and when the series came to an end it was not recommissioned. Chris Evans was not to win the war, but he did win this particular battle: it was widely felt that his show, *TFI Friday*, was doing more than enough to cater to the youth audience.

'*Unzipped* was a lot of fun and in some ways was a bit before its time,' says Conor McAnally. 'It only ran one series because it confused audiences and did not get the numbers it needed to guarantee another series. The other problem was that everyone at Channel 4 we were dealing with moved on during the period of production so we had no in-house champion for our cause. We are all still very proud of the shows but they kind of missed the mark at the time.'

And so another career black spot loomed for Ant and Dec. The boys were initially unsure what to do next as no immediate projects were forthcoming: they filled their time with stints on the summer holiday versions of *The Bigger Breakfast*, while doing appearances on the likes of *Noel's House Party*. 'It was so awful,' said Dec. 'As they opened the door we turned to each other and said, "What the fuck are we doing here?"'

But they were also beginning to draw up the initial plans for what was to become *SM:tv*. It wasn't a happy time for the duo, but it was, perhaps, fortuitous. Early failure, even more than early success, does a great deal to shape a person, and these career troughs undoubtedly impressed upon the boys the need to retain their humility.

And there were still some concerts to perform, albeit this time in the role of ringmaster. As ever, when times were tough – or indeed excellent – Ant and Dec headed home to Newcastle, where they were to head the Smash Hits tour at the Newcastle Arena. The party then moved on to the London Arena, where the duo compèred the show – 'They're all good-looking birds who can carry a tune,' said Ant of the female attendees – although they were almost overshadowed by the Spice Girls, then at the height of their fame. The evening had another resonance for Dec: he was reconciled with Clare Buckfield, while at the same time the boys managed to find time to publicise Aids and HIV awareness for the children's charity Barnardo's.

Nor did the lack of a recording career or a television show put the two off when it came to maintaining their profile. They managed to continue popping up on the nation's television screens, appearing on, among much else, Channel 4's *Light Lunch*, in which top chefs were invited along to cook for the presenters, Mel Giedroyc and Sue Perkins, and their guests. Cuisine seemed to be a theme in the approach to Christmas 1997: the boys also presented *Ant and Dec's Geordie Christmas* from a boat in the middle of the Tyne, as giant pies were catapulted in the air above them from one side of the river to the other. And their beloved Newcastle was able to share the limelight when they hosted *The National Lottery Live* from Newcastle's Quayside.

The new year saw a continuing busy schedule. In February Ant and Dec flew to Belfast to take part in *Making a Difference*, a BBC programme about stories of care and heroism during the Troubles. This was followed by an item on *The Big Breakfast* about herding sheep – apparently it is a cure for stress – although the item went slightly skewiff when the assembled sheep dogs utterly failed to herd the sheep anywhere near their pen. Nonetheless, this led to a further stint fronting the show with Melanie Sykes, of Boddingtons ads fame, as well as signing for a panto the following Christmas at the Sunderland Empire. Clare, Dec's girlfriend, was to be in the show, too.

The panto was to be *Snow White and the Seven Dwarfs* and, whatever Ant and Dec's real feelings about the current state of their careers, they put a good spin on it, to use a New Labour term. By the time they actually came to star in the panto, their careers were on the verge of being transformed, but at the time, despite their continuing television appearances, no obvious new path seemed to be presenting itself. Nonetheless, the two resolutely refused to complain, even though their actual roles had still to be worked out. 'Here we are, telling the press that we are going to be in a panto and having our pictures taken and then Billy Fane [the writer] says, "Well, lads, we better work out what you're going to do,"' said a cheerful Dec.

For he was determined to put a good face on it all. 'We have done little bits before in Christmas shows for charity, but this is our first real panto,' he went on. 'We have been offered panto every year for the last five years, ever since we left *Byker Grove*. But, since we started doing the music, we have been away from home a lot and the only time we have had to get back to the North-East has been Christmas. We have always said we'd be blowed if we had to work over Christmas. This year is different, because we have been concentrating more on TV and have given ourselves a bit more of a holiday. When our agent said it was time to think about panto again, we asked what was on offer and, when he said Sunderland, we jumped at it. It will give us the chance to be back home over Christmas anyway and we are really looking forward to it. I used to love panto as a kid. If you are enjoying it, chances are the audience will be enjoying it too.'

And so the steady drip, drip of television appearances went on. May saw the boys teaming up with former Newcastle United star Barry Vension in a quiz designed to go alongside the FA Cup, in which Newcastle was playing Arsenal. It certainly suited the football-mad duo. 'All season it has felt as though Newcastle's name is on the cup,' said Ant. 'We have cancelled holidays to see the game.'

None of this, however, was long-term stuff and Ant and Dec knew it. They might be genuinely modest, but they are also genuinely ambitious and both were well aware that if they were to stay on top of the game they had to find a decent and ongoing outlet for their talents. Guest appearances were fine (or not, in the case of some of the shows they did) but there is little worse than the perpetual guest star who was once a name in his own right, and Ant and Dec were determined not to end up like that.

And so the two had been working hard behind the scenes, coming up with an idea for an innovative children's show that would go out on Saturday mornings. By the end of the summer, news of these plans was beginning to leak out. There was a lot at stake here: the duo had to have a hit soon to remain among the big names in television, on top of which they had got to be seen to be more willing to toe the line. 'Beat the Barber', harmless as it was, had upset quite a few parents, as had their sly innuendoes and the occasional real lapse of taste. And for once the pair weren't going to be broadcasting alone: this time round they were to have a female co-presenter to help them cause mayhem – or rather, to keep that mayhem under control. That presenter was to be Cat Deeley, and the programme itself was to be *SM:tv*.

5

SM:tv

CAT DEELEY had recently been voted by readers of *FHM* magazine the seventh most beautiful woman in the world, which might have been an odd accolade when it comes to choosing a presenter for children's television, but it suited the boys down to the ground. 'Cat's a lot of fun and she's much better-looking than me first thing in the morning,' said Ant. 'And she's not afraid to tell us to shut up, because we've been known to go on a bit.'

And it was that, rather than her looks, which made her an ideal counterpart to Ant and Dec: 'If they mess about, they'll get the back of my hand,' she announced firmly. She was to prove the perfect bossy older figure to the two young anarchists she worked with, given to yelling at them, 'You're grounded, with no pocket money!'

Right from the start, the chemistry between the three was obvious. 'As soon as we came up with the idea for

SM:tv, we reckoned it would be great to get a gorgeous girl in the middle – and it was,' said Ant. 'We got hundreds of tapes in from girls but when we met Cat, we knew immediately she was the one. Her interview technique was to take the piss out of us straight away.

'She'd found out this embarrassing story about a night in a Chinese restaurant, when we were so drunk we fell off our chairs. Dec had been a bit abusive to this guy, so Cat pretended she had been his girlfriend. She said, "Hi, we've met before. I seem to remember you gave my boyfriend a bit of a mouthful." We couldn't remember a thing, so we were really apologetic. When she told us three hours later she was winding us up, that was it. She got the job.'

The new programme was to be 'purely fun', they said, harking back to *Tiswas*, one of the most successful children's programmes of them all, with a touch more anarchy and a nod in the direction of older viewers. There were to be cartoons, interactive competitions, sketches, games and comedy items – larks galore, in short. 'It's a programme I would have loved to watch as a kid, very heavily borrowing from *Tiswas* – that "anything goes" atmosphere,' said Ant. 'It's celebrating Saturdays – a great day when you're a kid. No school. You look forward to it all week.'

Dec was equally enthusiastic. 'I can remember getting up, running down on your own, an eight-year-old in your jim-jams, eating your cornflakes,' he said. 'I remember being there.' This was hardly surprising, given that it hadn't been that long ago – the two, now veterans of television, were still only 22.

'I was involved from the earliest time with Ant and Dec as we developed and pitched the idea and I have been the executive producer from show one,' says Conor McAnally. 'I have also produced and directed the show on occasions. The initial concept was that *SM:tv* would be about the lead-in to *CD:UK*. It was the prelude to the big pop party that would happen at 11.30am. So it was full of ideas about seeing bands arrive, talking with them when they rehearsed, sneaking looks in their dressing rooms and so on. The problem was that the big pop acts of the time would not come and play with us because we were new. No matter how wonderful Faithless are, they mean nothing to a nine-year-old kid, so we very quickly found these ideas were dying on their butts and had to invent new stuff.

'The pressure was huge both internally and externally [to beat the BBC]. There was a commercial imperative from ITV but there was also a major issue of pride for everyone involved in the team from stage hands to producers. We just had to make it work and we worked all the hours God sent until we managed to turn it round.'

With all that hanging on their shoulders, it was hardly surprising that Ant and Dec professed to being nervous. 'Expect the unexpected,' proclaimed Dec. 'We're not too sure ourselves what's going to be on the first show. We've already been warned about using sexual innuendoes and double entendres. I'm really worried I'm going to swear on live TV. I've been having nightmares about it.'

In fact, the boys were absolutely determined to make it work. Having left the BBC only to find that their stay at

Channel 4 was to be a brief one, they had a lot riding on *SM:tv*. They had also had a lot of experience of live broadcasting by now, and had enjoyed the experience. 'When we did *The Big Breakfast*, we found we liked live telly – it really gets your adrenaline going,' said Ant. 'So we jumped at the chance when we were offered a Saturday morning show.'

On Saturday, 29 August at 9.25am, the new show began. It was a bold move: ITV was pitting it against the BBC's *Live and Kicking*, at that time the undisputed king of children's comedy programmes and presented by Zoë Ball. But ITV was clearly determined to win the gamble: for a start, the new show came out when *Live and Kicking* was off air for its summer break, giving *SM:tv* a full month to win over viewers before its more established rival returned. Nigel Pickard, ITV's new Controller of Children's and Youth Television, was staunchly behind the new show, brightly announcing, 'It's called putting all your eggs in one basket.'

In fact, he was as determined as anyone to make the show work and to disprove the notion that 'you can't trust commercial television to do children's television properly'. Certainly ITV had a lot to prove: it had changed televisual direction almost constantly on Saturday mornings up till now, with the result that viewers had had nothing to adhere to. Apart from *SM:tv*, Pickard was also extending the remit of children's television to include more drama and comedy, in an attempt to move away from a diet consisting solely of cartoons. 'It's vital, and I'm telling producers this, that they have got to think more commercially about children's television,' he said. 'Outside of the pre-school programmes, all our shows must appeal to the 5–11 age group and not alienate anyone.'

And so the show began. Initially, however, it looked as if those eggs in that basket might all break. Presenting a live television show for three hours non-stop is a real test of nerve and at first the famous Ant and Dec chemistry seemed a little forced. *Live and Kicking* appeared to be winning with ease and it seemed as if, yet again, Ant and Dec had a vehicle on their hands that should have worked but didn't quite manage it.

But this time round they had a massive source of support: the ITV network. It wasn't just the boys who had a lot riding on this programme: it was also a battle between ITV and the BBC, and ITV executives lost no time in showing the pair they wanted them to stay. And so, over time, the duo began to lose their nervousness, to enjoy themselves – and viewers began tuning in. 'When we started, we soon learned that three hours of live Saturday morning television was a bit of a beast and we were up against the BBC,' said Dec. 'But ITV supported us and had more faith in the show than we did at times. We had meetings and we thought, Shit, this is it, but they were really positive.'

Ant agreed. 'Bad ratings, badly executed ideas,' he said of the first few shows. 'There were many anxious nights when I thought, That's it for us. Thank God ITV had the courage to say, "You've got a year to get it right."'

As the show began to gain ground, so everyone involved

began to enjoy themselves more. 'It was just a fantastic experience,' recalls Dean Wilkinson. 'I wrote it for four-and-a-half years and on the basis of that things have taken off. I have got a lot to thank them for. When they are good and they have got a good script they are just so much fun to watch. Their visual gags are always funny but they don't look funny on paper. They just make it work.

'When we were writing things like *Chums*, we always had a laugh. Ant would be a lot more innocent than Dec, and Dec would be a lot more devious when they play themselves in *Chums*. Ant is a bit more laddish than Dec. I used to play that up a bit. Taken to the extreme, Ant is slobbish and Dec is a pansy and showbiz. That was played up but in real life they are a lot more similar. They just want to do the job, get down the pub and watch the football.'

Life on the programme was certainly riotous. 'After one night's boozing after a recording we all went back to Ant and Dec's flat and another writer made the mistake of falling asleep first, so me and Ant wrote "I AM GAY" on his forehead in black marker,' says Dean. 'I remember he went to the toilet when he awoke in the morning and we were dying for his reaction when he looked in the mirror. After about 20 minutes he walked back out, the writing was gone and his forehead red raw from scrubbing. He calmly sat down and called us all a pack of bastards. Very funny.'

It helped that the boys continued to maintain a high profile through other television work. They fronted a programme introducing the highlights of that year's MTV awards and narrowly missed winning Male Personality

Award (for which they were jointly nominated) at the Northern Personality Awards, with the actual award going to Robson Green.

In their private lives the boys continued to thrive. They have often admitted to liking a drink a little too much, and this became evident when Ant was arrested after a brawl at a nightclub in Oxford. He was held for two hours before being released without charge, while his then manager, Newcastle-based Dave Holly, hastily defended his young client. 'An incident did take place, but the whole thing was blown out of all proportion,' he said. 'Ant is only guilty of being there when it happened. He'd been at the club with friends and one lad in there had been trying to be something special by having a go at Ant. He just ignored it, like he always does. This lad kept on and someone in Ant's party got involved, so the police were called. If it had been anyone else, I don't think the bouncers would have bothered, but, because Ant was famous, they called the police. He was nicked and ended up in a police cell for a couple of hours, but he didn't do anything – he wasn't chuffed, but it was just one of those things.' It was unfortunate timing. Not only was Ant getting *SM:tv* off the ground, he was also trying to rid himself of the image of bad-boy behaviour, as the two strove to broaden their appeal.

And they were certainly growing up. Now that Ant and Dec were firmly based in London, the two decided it was time to buy their own houses, rather than continue renting together – and so they bought two identical properties that are literally two doors away from each other in Chiswick, west London. 'We're both going to be living in the same area,' said Dec. 'But it's time for a change. We want to buy sofas and fridges.'

The move from a shared flat to two identical houses almost next door to each other wasn't planned. 'I knew a new development in Chiswick that was being built,' said Dec. 'There were two or three houses unsold, and when I went along to look at one of them I asked Ant to come along for his opinion.'

'I had a look at one,' said Ant. 'I went in. I loved it. Then we both said, "No, we can't do this – it's ridiculous."'

'It was a lovely sunny day,' said Dec, 'and there was a pub a few hundred yards away, and we sat by the river and had a drink and talked about how we both loved the houses, but couldn't move into the same street. But then we thought, Well, we're best mates, we socialise together, so what's the point of living at separate ends of town and spending a fortune on cab fares? And that was it. We knew that people would find this a very bizarre arrangement.'

But, as a concession to public opinion, the two decided that they would make an effort not to go on holiday together. 'It would be too much for some people,' said Ant. 'It would get them thinking we couldn't bear to be apart.'

But the two had as yet no plans to make honest women of their respective girlfriends, not least because they were still so young. 'I want kids,' declared Dec. 'I love children and definitely want some of my own in the future. But at the moment, I'm working to be financially secure.' Nor were they yet prepared to give up their laddish lifestyle. 'We still go on massive pub crawls,' Dec continued. 'After our

TV show, we go to the pub and drink until we can't stand up any more. It's a great laugh. Sometimes we knock back the booze with our guests. Terrorvision once tried to kidnap us …'

The light-hearted banter continued between the two, off screen as well as on, with Ant claiming that Dec had once made off with one of his girlfriends. 'He's kissed one of my girlfriends before!' he said. 'We went to this party and I went to the toilet and when I came back, Dec was necking with her.' The situation had not, however, been unduly serious – the pair remained friends.

In November that year *Byker Grove* celebrated its tenth anniversary, and the boys returned to their acting alma mater to take part in the celebrations, alongside other alumni, including Donna Air, Michelle Charles and Casper Berry. They also helped to publicise World Aids Day, and prepared to star in *Snow White and the Seven Dwarfs*. It was a very hectic schedule, involving commuting between London and the North-East, for the two had signed up for the panto before they knew they'd be presenting a Saturday morning television show. Nor had *SM:tv* yet found its feet.

'The Saturday morning show is a beast of a show, it eats up ideas and material,' said Dec. 'So we're here in the office from Tuesday to Saturday, we have to write the show and come up with ideas. I'm a little bit nervous about the panto, but only because we have to carry on doing the TV show. So we'll be up and down like yo-yos from London to Sunderland and Sunderland to London. And we'll be doing matinées on a Saturday. It's going to be a rush. The TV show is live and we come off air at 12.30pm, then it's a fast car to the airport and a quick flight up and get ready for the matinée. It's nice, though, as it's back in the North-East, near to home. That's one of the reasons we decided to do the panto. We've always wanted to do panto, but to be able to do it and be home for Christmas is great. That's important to both of us – to be at home for a family Christmas.' It was also remunerative – the two were to earn £12,000 a week each. Nor did they forget their social consciences: while up in the North-East they formally opened a new children's unit at South Tyneside Hospital in South Shields.

It was, funnily enough, that season in panto at the end of 1998 that proved the fillip the boys needed, in that it taught them again how to talk to their audience. And what their audience said was that the BBC was getting it wrong. 'They confirmed that what the BBC was doing was a bit patronising and just boring,' said Ant. 'They had a four-minute item on asthma.'

'Longer,' added Dec. 'They would literally do a seven- to nine-minute piece on asthma with an agony uncle.'

Ant came back with, 'But when I was a kid I hated that sort of stuff. I'd always rather watch cartoons or climb a tree.'

And so they battled on, only to find that matters improved considerably. 'We were a bit rusty at first and we got caught up in what most Saturday morning shows do when they're trying to beat the BBC: competing for the guests, the exclusive videos, the best bands, etc,' said Ant. 'But after Christmas, we stopped thinking about how to beat the Beeb and just concentrated on making a good show and having fun.'

It wasn't long before the viewers cottoned on to what was happening and started to tune in. And, to Ant and Dec's complete astonishment, they discovered it wasn't only children who were watching: it was young adults, too. A whole new genre of television was emerging called 'hangover TV': although the shows concerned were meant for children, they were also watched by 20-somethings recovering from the night before. 'I didn't realise the impact it would have on people who are our age,' said a bemused Ant. 'We go to pubs and get people of our age group mentioning stuff we've done that morning and saying the catchphrases.'

They weren't just saying the catchphrases: some of the boys' antics reverberated for weeks afterwards. 'One Friday night before the show, Dec knocked at the door holding a massive crisp, saying he was going to take it on the show the next day,' recalled Ant. 'He did and we were inundated with crisps, cornflakes and oven chips all wrapped up in cotton wool. My girlfriend had a crisp the other day and she screamed, "Is mine bigger than Dec's?" We see people in the pubs, looking at a crisp in their bag and then looking at us!'

'I think my favourite thing they did on telly was Captain Justice on *SM:tv*, which was Ant as a consumer rights superhero who fancied Dec,' says Dean Wilkinson. 'I don't know how we got away with it. One of my funniest memories is him trying to wrestle with Dec.'

It goes almost without saying that no sooner had the boys started on the show than they started running into trouble again with the odd gag that went too far. The pair were responsible for London Weekend Television receiving its first-ever warning from the Independent Television Commission for allowing sexual innuendo on to a children's television programme. Ant raised eyebrows when he read out a poem implying he'd like to get into the pants of Sabrina the Teenage Witch, although the man himself wasn't concerned.

'I'm amazed,' he said, when he was asked about Sabrina. 'The things they complain about are always the ones you think they'll never mind. We've done a lot worse than that and got away with it.'

Dec agreed. 'The worst one ever was one I never even realised I'd said,' he said. 'I was talking about watching the band Fat Les film their new video. But it came out as, "We've just been down to watch the fat lezzers in action."'

But, irate parents aside, it was part of their charm. They might push the boundaries, come across as too cheeky for words and even engage in a bit of out-and-out rudeness, but there was something reassuring about the boys. Whatever double entendre might slip out, you knew your daughters were going to be safe when those two were around.

Questions have often been asked about the secret of the duo's success, but the combination of friendship and professionalism has a great deal to do with it. 'A lot of that is experience,' says Dave Holly, who represented them until 2000. 'They know what makes them successful and they make sure they appear that way. The worst thing they could do is to change. People see them as 14- to 16-year-old Geordie lads – though I'm sure they're not quite like that now. Ant to me is a lot deeper than Dec. Dec is a jolly, cheeky chappy. He smiles a lot, he's more trusting. With Ant, it takes a long time for him to have confidence in people. It's wrong to say Dec is more superficial, but he's more easygoing. Ant's a thinker. He's just a bit wary of who he says things to and when.

'They've been together for so long they can read what the other is thinking. In their early days in the music business they were sharing rooms, working with each other day and night. I've never, ever known them to fall out. They discuss things, but they don't punch each other's lights out. When they're writing, one starts it off and the other carries it on, like songwriters. It's a team effort. They've got a similar sense of humour and, because they're together all the time – meeting the same people – they are, to some degree, at one with one another.'

As it became established, *SM:tv* soon began winning hands down over the competition. It was beating *Live and Kicking* in the ratings war, sparking rumours that the BBC was all but waving blank cheques at Ant and Dec to take over presenting their humbled rival. But the duo, still smarting from the BBC's treatment of *The Ant and Dec Show*, were unmoved.

They also began to talk about the dark days, the period during which their careers had appeared to stall. Unusually for the two, they started criticising other celebrities, most notably Vanessa Feltz, with whom they'd appeared on *The Big Breakfast*. 'She was fairly nasty to us,' said Dec.

'Though not to our faces,' added Ant. 'She still doesn't realise we know what she said but we were told.'

'When we've been with her, she has been very nice to

our faces, but we know she has said things,' Dec went on.

Vanessa herself was hurt by their remarks. 'I'm nonplussed,' she said. 'I wouldn't dream of saying anything horrible about Ant and Dec. I think they're brilliant. In fact, my children do, too. I took them to *SM:tv* and they had a fabulous time. Whoever is telling them these things isn't telling the truth.'

She wasn't the only celebrity to profess admiration for the boys. As the show continued to garner adult fans, so an increasing number of established names began to heap praise on the two, among them Boy George, who had been invited on to *CD:UK*, a chart show also hosted by the boys which ran straight on after *SM:tv*. 'Last Saturday I was a guest on the pop TV show *CD:UK*, fronted by the charming twosome Ant and Dec, the pop world's answer to Morecambe and Wise,' he wrote. If there was any doubt as to the national affection in which Ant and Dec were held, that doubt was now dispelled.

The two, along with their show, were now so popular that they were causing serious ructions over at the BBC. Zoë Ball and Jamie Theakston were leaving *Live and Kicking*, which meant that the Beeb not only had to find two new replacements but also to work out some way of winning viewers away from *SM:tv*. There was to be a lull over the summer while the powers that be decided what to do. *SM:tv*, meanwhile, wasn't even slightly unnerved. 'We will be ready for them,' said a spokesman for the show, 'and it has to be an advantage that we will keep going throughout the summer. They will have to come up with something very special to get back to where they were. It's become a tired old format.'

That was true enough, but *SM:tv* did not only have the advantage in that it was a livelier show: more than that, it had presenters who were fast turning into national treasures. And yet, even now that their careers were so firmly back on track, Ant and Dec remained exactly as they always had been: level-headed and refusing point-blank to let their stardom turn their heads (much like Morecambe and Wise, in fact). The two still came across as down-to-earth Geordies, albeit ones who were very aware how lucky they had been. 'Free CDs!' gloated Dec to an interviewer who visited the boys at the *SM:tv* studio and found himself surrounded by posters, pin-ups and, of course, pile after pile of CDs.

But behind the laddishness lay two increasingly astute performers. They had been lucky and knew it, but they were determined to hang on to what had come their way. They were constantly on the lookout for new ideas and opportunities, as Dec revealed in an interview in 1999. 'Well, um, like, we have talked about doing a sitcom, yes,' he said. 'It's split between Newcastle and America, with Ant and me doing a kind of *Likely Lads*. Not a *Men Behaving Badly*, because Martin Clunes and Neil Morrissey have already done that very well and it wouldn't be right for us anyway. Besides, it's not for four or five years yet. Plenty of time to get it right.'

The industry was also treating the duo with increased respect. Like so many former child stars, they initially found it difficult to be taken seriously as adults, a situation that was beginning to change. 'Ah, BBC meetings for *The Ant and Dec Show*!' Ant recalled. 'We would go in with an idea and we'd explain the idea and they would look at us and then look at our producer and he would repeat the exact same idea and they'd say, "Ha, ha, now that's a good idea! We like that!" That used to really nark us.'

Their treatment at the hands of the BBC had clearly created wounds that ran deep. They had still neither forgiven nor forgotten what had happened to *The Ant and Dec Show*, and were keen to tell everyone about it, too. 'The papers said we'd been dumped but actually the BBC were surprised when we said no,' said Dec. 'If it's going to take another five years for some people to come around to the fact that we have opinions that ought to be listened to, then I'm prepared to wait. I would rather not shout, "Give us some respect." I would rather just let them catch up on their own.' The point was clear: Ant and Dec might have been performers on children's television but, when it came to running their careers, they were as grown-up as the greyest heads in the industry.

They also got irritated that other performers, such as Chris Evans, got credit for being the only madcap, anarchic performer on television, when the boys were doing their bit, too. The difference, of course, is that Evans was aiming for an adult audience, while Ant and Dec, despite their increasing host of grown-up aficionados, were still on children's TV. 'That is annoying,' admitted Dec. 'There are people who constantly get credit for things we have done. It doesn't really bug us, but you can't help but wish that one day somebody will recognise what you do and tell others. I mean, I watched the last series of *House Party* and [Noel] Edmonds looked tired. He spent too much money on weak ideas. If you're not having fun, stop doing it. When pop music stopped being fun, we gave it up.

'Like a lot of people in TV, Edmonds is too close to TV. That's the thing I love – being able to cut off from being a performer and watching, 'cos I love telly. Ironically enough, Edmonds was a hero of mine when he did *Swap Shop*. I used to rush downstairs for it every Saturday morning. Now I do the same thing as him and I think of how there are other kids like me waiting in their pyjamas. We get letters saying, "I love your show and enter all the competitions." It's an inspiration.'

As it became increasingly obvious that Ant and Dec were becoming mainstream stars, with adults as well as children for fans, so their opinions tended to be sought out when anything pertaining to Newcastle arose. In the summer of 1999 it was revealed that Newcastle, following in Manchester's footsteps, was planning a gay village. 'A gay community already exists in Newcastle but a lot of their spending power is disappearing to other parts of the country,' said council boss John Miller.

'The last thing we want to do is create a ghetto and put up barriers. We want an area where everyone feels welcome. Manchester's Canal Street would be a good model for us to follow but we already attract tourists from all over the world, so our gay village may become as trendy as Miami or San Francisco.'

And what did Ant and Dec think? 'It's one of the best

cities in the world to party in, and anything that brings people here is great with us,' they said.

The boys themselves, of course, were still with their girlfriends and had been known to admit that the two girls had a lot to put up with. 'Getting up at 5.30am every Saturday to do the show has killed Friday nights,' Dec confessed. 'We said once that we had to have a sex ban on Fridays to help us get up in the morning, so every weekend the crew greet us saying, "You two still not getting any then?"'

6

With Friends Like These ...

PUBLICLY, THE two continued their good-natured banter but, as ever, behind the scenes they were carefully planning their next move. Having very publicly trounced the BBC, which had not only lost them to ITV but also had seen its own children's television outclassed on every level by the pair, Ant and Dec were by now ready to kiss and make up, so to speak. They were offered the chance to host Radio 1's *Breakfast Show*, but turned it down, one very early morning a week clearly being enough, but instead did a pilot for the Beeb for a show called *Friends Like These*. It was Ant and Dec's first adult show and both they and the BBC were pleased with the result. 'I think they liked it. And we certainly enjoyed ourselves,' said Dec.

Not everyone was pleased: for a start, ITV was none too thrilled to learn that the boys might be 'ready to rhumble' with a rival channel. 'They recorded the BBC pilot show called *Friends Like These* while they were on holiday, but Ant and Dec are under contract to *SM:tv* until August 2000, and I cannot see them having time to do both,' said Simon Jones of Freud Communication, which acted as a spokesman for *SM:tv*. ITV itself, meanwhile, had awarded the boys a new contract worth £500,000 each. But it would have been unwise to be too insistent on keeping Ant and Dec to themselves. Now that the boys really were being taken seriously, they had become extremely sought-after commodities – and, as they had showed in their earlier negotiations with the Beeb, they weren't afraid to walk away if they didn't get the deal they wanted.

It was soon confirmed that Ant and Dec were going to present the new show. It was exactly what they had been looking for: prime-time adult television going out on Saturday night, in which members of the public would nominate friends and family members to perform mental and physical challenges to get into the final. 'They are the stars of the future,' said a clearly delighted David Young, Head of Entertainment at the BBC. In fact, as everyone had now realised, they were the stars of the present as well.

Ant and Dec themselves were absolutely delighted. 'It could be the start of something big,' said Ant. 'We've just made the pilot, but the BBC looks keen to take it up. It's a game show with an added twist. Two sets of five friends are set mental and physical challenges to get into the final and win a dream holiday. One team gets eliminated and then we pick two friends out of the remaining five who are set questions about each other and their families. If one gets an answer wrong, they lose the holiday for the other. The BBC approached us with the idea, and we were really flattered. Being on Saturday evening television is a big thing.'

And, of course, the boys were asked how they would do if one were asked personal questions about the other. The answer surprised no one who knew them. They had now been friends for over a decade, were seemingly inseparable on screen and off, had shared a flat together for some years and now lived almost next door to each other. 'We did some questions for ourselves,' said Ant, 'and I think we do know just about everything, including each other's parent's maiden names.' If ever a double act were the double act to front a programme about friendship, it was Ant and Dec.

In many ways it seemed like all their wishes had been fulfilled at once. They had not only won the ratings war with the BBC with their Saturday morning show but were also now appearing on prime-time telly at the same time. And still the boys didn't let it go to their heads, hero-worshipping away as they always had done when meeting someone who was, after all, a fellow celeb. 'We were at an ITV do a couple of weeks ago and Des Lynam was there,' confided Ant. 'On *Match of the Day* he was Mister Cool. It took me ages to pluck up the courage to talk to him. We had a great chat.'

It seemed as if life couldn't get better. *SM:tv* was now so popular that it was attracting not only fans of all ages but guests of the highest calibre. The boys were stunned and delighted. 'We were over the moon at overtaking *Live and Kicking* in the ratings,' said Ant. 'When we first started, we were up against Zoë and Jamie. They were an institution and had massive guests. Now we're getting big names on. Sting was a great laugh and Jay Kay from Jamiroquai has asked if he can be on our *Chums* sketch show. The Pet Shop Boys did the same.'

And then, of course, there was the new show. If the boys were feeling that revenge is sweet, they had the common sense not to show it, and merely talked about how strange it was to be back at the BBC. 'It was weird going back there and filming again in front of an audience and working with a lot of the crew we used to have on *The Ant and Dec Show*. Weird but nice,' said Ant.

It was clear: the BBC had at last been forgiven – and was very unlikely to upset two of its star performers again.

If all that were not enough, the boys' off-screen lives began to return to some degree of normality. Although Ant and Dec were now arguably more famous than they had ever been, they were famous as television presenters, not pop stars, and that meant no more screaming tweenies. 'We can go out drinking with mates now,' said a clearly relieved Ant. 'We couldn't before, when all the pop thing took off, as we got mobbed.'

What could go wrong? Well, something had to and, in one critic's eyes at least, it turned out to be the new show. After the much-heralded launch, the first in the series came out and garnered one of the most vituperative reviews Ant and Dec had ever received. 'It was boys against girls, with two teams battling it out for the holiday of a lifetime,' it began. 'Last night that was the Cayman Islands and, judging from the opening shots of Ant and Dec relaxing on a beach and the OTT praise for both the resort and the hotel, I reckon the two Geordies had already had theirs at our expense. But they paid for it in the end because their show stinks.'

It might have been disheartening for the boys, not least because this was their first proper venture into prime-time adult broadcasting, but they were not unprepared for something to go wrong. They had been in the business for over a decade now, and had seen shows fail before, on top of which they knew just how competitive the industry could be. 'If you have been successful, there are always going to be those waiting to see you fall flat on your face,' said Dec. 'But then there is pressure on everyone, no matter what they do.'

Anyway, the two were in a much stronger position vis-à-vis the BBC than they had been formerly, and Auntie wasn't about to let the boys get away again. Nor did the majority of the other critics agree. On top of that, the idea had originally come from the BBC and not Ant and Dec. David Young, BBC Productions' Head of Light Entertainment, and the brains behind the show, was solidly behind it all, as indeed he would be. 'You don't need to spend thousands and thousands of pounds on sets like *Gladiators* and *Ice Warriors* for a programme to be gripping,' he said.

And it turned out that the viewing audience quite liked the show, which did, after all, manage to combine attractive presenters with a genuine challenge. Young was clearly relieved, and pointed out that Ant and Dec were just right for the slot, as women fancied them and men wanted to go for a beer with them. 'They are wholesome and a bit naughty,' he said.

Young himself came up with the idea for the show while watching the 1998 World Cup. 'During England's match against Argentina, both David Batty and Paul Ince missed penalties and I have never seen such tension,' he said. 'I thought if only I could get that into a TV show.' In fact, he managed to do that so well that the pilot ended up with a slot involving threading needles. It was a brave move. 'Everyone said it wouldn't work, and even on the night I had another game in reserve,' said Young. 'Up to the very last minute I was going to change it, but the two producers said no and it was the right decision. When you see the contestants' hands shaking, and everything depends on it, it works.'

It did indeed, and, despite that bad fairy of a critic, a ten-part series was commissioned. This was a relief to the boys, who were increasingly keen to be taken seriously, a desire that wasn't always fulfilled everywhere they went. 'We still get kids coming up to us in supermarkets singing "Let's Get Ready to Rhumble",' admitted Dec. 'I just shout, "Darling, that is so 1996."'

It soon appeared that the gamble taken by all involved was going to pay off. Ant and Dec were as pleased as anyone: they had been receiving quite a number of proposals through their production company and weren't afraid to turn the bad ones down. 'We were approached by this one bloke who had a great idea for a late-night show,' said Dec in one interview. 'We would have been sharing this flat and talked about birds and cars, drink and eat curry. We thought that would be great fun.'

'Yeah, great fun,' said a sarcastic Ant.

'I've got this brilliant idea about going to different pubs each week and seeing how much we have to drink until we fall over. I think that would be brilliant,' said Dec.

'Nah, that's awful,' said Ant.

'Go on, tell him what your idea is then.'

'No, I can't, it's a public place. What about badger baiting?'

Of course, Ant and Dec weren't right for the show just because they appealed to men and women alike: it was the depth of their own friendship that came through, a friendship that was utterly genuine. 'We've never said to each other, "Let's be dead chummy to keep our TV careers going,"' said Ant. 'People would soon see through that. We've just been very lucky to have so much in common. We hit it off right from the start. And our girlfriends get on well together too, thank goodness.'

'Unlike me, Ant is really cool under pressure and always manages to keep things in perspective,' said Dec. 'He's a calming influence on me.'

'Dec is very understanding and good to talk to, so I'll see him down the pub and he'll always sort my problems out,' said Ant. 'But he does have this weird habit of always thinking he's only had three pints, when he's actually had eight, plus a couple of bottles he drank at home.'

The two girlfriends were also remarkably relaxed about the strength of the friendship between Ant and Dec. 'They think it's hilarious,' said Ant.

'If I go shopping with my girlfriend,' said Dec, 'and we meet up with Ant and his girlfriend later to have a pint and catch up, they're like, "Are you happy now? Back with your friend?"'

And they were utterly aware of how fortunate they were that the show had come along just as they realised they would have to make a move into adult telly. Asked if they were nervous at the prospect of making the jump, Dec replied, 'Not really. We didn't say to ourselves, "Right, come February 2000 we'll move into prime time." It's just that shows like this don't come along every five minutes. There are bound to be those who haven't seen our other shows or seen us on *Top of the Pops*. They will switch on and say to themselves, "Who are these two?" But we're looking forward to that, to winning them over.'

And as for having not one, but two hit shows on their hands, the pair were relaxed about the future. 'Things are going so well for us at the moment and both the BBC and ITV are allowing us to carry on,' said Ant. 'How long we can carry on doing that I don't know.'

For as long as they wanted, would seem to be the answer. The BBC was hoping they could conquer Saturday night television just as they had already conquered Saturday morning TV, and was keen to do as much as possible to promote the show. As with any successful television programme, far more planning had gone on behind the scenes than was immediately obvious. The challenges set for the contestants might have sounded trivial but, given the context of the show, turned out to be genuinely exciting.

They were also extremely wide-ranging. 'The games vary from the basically simple to the downright scary,' said Ant. 'For instance, we've got threading a needle and parking a car with a handbrake turn. But even the simple ones can make you sweat, especially if you're the last to go and your team mates are depending on you. It's all down to picking people for what they're best suited to.'

But, as the boys' fame grew, they remained resolutely anti-celebrity, avoiding West End members' clubs and keeping their social lives revolving round the local. 'We're not that showbiz – we don't really do the parties,' said Dec. 'We'd rather go to the pub.' They were even members of a local pub quiz team called the Crabladders. 'We're rubbish,' said Dec, who went on to explain what a crabladder is by pulling up his shirt and pointing at the strip of hair that descends from the navel. 'It's this bit here, look. I think it's a Northern expression. Anyway, we're bottom of the league, but it's a good laugh.'

That lack of pretension endeared them to fans and colleagues alike. It is incredibly unusual in the entertainment industry to find people who inspire as little criticism as do Ant and Dec, but the fact remains that no one has a bad word to say about them. 'We learned early to get on with it; as kids on *Byker Grove* it wasn't possible for us to muck around,' said Ant.

Nor did they make the mistake of believing their own publicity. 'It's funny,' said Dec. 'I don't really think of us as TV presenters. I think of TV presenters as responsible people who show children what to do with empty Fairy

Liquid bottles. Not a couple of blokes who don't mind telling kids to shut up.'

David Young, unsurprisingly, is effusive in his praise. 'Utterly professional,' he says. 'They're really nice guys, very intelligent. We didn't want old-school light entertainment, we didn't want spangly jackets. We wanted something that would pull back that 16- to 34-year-old audience that probably didn't really like Saturday night TV, that had been disillusioned with it. And it seems as though Ant and Dec will be able to do it.'

Indeed they would. When the programme was only halfway through its initial run, it was clearly proving to be such a success that it was recommissioned for a second run, to go out in the autumn. The biggest nobs of them all at the BBC professed themselves pleased. 'Peter Salmon, the BBC1 Controller, is absolutely delighted with it – it's done really well and it's a great show,' said a BBC spokeswoman. 'It's very unusual to commission more than one series at a time, but the very fact that he is already thinking about a third one is a clear indication of its success.'

Back on Saturday mornings, the boys also continued to produce the goods for *SM:tv*, although they continued to skate on perilously thin ice. On April Fool's Day 2000, Dec appeared to collapse on set just as the programme switched to a cartoon: ten minutes later, when the cartoon was over, a radiantly healthy and beaming Dec told viewers it had all been a prank. The nation was not amused. Hordes of worried children had phoned and emailed the show before Dec had been revealed to be in robust health, forcing Conor McAnally, the executive producer, to apologise for the stunt.

'Dec fainting was an April Fool's joke and was very much in the spirit of the show,' he said. '*SM:tv* always strives to thrill, surprise and delight its audience and Dec was back on air within eight minutes to reveal that it was an April Fool sketch. We did not intend to cause offence and would like to apologise to anyone who was upset by the prank.'

But the boys revelled in the fact that, as the show went out on ITV, they probably had more leeway than they would have had with Auntie. 'The BBC have this responsibility to do sensible public broadcasting, whereas we've got the luxury where we can dress up and play these stupid games,' said Dec. 'We wanted to recapture the days of *Tiswas*.'

'*SM:tv* is just us having a laugh, taking the piss and being quite comedic,' said Ant.

Certainly items such as 'The Stripping Vicar', featuring a vicar who couldn't resist taking his clothes off every time he heard the words 'strip' or 'get them off' in the context of normal conversation was very close to the bone.

So what of their responsibility as role models? 'To tell you the truth, it tends not to cross my mind too much,' said Ant. 'I'd rather be seen as the cheeky older brother than a parental figure telling them what to do. We get a lot more respect for being in touch and being on their wavelength.'

However, the pair knew there were some boundaries they must not overstep. 'At the time the programme goes out, we wouldn't use any strong language,' said Dec. 'Even mildly strong. And there is no way we could ever make references to drugs.'

'Having those restraints makes it a bit more cheeky,' added Ant. 'If we were allowed to get away with anything, it wouldn't be so much fun.'

Despite the lightness of the banter, the boys clearly had given some thought to what was or was not responsible. Ali G, aka Sacha Baron Cohen, had recently been criticised for having glamorised drugs, an accusation the boys considered ludicrous. 'There are some people who said *Trainspotting* glamorised heroin,' said Dec. 'I watched *Trainspotting* and I found it quite disturbing. Anyone who wanted to try heroin would be put off. You get these pressure groups and organisations. We've experienced the sharp end of the tongue of Middle England with our cheeky, suggestive humour. People write in to say, "My children will certainly not be seeing this again."'

Another possible fount of controversy was the Pokemón cartoon featured on the show. Pokemón cards had become a near addiction for some young teenagers, and had been banned in some schools because the owners of those cards were far too busy swapping them with one another to concentrate on anything else, which was in itself a reason in some quarters for keeping Pokemón off the show. But it was in the course of an interview that Ant and Dec learned for the first time that there had been a Pokemón-related stabbing in an American school. Both were clearly shocked.

'I didn't know that,' said Dec. 'That's unbelievable. Anything like that is obviously quite worrying.' There were quite a few pauses as he spoke, as he clearly sought to present the case for the defence with great care. 'Those sorts of thing obviously shouldn't go on, but I don't see it as a reason to stop. If we're not showing the cartoon, then someone else is going to show the cartoon. It's the same as teenage girls get with boy bands: the shaking around, the putting themselves in dangerous positions.

'I think far more bullying goes on because of pop bands than Pokemón. You see those girls hanging around concert venues and hotels, little groups all bitching at each other and fighting. And the Pokemón craze will peak out like every other craze.' Dec, of course, knew what he was talking about: it had been after a PJ and Duncan concert that one of the duo's own fans had had her arms broken by jealous rivals.

Someone else who found herself the target of envy was Cat Deeley, because of her proximity to the boys. She accepted it with good grace. 'Yes,' she said, of teenage fans of the duo. 'They stop me in Safeways and ask if I'm in love with Dec. I tell them, "Yes, I'm hopelessly in love with him." I'm not, of course, I think he and Ant are great, really nice boys – and very protective.'

She also revealed that, despite her bold auditioning tactics, she had actually been extremely nervous when first up for the show. 'I was scared when I walked into the studio,' she confessed. 'It was huge, with smoke machines, stages, star curtains and lights and it was, "What have I let myself in for?" I'd talked a good game to get there, but I suddenly realised I was with the big boys. I was practically hyperventilating. But when I go into work every Saturday at 5am I tell myself that everything I do I must do with total commitment. If I were half-hearted or scared it would show. I've had to do some daft things, but I've discovered that if I can give it my best shot people will laugh with me.'

It seemed fitting that at this high point of the boys' career they returned to their old alma mater, *Byker Grove*, to film a special episode that was due to go out in the autumn. It was like stepping back in time and a salutary reminder of quite how far they had come. 'Being back in the Grove was fantastic,' said a clearly delighted Ant. 'It was amazing how easily we slipped back into PJ's and Duncan's shoes.'

Dec was equally thrilled to be back where it all began. 'It was great to see some familiar faces and catch up on seven years of *Byker* gossip,' he said.

The current *Byker* crew were impressed by the boys. 'They're such good crack,' said the show's current producer, Morag Bain. 'I'd never met them before and wondered what they would be like. But they're still so down-to-earth and mucked in with everyone. We had a great laugh with them.'

One of the show's then stars, Alexa Gibb, agreed. 'I thought they might look down on us, but they were really great,' she said. 'There were no airs and graces, they were just lads.'

But they were adult stars now, not child performers, and increasingly successful ones at that. In May 2000 *Friends Like These* won a coveted Bronze Rose in the gameshow category at the prestigious Rose d'Or festival in Montreux. Now everyone was beginning to want a piece of the duo:

Avalon management agency, which had the likes of Frank Skinner and Harry Hill on their books, made a concerted effort to sign them up, saying that the pair weren't benefiting as much as they could do from their current management. Not everyone agreed.

Ant and Dec now had both Saturday morning and early Saturday evening pretty much in the palm of their hands: as one industry insider observed, there was no need for them to take on a late-night Channel 4 slot in which they could swear a little, before spending three weeks slumming it at the Edinburgh Festival. That would also have slotted them back into a niche – an adult niche, admittedly, but a niche nonetheless. They were far too canny to go for that. To survive for a long time in the television industry, it is essential to maintain the broadest appeal possible, and telling a few unfunny jokes with Frank Skinner wasn't what either saw as their future path.

And, as the situation was, their influence was already extraordinary, with every location that appeared on their show promptly deemed a must-go tourist location by the great British holidaymaker. This was clearly in evidence after the islands of St Kitts and Nevis were featured in one episode: the following week, the St Kitts and Nevis Tourism Board was inundated with enquiries at the London International Dive Show; it estimated UK arrivals could rise by as much as 20 per cent.

As the duo's popularity soared ever higher, ITV had clearly learned from the BBC's mistake. It was determined not to lose its golden boys, and signed a golden handcuffs deal with them, estimated to be in the region of £800,000. 'It's true the boys have signed for the third series and there is no date when that will finish,' said their agent, Simon Jones. 'The series will run as long as it can. Ant and Dec were over the moon with the deal. They have great fun when filming and the deal means they can carry on having fun.'

It also meant that they could carry on making a great deal of money. Both have always been keen to play down their actual wealth, but there is no question that it was growing. It was a staggering amount of money to be earning at the age of just 24, especially given their working-class backgrounds, and yet another indication of the high regard in which they were held both in the industry and by their fans.

The BBC was all too aware of what it had lost. Chris Bellinger, Head of Children's Entertainment, was quite open about the fact that he was very sorry Ant and Dec were no longer doing children's TV at the Beeb. 'They have grown with the audience, they understand the audience and occasionally, yeah, they do seem to overstep the mark with their cheeky banter but, hey, that tends to be inevitable with live shows,' he said.

The hundredth episode of the show sparked a whole glut of admiration, including praise from, of all people, the actress Helen Mirren. 'I think they're geniuses, I really do,' she proclaimed. 'And so cute. Whenever I'm in England I get up early on Saturdays so I can watch their show in peace and just enjoy what they do. I think my husband is getting a bit jealous.' It was a defining moment. When Helen Mirren admits she gets up early to watch your show, then you are truly hot.

Other projects bubbled away in the pipeline. There was that potential film set in the music industry, still shelved but not forgotten, and the possibility of a sitcom, when and if time would ever allow. 'We've been working on a sitcom for nearly two years,' Ant revealed that spring. 'It's about two blokes abroad, that's all I'm saying. It's something we keep coming back to. We still love the idea, so it will happen, but it could be in six months or six years.'

Something else that was very much on the back burner was marriage. Lisa had by now moved in with Ant, and Clare, although she lived elsewhere, remained very much a feature in Dec's life. But both couples had been together for years now, prompting reporters to ask if they were ever going to get around to making it up the aisle? 'Not likely! Don't say it too loud,' said a slightly panicky Dec. 'Don't give them ideas. We're both still very happy and taking it as it comes. Seriously, we've got plenty of time for that and the girls are of that opinion as well. They've got their own careers and want to do their own thing. Clare has just bought her own flat. There's plenty of time for all that. We both fully intend doing it some day, but not just yet.' Of course, the two were also still very young – and very, very busy with their careers.

There remained one other question hanging over the boys and one that is there to this day: would they ever split up? They have talked about it. 'We both know at some point that one might want to go off and do something on their own, but we're cool about that,' said Dec. 'We've been offered solo stuff, but it hasn't really been right for us.'

Ant sounded slightly less sure. 'We're happy as we are,' he said. 'Besides the first job we ever did without the other would feel like we'd had our right arm chopped off.'

Anyway, why destroy such a successful partnership? As the end of 2000 rolled round, it was announced months before such a proclamation usually took place that Ant and Dec would be presenting the Brit Awards the following year. For this the boys were to be paid a cool £15,000. Each. 'The organisers don't usually look this far ahead when choosing the presenters but they know Ant and Dec are hot properties at the moment,' said an ITV source. 'They want to get them early so there's no chance of losing them. They figure that by March next year they'll be even bigger than they are now. It's a great choice and it's great they've agreed.'

He was certainly right there – Ant and Dec were getting bigger with every day that passed.

7

Nothing Succeeds Like Success

IT WAS clear by now that the boys' future was assured. They had not only programme makers but also rival channels battling it out for them, with the BBC desperate to hang on to the act they so recklessly lost a couple of years earlier and ITV equally desperate to make the boys entirely its own. And so, in November 2000, ITV finally pulled out all the stops and made the pair an offer they really couldn't refuse: £1 million each. It worked, and the boys announced that, after two successful seasons, they were leaving *Friends Like These*.

'It's a real shame they are leaving us because we think they're great,' said a BBC spokeswoman with commendable restraint. 'The door is always open for them to come back to the BBC.' Behind closed doors, of course, it was quite a blow. The then BBC Director, Greg Dyke, had proclaimed himself a fan, and while a third series of *Friends Like*

These did go out, presented by Ian Wright, it somehow lacked the magic.

ITV, meanwhile, was absolutely delighted. 'We're thrilled to be cementing our relationship with Ant and Dec,' said a spokeswoman for the channel. 'They are enormously popular and have shown themselves to be hugely talented across a range of different programmes.'

Ant and Dec themselves were extremely diplomatic and refused to rule out the possibility of working with the BBC again. 'Ant and Dec have a load of offers in front of them and unfortunately they can't do them all,' said a colleague. 'They are very much in demand and have been very successful in what they have done so far. It has been a hectic time for them, and they are now very much in the spotlight. I cannot reveal exactly what the new project is, but it is one they have been talking about doing for a while. They are determined to develop some of their ideas and unfortunately that has meant they are unable to carry on with *Friends Like These*. However, reports they have left the BBC are inaccurate. As far as I know, they have every intention of working with them again in the future, they have certainly not indicated there has been any major fallout.'

Nor had there been. Ant and Dec themselves were far too canny to involve themselves in a row: it was simply that they were now in the hugely fortunate position of being able to pick and choose the work they did. *SM:tv* was now getting 2.5 million viewers, against only one million for *Live and Kicking*, and it was almost entirely due to the two young presenters. Very fittingly, they finished off the year by winning two awards at the Children's Baftas: *SM:tv* won the entertainment category and the two were also given the special Kids Vote award, chosen by a panel of their adoring young fans.

The duo were jubilant. They were determined to press ahead with the sitcom they had been talking about for years, to say nothing of taking on more presenting roles – some of which were to make them even more high profile. The wounds from some of the early shows that hadn't quite worked were completely healed and Ant and Dec could now be said to have finally overtaken Chris Evans in their surreal and anarchic brand of TV.

In the spirit of the moment, Dec offered to buy his parents a £300,000 new home. They refused, saying they wanted to stay in their old council house. 'This is home to us and it always will be,' said Dec's mother, Anne. 'Dec's bedroom is just the same as when he left it. I keep it that way for him when he comes home to visit. Declan could afford to buy somewhere for us and has offered to do that but we don't want him to. It is his money and he worked hard for it.' He certainly had – and there was still a great deal more work to come.

Ant and Dec kicked off the New Year in as appropriate a manner as possible: by celebrating it on television. They had been asked to do a special Millennium show which was to have been pre-recorded, until at the last minute it was decided that it should go out live. The boys sailed fairly close to the wind on this one but managed it nonetheless: they began celebrating New Year's Eve in Newcastle, travelled down to London through the night and went straight on air. It is a testament to quite how deft they had become as performers that they managed to do the show at all, given the state they were in. Despite being given to boasting about how much they drank, they usually confined their drinking to after hours. This time it was almost part of the show.

'So we're in Newcastle at midnight, living it up down by the Quayside, and this big van comes to pick us up,' Ant recalled. 'So we got a crate of beer, drove all the way to the studio and went straight on air.'

'We were drinking Buck's Fizz between the cartoons,' said Dec. 'But, by 12.30, we'd started to sober up.'

'It wasn't pretty,' said Ant. 'Especially when you're pretending to be a Pokemón character.' It was an experience they didn't try again.

As Ant and Dec began to plot the next stage of their joint career, the Brit Awards loomed large, giving them a chance not just to revel in their massive popularity but also to show, yet again, just how down-to-earth they are compared with other big acts. Much good-natured teasing ensued about the diva-like demands of some of the world's biggest stars, people that Ant and Dec were now certainly mixing with in a professional capacity, even if they still maintained a lower profile in their private lives.

'The bigger the artist, the nicer they are,' said a charitable Ant. 'U2 came on our Saturday morning TV show and they were lovely. Then you get big American female singers like Jennifer Lopez, who haven't been

Above: Anthony McPartlin (*left*) and Declan Donnelly (*right*), fresh-faced and unaware of the huge success story that lay around the corner.

Below: The beginning of a marriage made in heaven.

Above: Playing their *Byker Grove* alter-egos, PJ and Duncan.

Below: All in the name of showbusiness … Dec (*right*) pictured while filming *Byker Grove*. His co-star is Brett Adams, who played Noddy in the series.

The cast of *Byker Grove* on a weekend away in Keilder.
Above: Dec with production secretary Dee Wood.

Below: Dec pictured with Jill Halfpenny who also cut her acting teeth in *Byker Grove*. She went on to play Kate in *Eastenders* and after winning *Strictly Come Dancing*, she landed the lead role of Roxy Hart in the West End musical *Chicago*.

Above left: Ant immerses himself in one of PJ's storylines.

Above right: Dec gets into the Christmas party spirit.

Below: Ant and Dec join other members of the *Byker Grove* cast, both past and present, to celebrate the 10th birthday of the show.

Above: It was Ant and Dec's parts in *Byker Grove* that led to them becoming a real-life pop duo.

Below: The lads celebrate after signing their record contract in November 1993.

Above left: Oh yes they did! Starring in *Snow White*, Christmas 1998.

Above right: Dec with his brother Dermott.

Below: Ant, Dec and Robbie Williams prepare for their New Year's Day show on Radio 1.

Above: Two stars who have not forgotten where they came from – opening the Gala Field Centre in Newcastle upon Tyne, a real-life Byker Grove.

Below: Causing mayhem and mirth wherever they go – appearing on Channel 4's *The Priory*.

You can take the boys out of Newcastle …
Above: Modelling one of the strips of their beloved Magpies.

Below: Switching on the lights in Newcastle City Centre.

Inset: Dec visits his old school, St Michaels R.C. School in Elswick, to present prizes to pupils.

around long [this was 2001] and they are notoriously difficult. I read stuff in the papers about what these divas demand and I think, That doesn't happen, but it genuinely does. That's the big thing people down the pub want to know – how many dressing rooms did she have on *Top of the Pops* when we presented it? We have to put our hands up and say Jennifer Lopez had 15 dressing rooms – she had 40 people with her, she had four chefs. We asked for a plate of biscuits in our dressing room and we still haven't got them. People like Jennifer are too cheeky – how can you ask for all of that? I got a PlayStation in my room when I was doing one show and I thought I was on to a winner, but it didn't work.'

Jennifer Lopez is, as Britney Spears once famously remarked, the diva who gives diva lessons to other divas, but the point was clear: the difference in style couldn't be more acute. Ant and Dec may have been millionaires by now, although both denied it, massively famous and even more massively popular, but both remained firmly fixed to their Geordie roots. Nor did they run wild with money. 'We are not massively extravagant, but we're not thrifty either,' said Dec. 'We're pretty sensible with money, really. Neither of us had a lot when we were growing up and having to struggle makes you more careful when you reach this position.'

And, although they were by now seasoned performers, both professed to nerves about the upcoming awards.

'When our management phoned us to say we'd been offered the Brits, we were like, "Yeah, yeah!"' said Dec. 'As a presenting job, you don't get a bigger night. It's always the scariest one. It's known for controversy, people getting on stage and this, that and the other. People keep saying, "What will you do if this happens?" We just don't know. But we don't want to be remembered as the most boring Brits – I might have to shout out, "Show your arse" to Ant if it's too quiet.'

As their fame increased, though, the boys were beginning to show an uncharacteristic sensitivity to one small problem: their fans, much as they loved them, couldn't always work out which one is which. (For anyone who has read this far and still isn't sure, Ant has the higher forehead and Dec is the shorter, cuter one.) They could laugh off being called gay, but seemed quite genuinely hurt at being deemed interchangeable. 'The worst is when people argue with you about who you are,' said Ant. 'I've told people I'm Ant and they say, "No, you're Dec." It does get quite upsetting and I sometimes wonder if people are going out of their way to call me Dec.'

It seems unlikely that they were, but Dec felt just the same way. 'I was talking to a shop assistant last week who said, "It's great to see you, I'm a really big fan, I've watched your career. Say hello to Ant for me." I thought he knew who we are, then he ruined it by saying, "Good to meet you, Ant."' It wasn't that high a price to pay for their fame, but it clearly rankled, and it was to continue to do so as the years went by.

They were keen, too, to show that, despite the famed closeness, both had a life of their own. 'We hardly ever fall out,' said Dec. 'We get a bit ratty with each other after a drink but we don't remember it the next day. If we do have a disagreement, we'll always sit down and discuss it. We spend a lot of time together at work, then we go out together. But we don't spend all day, every day together. We've got girlfriends and do separate things. I'll go away for the weekend with my girlfriend and Ant will go away with his. The four of us don't always go out or on holiday together. I keep hearing how we've got this out-of-the-ordinary relationship, but it's not like that. We both lived in Newcastle, but there was a whole bunch of us that were mates. Then me and Ant came to London, so we shared a flat.'

He might have been feeling a bit defensive, but Dec was wrong: they did and do have an extraordinary relationship. Even the great Morecambe and Wise, to whom Ant and Dec are now so often compared, didn't actually socialise together. Like Ant and Dec, Eric and Ernie met when they were still children and formed an extraordinary closeness and friendship but, because they spent their entire working lives together, they offset that by spending their private lives apart. Not so Ant and Dec. The bond between them is as unusual as it is deep.

In another interview the closeness between them was obvious when they were talking about their friendship:

> *Ant: Adult media is always looking for a seedy side …*
> *Dec: … or you get the thing that something obviously happened in our childhood that's made us cling to each other …*

Ant: ... whereas we're just pals. The teen mags just accept that we are happy-go-lucky fellas but the adult press ...
Dec: ... are like, 'Why are you such good friends? Why?'
Ant: Is it family life?
Dec: We've struggled to find a profound reason why we are such good friends, but I don't know if there is one. Maybe there is one, maybe I'm pooh-poohing something important. But I think we're still two quite simple, I don't mean simple as in thick ...
Ant: I think we're just quite easily content.

When not analysing their friendship, the two were clearly increasingly excited about the big night ahead. They had actually been to the Brits before during the course of their singing career, when they were nominated for the best newcomer award, which they eventually lost to Oasis – 'We travelled to the Brits in an ice-cream van,' said Ant, 'and got stuck in traffic, so by the time we got there all the photographers had gone. We climbed out of the ice-cream van really excited and no one cared!' – and professed themselves delighted they were now actually hosting the show. 'We both remember sitting there that night,' said Dec, 'and Chris Evans was hosting it and we were both saying, "I'd love to host this one day."'

That day had come. Now attention turned to what the boys would be doing and wearing on the big night. Did they have any lucky charms? they were asked. 'No,' said Dec. 'I used to have lucky socks, but I wore them to the FA Cup Final and Newcastle got beaten. They're at the back of my sock drawer now.'

'I'll wear white underpants,' said Ant. 'They're not lucky but I just prefer nice white pants rather than dark ones when I'm on telly.'

'Why?' asked Dec.

'I don't know,' said Ant. 'I just always do. They don't have to be completely new. I'm not like Ian McShane in *Lovejoy*, where in every shot he would be wearing a brand-new white T-shirt under his shirt. They just have to be white.'

'Well, I never knew that!' said Dec.

In the event, the evening went off smoothly and was actually dominated by Robbie Williams, who won three awards; Geri Halliwell looked alarmingly slim and made an alarmingly cheap remark as she presented an award to Robbie with the words, 'According to the press he has been giving me one, so now I'm going to give him one'; and Eminem put in his usual foul-mouthed performance.

Ant and Dec also discovered some unlikely fans: Coldplay, the British group whose lead singer, Chris Martin, is now married to Gwyneth Paltrow. The band won two awards, after which Chris remarked, 'The *NME* awards meant more to us because we're more "into" the *NME*. But the Brit Awards were fine, because we got to meet Ant and Dec. We're big fans of theirs!' It was high praise indeed. And the Ant and Dec golden touch seemed to have rubbed off on the programme itself: a month later the Brit Awards won the TV Music and Arts Programme in the annual Showbiz Awards.

Barely minutes after their triumphant appearance, the two scored yet another success. In March 2001 the BBC finally bowed to the inevitable, and announced it was axing *Live and Kicking*. Ant and Dec had won the Saturday morning ratings war. 'It was a difficult decision,' said Nigel Pickard. 'Everyone worked really hard on the show and it had a successful run over the last eight years but recently it has not performed as it once did and we are looking to the future with a fresh Saturday morning show for the autumn.'

It's one thing to beat a rival programme in the ratings war and quite another to be so massively successful that your rival is taken off air altogether. It was an absolute triumph for the two and, given that *SM:tv* was very much their baby, a true confirmation that they weren't just performers: they had brains and ideas, too.

SM:tv was more popular than ever, not least because Ant and Dec weren't afraid of mixing it with the children. The infants on the show weren't held at arm's length and treated with caution: rather, Ant and Dec almost descended to their level and acted like children, too. That old adage that you should never appear with animals and children was suspended in their case, not least because they came across as overgrown children themselves. One feature that brought that out in particular was a slot called 'Wonky Donkey', in which callers had to guess the rhyming identity of a cuddly toy. Dec would get increasingly frustrated as a poor child continued to get it wrong: 'It's got to rhyme!' he would bellow. 'Are you thick?'

Another segment of the show was called 'Challenge Ant'. A child would be called on to ask Ant a series of showbiz-related questions, for which he or she would receive small prizes. Then the child would get the chance to gamble all his or her winnings on a 'Killer Question'. If Ant got it wrong, he would have to put on a dunce's hat and endure a taunting song, in which the audience would chant, 'You're thick, you're thick ...' and the child would get a bigger prize, such as a DVD player. But, if he got it right, the child would be sent home empty-handed.

Some adult viewers questioned this, but the children seemed to emerge relatively unscathed and the audience loved it. 'We've been criticised for not being nicer to the kids,' said Conor McAnally, the show's executive producer. 'But the crucial thing is not to be patronising. If we run a game where the child gambles something and he loses, he gets nothing. As well as teaching them a valuable life lesson, there's also a big element of humour. When a kid loses, it's very funny.' No one appreciated this more than the show's adult audience. 'People sit there at home thinking, Yeah, serves you right, you smart little ...,' McAnally went on.

Everyone involved had reason to feel proud. *SM:tv*'s 2000 Christmas show featured a special edition of *Chums*, the spoof of *Friends*: it pulled in 3.5 million viewers, more people than were watching *Friends* itself. 'It's an extraordinary achievement,' said McAnally. 'We knew from the start that we'd try to take this different approach, try to do something we felt nobody else was doing. At that time, *Live and Kicking* was dominant. ITV had a 28 per cent share of the figures, with the BBC on 40 per cent. Our objective was to get level pegging. Now the whole thing's reversed. That's more than just a successful TV show, that's a phenomenon, a whole culture shock.'

Of course, not everything ran smoothly. The previous December they had run a one-off *Secret Camera Show*, as a segment in *Unzipped*, which included shots of naked buttocks and what appeared to be a woman expressing milk from her breasts. That got 39 complaints to the Independent Television Council, 32 of which were upheld.

And then their co-star Cat Deeley came in for some stick as well, not least when she was photographed with one exposed breast. The boys were merciless about it. Asked if they'd seen the pictures, Ant exclaimed, 'He cut it out! It's plastered all over the walls of his house. Wall-to-wall pictures of Cat! "No, Cat! Don't go into his room!"'

'It's not true,' protested Dec. 'When stuff does come out about her, she'll come into rehearsal and no one will say anything – we just get on with it. But this time she goes, "So … I presume you've seen the picture?" And we were trying so hard to keep a straight face, but we started pissing ourselves.'

The boys remained as good-natured as ever and didn't gloat about *Live and Kicking*'s demise. Instead, Dec returned home to his parents, where he took the opportunity to visit his old first school, St Michael's Roman Catholic Primary, in Elswick, where he presented reading awards to children and their parents. The visit was a surprise, eliciting yells of joy from the 200-odd pupils present when Dec entered the hall. 'I can't believe everything is so small,' said Dec. 'I know I haven't got that much bigger but it feels as though I am in the Land of the Giants. It all came flooding back, I can remember like it was yesterday. I can remember the quiet corner where I used to have a nap after drinking my milk. It was great to see their faces light up, I am glad they knew who I was – they normally think I am Ant.' There it was again, that little niggle, but Dec took the sting out of it by adding, 'He is tucked up in bed at home at the moment being looked after by his mam because he's come home for a few days as well.'

In fact, both boys had a well-developed social conscience. That summer Dec was to become, alongside the ex-MP and Governor of Hong Kong Sir Chris Patten, a patron of St Cuthbert's Care, a charity set up to help orphaned and abandoned children. His religious faith remained strong, too, and he wasn't afraid to talk publicly about the importance of prayer and confession.

Back in London, the boys were about to embark on their latest venture, a Saturday night offering called *Slap Bang*. They were taking a break from *SM:tv*, with the result that there was much joshing on the subject of that Friday night abstinence. 'We'd introduced a sex ban to stay fresh for our *SM:tv* show on Saturday mornings,' said Dec chirpily. 'But now we're going out live at 6.30pm with *Slap Bang*, we get a long lie-in for a change, and it's going to be nookie all the way.'

Not that they could resist a few more gay jokes at their own expense. 'That makes us laugh,' said Ant, of the gay rumours. 'We camp it up a bit on the show, but we've never got off with one another.'

'Well, there was that one time in the back of a taxi,' said Dec. 'But we were very drunk.'

'Oh yeah, it was lovely,' said Ant. 'He booked me into a nice hotel, there was champagne, everything.'

In fact, the two were still firmly involved with their girlfriends, although there were signs that Ant's relationship with Lisa was possibly stronger or more serious than Dec's with Clare. Indeed, there had been rumours that they had split up, although that was not true and upset Dec. 'Work is very big in our lives, but love is of equal importance,' he said. 'We've both been with our girlfriends a long time – Ant says we should get a loyalty bonus – and I think the secret of staying together has been to do everything they say.'

'The key to a long and happy relationship I've found is to not answer back ... and to buy them loads of shoes,' said Ant.

'I had my parents and friends calling up saying, "Why didn't you tell us?" [about the split with Clare] but we're still a couple and it's all fine,' said Dec. 'Ant was a good friend when I was upset by the split rumours. We're not so laddish that we can't talk to each other about our relationships and other sensitive issues.'

Meanwhile, preparations for the new show were well under way. 'I had created a show called *Celebrity Bar & Grill* as an Ant and Dec sitcom vehicle which I pitched to the network,' says Conor McAnally. 'They were interested but the whole thing went through a huge process of evolution which finally resulted in *Slap Bang*.'

Clearly, the hope was to emulate the success of *Chums*: there was to be a spoof of *Cheers*, entitled *Beers*, set in Ant and Dec's local pub; a segment entitled 'Formula Six and a Half', in which children were to race one another in mini grand prix cars; and 'Challenge Ant', in which OAPs, rather than children, asked him questions. In other words, the show was supposed to be an *SM:tv* for adults, which should perhaps have rung warning bells, given that *SM:tv* was itself already extremely popular among adults. But hindsight is a wonderful thing.

And, despite the success of *Friends Like These*, Ant and Dec had still not quite conquered prime-time television. They were still primarily considered to be children's entertainers, and both were well aware that, if they wanted to stay in the business over the longer term, that was a jump they were going to have to make. But, with a couple of near misses, programme-wise, behind them, they were also playing down their next move.

'I keep reading that doing prime time is our coming of age, and that we're making a leap into the world of adult TV,' said Dec. 'But we've never once said that's what we're doing. It's not as if we've changed or gone all grown up and are going to start being all serious and highbrow.'

'We're going for the same sort of audience we do on a Saturday morning,' said Ant. 'A family one. In the mornings, mum and dad potter around while watching us with the kids. Then there's the 20-something hangover lot watching us. Everyone goes off and does their own thing before coming back together at tea time. And that's where we come in. We're not trying to do serious stuff like *Millionaire* or *The Weakest Link*. It's just a bit of a laugh, really.'

But what everyone involved seemed to have forgotten was that prime-time television wasn't the right place for what was in essence still a children's show but with grown-up participants. Adults might watch children's television on Saturday morning, but they don't want to do so on Saturday night, which is why, for example, *Sabrina the Teenage Witch*, another children's show popular with young adults, has never been scheduled in prime-time television. But, at the time at least, everyone's hopes were high.

Ant and Dec themselves were determined to make a success of it. 'A few years ago, light entertainment was almost a dirty word,' said Dec. 'People thought it was uncool and preferred alternative comedians. But it's coming round again, although there's no one of our generation doing it. So hopefully it's the area we'll be able to monopolise – and make loads of money.'

On that last point at least, he wasn't joking. Dec has spoken in the past about going cold with horror when reading about a celebrity who once earned millions and now had nothing, and he and Ant were determined they weren't going to end up like that. All too aware of the fickle nature of television, both had by now employed the services of a financial adviser and were quietly building up a portfolio of investments. Neither was flash with his cash. 'I'm not extravagant,' said Dec. 'It must be because of our working-class backgrounds. It's not in our nature. I think it's extravagant just having a cleaner. I used to go around picking certain things up I didn't want her to see before she came. No, the most I've bought is a house, a car – just what normal people do.'

And so a great deal was riding on this new show. Conor McAnally, like everyone else, expected it to be a success, not least because of its two presenters. 'Performing large-scale live entertainment programmes is what they do well,' he said at the time. 'They are in a class of their own. Unlike others, they have a real relationship, they've lived in each other's pockets for the past 12 years and they think each other is the funniest guy on the planet. They are grounded; if they were all starry the public would pick up on it.'

They were prepared to make idiots of themselves as well: the show featured them taking the mickey out of pop stars, including Sir Elton John and George Michael. Ant played the current-day George, who travelled back in time to meet his younger self, played by Dec. Given that this was the early 1980s, Dec donned a Wham! T-shirt, an eighties wig, white tennis shorts and, just as George Michael had done, thrust a shuttlecock down his shorts. 'Obviously I didn't really need the shuttlecock down the trousers but I wanted my George to be historically correct,' confided Dec. Madonna and Michael Jackson were similarly lampooned.

And so the show began. Another unusual feature was that it went out live, something that hadn't been done for some time on Saturday night television, in the hope that it would add an extra layer of excitement to the show. It didn't. The first episode, which featured the boys' fan Helen Mirren, was pronounced 'pure drivel' by one critic and unfortunately the ratings said much the same. Over on the BBC, *Dog Eat Dog*, fronted by Ulrika Jonsson, pulled in 5.4 million viewers, while *Slap Bang* managed only 4.2 million. If that were not enough, soon afterwards Ian Wright took over hosting *Friends Like These*, which went out at exactly the same time as *Slap Bang*. It got 4.7 million viewers, as opposed to Ant and Dec's 3.5 million. Increasingly concerned ITV bosses moved *Slap Bang* to an earlier slot in the evening.

If the boys were concerned, they weren't showing it. They were getting high-calibre guests: Robbie Williams appeared on the show and seasoned actresses like Anita Dobson and Claire Goose were regulars. The audience, however, was not impressed: ratings now fell to three million, with one or two of the unkinder spectators of what was clearly becoming a debacle snidely muttering that the boys were getting their comeuppance for defecting from the BBC.

'I think its strengths were that it was funny and very slick for a live entertainment show and Ant and Dec were both excellent in it,' says Conor McAnally. 'Its main weaknesses were that it was playing to an audience who weren't yet familiar with Ant and Dec's relationship and therefore didn't get some of the gags. The show was probably pitched too young. The Saturday evening audience has a huge proportion of people over 50 and there wasn't much in the show for them. The constant schedule shuffling didn't help it much either.'

But when *Slap Bang* came to the end of its first (and only) run in July 2001, industry insiders, especially those at ITV, were cautious in the extreme when talking about the show. No one wanted to admit openly that it had been a failure, not least because no one wanted to antagonise Ant and Dec themselves. By this time it was accepted that, while they might not have pulled it off with one particular show, chances were that they would make up for it next time round, and so to criticise them in public might lead to them running off to yet another channel.

ITV bosses wouldn't even admit the show wouldn't be coming back. 'We are definitely doing more,' said Claudia Rosencrantz, ITV's Controller of Entertainment. 'It needs work on it. I thought parts of it were incredibly funny.' Perhaps they were, but the audience, the most important arbiters of TV success, did not, alas, agree.

8

Pop Idol

AS THE boys, not for the first time, began to reassess the situation, one thing was clear: they had made the transition from children's television presenters to adult entertainers, even if *Slap Bang* had not quite gone according to plan. They were now serious players in the television industry, and they knew it. 'The turning point was in our local pub,' Dec recalled. 'Before, we'd have blokes carrying their three pints back from the bar and they'd be shouting, "Oi! Are you ready to rhumble? Wankaahs!" Well, now they're shouting, "Oi! Wonkey Donkey!"'

And they still had *SM:tv* to fall back on. The two were getting naughtier than ever, quite deliberately getting as many double entendres into the show as they could, and, given the nature of some of them, it was hardly surprising people sometimes thought they were gay. 'We did a good one where I was an airforce wing commander, and I was enjoying breakfast with my pilots,' said a gleeful Dec. 'And I was saying, "If I can't slip my two favourite airmen a sausage in the morning, there's something seriously wrong."'

Nothing seemed to faze them. When Slash said 'fuck' on the show, they managed to make light of that, too. 'I was on the other side of the studio when Cat was interviewing him,' said Ant, 'so through my earpiece all I heard was, "We've had a fuck! We've had a fuck!" I was like, "What? In the gallery? During a live show?"'

Despite sailing so close to the wind, and despite the disappointment surrounding *Slap Bang*, Ant and Dec were becoming, if anything, even more popular. The problem with *Slap Bang*, of course, was that the formula wasn't right, rather than that the presenters weren't, which meant that the two escaped relatively unscathed from the proceedings. 'That [the failure of the show] kind of threw into doubt their ability to make the crossover, but maybe *Slap Bang* was too much like a slightly more grown-up version of *SM:tv*,' said Roger Fulton, deputy editor of *TV Times*. 'It just didn't work and it was quite embarrassing at times. But as presenters, they are terrific. There's no doubt that they have got a lot of personality and an appeal that works across the generations, but what they need is the right show.'

They didn't really need to worry – Chris Tarrant had a very similar problem when he tried to produce an adult version of *Tiswas*, and he certainly made good in the end. And other projects were flooding in. Proof, if any were needed, of quite how well the two were doing came that summer, when

Prince Charles invited them to Highgrove to do an interview with him. Part of it was to be screened on *SM:tv*, before going out in full the next day as part of a three-hour special on Party in the Park, the Prince's Trust concert.

'I suppose Ant and Dec are rather a surprising choice, but it came from the desire to reach those people who might not watch David Frost,' said Tom Shebbeare, chief executive of the Prince's Trust. 'It was great to see how the Prince can identify with people of that age group and get on very well with them. Our target group might never have heard about the Trust but they might listen to Ant and Dec and realise what the Trust could do for them.'

In the event, the interview went swimmingly, with the Prince confiding he was a great fan of Catatonia and Tom Jones, highly diplomatic choices inasmuch as both hailed from Wales.

And so the march towards adult presenting went on. There were rumours that *Slap Bang* was to be recommissioned for a second series, but these turned out to be untrue, as well as rumours that the two were considering leaving *SM:tv*. This was much closer to the mark, although no one wanted to admit it as yet. 'To be honest, I don't know how much longer Ant and I will be at *SM:tv*. It's not up to us any more,' said a slightly disingenuous Dec. 'It's up to ITV boss David Liddiment. It's his decision where he will place us, so I'm not sure what will happen at *SM:tv*. Our fate rests in ITV's hands.'

In fact, the boys were reaching a level where they could pretty much name their price. It was almost inconceivable that ITV would really want to lose a children's Saturday morning show that had beaten the BBC for the first time in a generation, and nor would it want to upset two of its biggest stars. The real people who had a say over what Ant and Dec would do next were Ant and Dec. And they knew what they wanted to do. They wanted to grow up.

Ant and Dec's next project could have been put together with them in mind. There was to be a new television series in which a panel of judges would put some hopeful youngsters through their paces and at the end of it the winner would become a singing sensation. The programme was, of course, *Pop Idol*, and who better to host it than two of the most popular presenters on television who had themselves had a singing career? Step forward Ant and Dec – and this time the programme was to go on to be a resounding success. Despite doubts from some quarters, the show had that most essential of attributes: a good formula. All it needed was a good team, and Ant and Dec were the perfect choice to front it.

The boys themselves made light of their previous singing career. 'We will probably be telling them how not to go about making it in the music industry,' said Ant.

'Everybody who takes part seems nervous,' added Dec. 'But there are some people who seem to be able to handle that and give a brilliant performance, so I suppose they could have what it takes. There are quite a few people where you think, My God, why did they get out of bed this morning? Some of them were a bit deluded.'

'But the judges told them that,' said Ant.

'Our job was just to chat to hopefuls,' said Dec. 'And we

had it all – the tears, people getting angry, people wanting to go back in and do it again or to have an argument with the judges. If you wrote any of what happened, people would say it was too far-fetched. But I tell you what – there is nowt so queer as folk.'

'We only sat in on a few auditions, just to see the judging process, and then we were at the back, out of view,' said Ant. 'But there were times I was in hysterics. I wouldn't have laughed in front of them, because that could destroy someone's confidence, but one time we were laughing so much we were told to get out. I know we make fools of ourselves on a regular basis, but we're paid for it!'

And how, they were asked, would PJ and Duncan have fared? 'I don't think we would have got past the first stage,' said Dec. 'We wouldn't have got a recall.'

'I think you are being a bit hard on yourself,' said Ant. 'On all our records, he used to sing and I used to gently rap. I got away with it for a few years.'

And what would Cat Deeley be like as a pop idol? 'She's got everything,' said Dec. 'She's got the looks and personality, but she can't sing a bloody note.'

'I don't think we will be stepping back into our musical shoes,' said Ant. 'Pete Waterman asked about doing something new, but it hasn't made us yearn to be pop stars again.'

If their stories about the auditions can be believed, the boys saw some very eccentric sights among the array of would-be pop stars who paraded in front of them. 'There were singing Elvises in full costume,' said Ant.

'With one leg,' said Dec.

'Aye, with a wooden leg,' said Ant. 'There was one girl wearing a lacy top and we jokingly said, "Are you wearing your mam's net curtains?" And she said, "Yeah, I am!" She'd cut down her mam's net curtains and sewed sleeves on to a T-shirt ...'

'She said, "If I don't get through the audition, I've got to sew them back into a pair of curtains,' said Dec.

Ant added, 'She didn't get through.'

There was more. 'Then there was the 48-year-old Indian man who couldn't speak English,' said Dec. 'He didn't want to sing, he just wanted to recite Hindu poetry.'

'I'm sure he just wanted to lech at the young girls,' said Ant.

'We told him he was too old to audition,' said Dec, 'so he said, "Right, I'll just sit here", and he sat in the corner looking at all the girls.'

'There was one guy,' said Ant, 'with a big tache and glasses. He was more than 30 and we said, "Well, you can't audition but you're more than welcome to sing now in the registration hall." And he started singing "Any Dream Will Do". We joined in with him and had a bit of a singalong, and afterwards all the kids really applauded.' Was he any good? 'No!' said Ant. 'But he had bottle. These people have seen *Popstars*, so they know that, if they're weird or wacky, they're more likely to be given airtime.'

And if anyone were in any doubt as to Ant and Dec's suitability to front the show, the pair topped it all off by being named as Britain's most popular entertainment presenters at the National Television Awards.

Of course, the cuddly twosome provided a wonderful contrast to Simon Cowell, whose role on *Pop Idol* sometimes seemed to come perilously close to trying to make the contestants cry. Ant and Dec brilliantly set themselves up to side with the youngsters appearing on the show, rather than the judges, and weren't afraid to berate Cowell for his harshness. 'Oh, that Simon Cowell is a nasty piece of work,' said Ant. 'There is an element of truth in everything he says, but he doesn't have to say it so harshly.'

'It is so uncalled for. We have told him off,' said Dec. 'We say, "Simon, you don't have to say that." And he says, "Yes I do." He says we are presenting *Pop Idol*, not *Very Nice Singing Idol*. He says he doesn't want to lie.'

Professionally, everything was back on track, but in the boys' personal lives it was a different story. Ant and Lisa were still blissfully happy together, but Dec and Clare were still experiencing problems, and so split up briefly, before deciding that they wanted to be together after all. 'We had a break,' admitted Dec. 'She was going off to do a play and we realised we had been together for eight years. We were questioning why we were still together. So I told her to go off and do the tour. We would not get in touch and she could do anything she liked. I haven't asked her if she did – that was the deal. But we agreed that, if we were still looking forward to seeing each other at the end of the tour, then we would be together for the right reasons.'

In the event, the couple were reunited, but Dec's lack of concern over what Clare had been doing while she was away did suggest that this was one relationship that wasn't going to go the distance.

Further signs that all was not well came in October 2001, when Dec committed his one and only transgression to date. After a lifetime of avoiding celebrity pratfalls, poor old Dec found himself in the clutches of a lap dancer – and one who had already publicly talked about her profession in a Sunday newspaper. It all began when Ant and Dec visited Secrets nightclub in London. Ant seemed faintly amused by the whole set-up, while Dec was quite clearly carried away by the whole experience. During the course of the evening he actually spent £800 getting the girl to dance – about as out of character for one so fresh-faced and so careful with his money as it was possible to get.

The dancer was called Tina Benson, although she danced under the name of Fame, and Dec wasn't her first encounter with celebrity – she had form. Richard Branson had also been on the receiving end of her charms, although only on the dance floor, while she had happily boasted about a threesome with Robbie Williams and a fling with *Royle Family* star Ralf Little. It is unlikely that Dec was aware of this past – otherwise he would have realised that Tina was only too happy to talk about her night in his hands.

'I couldn't believe it when Ant and Dec came in with a bunch of friends,' she said. 'I recognised them straight away and was very pleased when Dec asked me over to their table. They both seemed very nervous at first and needed a few drinks to help them relax. We sat at the table and just talked for a while. We got chatting about our personal lives, and we just clicked straight away. Dec told me he had recently split up from his long-term girlfriend and I told him I had also broken up with my boyfriend. He was very charming and told me he loved blondes and said I was very beautiful and wanted me to dance for him. I explained the rules to him and told him that, if he wanted a dance, it would cost £10, £15 to take my top off or £20 to strip completely. He gave me this cheeky chappy grin and asked if I would strip for him. After that he just kept waving £20 notes at me and getting me to dance naked for him. It was fantastic.'

Bystanders couldn't believe what they were seeing. Not only was Dec famously clean-living, but, more to the point, he had never made a blunder like this before. The boys had been impeccably behaved during their years as pop stars and had never once taken advantage of the many fans willing to throw themselves in their path. But Dec was clearly enjoying every minute of it. 'Dec was splashing around a lot of cash,' said one of Tina's fellow lap dancers. 'He wanted Tina to perform for him and him only and gave her £800 to spend the whole evening just with him. Dec was loving every minute of it. He was sitting there with this fixed grin on his face and his eyes were on stalks. Normally the girls move around the tables dancing for different men, but Dec only wanted Tina. She was loving the fact that he was a star and only wanted her to dance for him. Tina stuck to him like glue for the rest of the night until the club closed.'

Actually, she stuck with him later still: the two repaired to his house and the following week she gave an even more lurid account of what had gone on between them. Suffice it to say that everyone appeared to have enjoyed themselves until the next morning, at least, when Dec sobered up and realised what he'd done. Not only that: it appeared Tina wanted more than just a night of fun. She had hoped for a singing career herself, and by her own admission wondered if Dec might be able to help. 'I wanted to ask Dec about getting me on his show, maybe as a backing dancer or something,' said Tina coyly. 'I've got his number and we are good friends but I would feel embarrassed about asking him, it wouldn't be right.'

It says something about the world in which we live that a lap dancer would be perfectly happy to sleep with Dec hours after meeting him and then reveal all the gory details in a newspaper afterwards, but would be far too shy to ask for help in her career, but there you have it. Anyway, Tina couldn't have chosen a worse way to go about it. Dec is a good Catholic boy, who would have been ashamed of his actions and appalled by the publicity they attracted, on top of which his relationship with Clare, rocky as it sometimes seemed, wasn't yet over for good. Shortly afterwards Tina claimed that he rang her and told her he had been reunited with his ex. As for Dec himself, unsurprisingly, he has never wanted to dwell on it and would only say, 'I have been to confession and I am forgiven. The whole thing brought Clare and me closer together.' He clearly learned his lesson: there has never been a similar episode since then.

Ant and Dec were still suffering from that other, growing frustration: people were still not able to tell them apart. Both were clearly beginning to find it increasingly irksome. 'On *SM:tv*, we have segments like "Challenge Ant", which is me being challenged, and "Dec Says", which is Dec reading out letters,' said Ant. 'There's another called "Ant's Songs", where I sing songs kids have sent in. All these are pointers to the fact that I'm Ant and he's Dec. But people still get it wrong.'

'We have this cunning plan which you may not have noticed,' added Dec. 'Whenever we're on telly or in photos we always stand so that, left to right, it's always Ant and Dec. But at the end of the day, I don't know which one's Hale and which one's Pace or which one's Mel and which one's Sue.'

But then even journalists sometimes got it wrong. Reading through interviews the boys have done over the years, it is not unusual to see Ant described as one of seven children, with a brother who is a priest, while Dec is described as coming from a broken home. In such cases their details have, of course, been mixed up.

It seemed utterly fitting that in November 2001 Ant and Dec attended the première of *The Play What I Wrote*, a tribute to Morecambe and Wise. Dec had long boasted that he knew all the great comedy duo's routines off by heart, and by this time Ant did, too. The play had become famous for featuring a mystery guest every evening, which gave the boys plenty to muse upon, given that Cat was there, too. 'We've been snubbed,' said Ant. 'Cat was asked to see the show so she could think about doing a cameo, but they haven't asked Dec or me yet. She'll probably take the role and it will launch a glittering stage career. In five years' time, she won't remember who we are.'

Dec, meanwhile, declared himself delighted to be paying homage to his heroes. 'I've been a fan for years, collecting annuals and sheet music off the internet,' he confided. 'I only had one chance to meet Ernie Wise, after a *This Is Your Life* show a few years ago, but I was too nervous and bottled out.'

As *Pop Idol* began to soar in the ratings, the boys made an extremely canny decision: they were to leave *SM:tv*. That transition to adult television had worked: while they might not, as yet, have found the suitable format for them and them alone – *Pop Idol* worked, but it wasn't actually a vehicle for the boys – it was clear they would soon be able to bridge the gap. And the boys were well aware of that showbusiness adage: always leave them wanting something more. *SM:tv*, which had by now garnered 14 awards, had been a stunning success and an enormous achievement and it was very sensible to leave while it was at its peak. *SM:tv* had even prompted no less a figure than Bono to announce to the boys, 'You are one of the great couples of our time.'

So the announcement was made. 'We have always loved doing *SM:tv* and *CD:UK*, so it was always going to be a hugely difficult decision to leave the show,' said Ant. 'We always said we wanted to go out on top and, after much thought, feel that this is the time for us to move on. As co-creators of the show, we are immensely proud of what *SM:tv* and *CD:UK* have achieved.'

An indication of quite how successful *SM:tv* had been came in the guest list for the final show: Mariah Carey, Robbie Williams, Hear'say, Dane Bowers, Denise Van Outen and Samantha Mumba were just some of the big names who appeared.

Some rather unusual fans took it really quite badly. 'The other day I was at the airport and this old lady came up and had a go at me about it,' said a slightly astonished Dec. 'She thought it was out of order for us to leave. My sister won't even talk to me – she has been in tears. And people stop me in the street and tell me they are really angry with us for leaving. It's amazing the reaction we have had.'

Everyone involved was equally upset. 'I remember the last *Chums* where Dec and Cat got married,' says Dean Wilkinson. 'The episode finished and I suddenly burst into tears. I thought, I'm not gonna be writing with Ant and Dec again.'

To date he was right, although the boys did help him further when they penned a foreword to one of the books in the *Legends of Arthur King* series, an act, according to Dean, that was almost certainly a factor in its success.

It was decided that the show would continue, now hosted by Cat and James Redmond. Tess Daly and Brian Dowling came on board soon afterwards. Cat, while putting a brave face on it, was also clearly saddened by the news. 'We went for a farewell drink before the last show and that was when it hit us,' she said. 'It's the end of an era and they're always sad. But we've lived in each other's lives for three years now, so we'll go out and keep in touch. We might even work together again because there's such good chemistry.'

Ant and Dec themselves certainly had no shortage of

offers of work while they decided what their next big move would be. They were to present the Record of the Year 2001 in December, on top of which an NSPCC poll, conducted among children to see who they would most like to be their spokesman on issues such as bullying, child abuse and education, put them on top, with more than 40 per cent of the votes. This tribute actually reduced Ant's mother to tears.

'A helluva lot of responsibility, I don't know whether I would like to take it, although my mam was over the moon,' he recalled. 'She said, "This is such an honour, son." But we take our responsibilities towards our younger audience very seriously. We never refuse to sign an autograph either – it only takes a minute to say, "How ya doing, pal?" Then they skip away happy. It's hardly a pain in the arse.'

'We'd never set a bad example,' added Dec. 'We sometimes get drunk in our local pub, but that's about it.'

In truth the two were in some ways wise beyond their years, and both believe that might have had something to do with the strength of their friendship. Asked about their domestic set-up, Dec replied, 'My house is all magnolia and oatmeal coloured, which might sound a bit middle-aged, but I think it's because we've had our ups and downs – we had to grow up quick – much of it has been insecure and sporadic. What Ant and I crave is a little consistency. That's why we've been constants in each other's life.'

'We wanted a bit of security,' added Ant. 'We want to have a mortgage, a home and enough money to feel secure for the rest of our lives.'

Projects continued to pile up, with one in the pipeline

that was particularly close to the boys' hearts. Now that they were associated again with the music business through *Pop Idol*, the Football Association had them in mind to record the official England anthem for the 2002 World Cup. The song hadn't yet been written, but FA bosses were determined that it should be the duo who would sing it. 'Ant and Dec are the ones we want,' said an FA insider. 'They're massive Newcastle supporters and know a lot about football. And they're also the most popular people on TV. We're hoping to recreate the buzz David Baddiel and Frank Skinner's "Three Lions" had during Euro '96. That sold a million and we think that, with Ant and Dec's appeal, they could beat that. We made a mistake for the last World Cup when we got the Spice Girls to sing the official song. But we're sure that, with Ant and Dec, we'd be on a winner.'

Even before the boys were officially approached, it was fairly certain that they would want to be involved. 'They worship Newcastle,' said a friend. 'When they were kids, they wanted to play for the team. They were never good enough. But this would be the next best thing.'

As *Pop Idol* continued to be a national obsession, it also threw up remnants of the boys' pasts. In January 2002, when Hayley Evetts made it to the finals of the show, she revealed that she had actually first met Dec in 1996 at an awards bash, when she had been pictured hugging him. She appeared almost as excited to renew her acquaintance with her hero as she was to make it to the finals of *Pop Idol*. 'I used to have a crush on Dec when he was in *Byker Grove*,' she admitted.

A friend of the singer went one step further. 'Hayley was completely obsessed with Dec – she really fancied him,' she said. 'She could not believe her luck when she finally got to meet him backstage after a Smash Hits awards bash. The pair of them got on particularly well that day. There was some chemistry between them. Sadly, though, both went their separate ways after that night.' They went their separate ways again after *Pop Idol*, too, not least because they both had partners now.

Hayley was duly voted off the show and Ant and Dec were forced into a diplomatic role, apologising to the audience when Simon Cowell swore at Pete Waterman during a heated debate about the abilities of Darius Danesh. Meanwhile, over at *SM:tv*, ratings were beginning to suffer in the wake of the boys' departure: by the end of January 2002, less than a month in with the new team, the show had lost a quarter of its viewers. Rather wisely in the circumstances, Cat decided to leave, too, although she was staying with *CD:UK*. 'I have been offered exciting projects, and I was torn between these and leaving the show I loved,' she said. 'By continuing with *CD:UK* I can still be part of the great team and concentrate on new projects as well.'

On Saturday night, however, viewers were turning on in their droves: *Pop Idol* had more than nine million people watching regularly, and that rose to ten million as the last show in the series drew near. The programme was fast becoming a national obsession. As the final show approached, the contestants were narrowed down to three: Will Young, Gareth Gates and Darius Danesh. The three were now attracting almost as much attention as the judges and hosts, with dark mutterings about a North/South divide influencing the voters (the North favoured Gareth, the South Will). In fact, the threesome became so popular that they were whisked away to Ireland to perform as a supporting act for S Club 7 – a concert that was, almost inevitably, hosted by Ant and Dec.

An unfortunate reminder of *Slap Bang* popped up at this point. The Broadcasting Standards Commission publicly reprimanded the duo for an item in which Dec pulled a plastic toy pistol from his pocket and pretended to shoot a departing Bill Roache, aka Ken Barlow in *Coronation Street*. He had been referring to him as Ken, not Bill, with Roache pretending to get annoyed and storming off the set. Parents across the land weren't pleased and a viewer complained.

'The hosts were primarily known for their work as children's television presenters and younger children and teenagers would have been drawn to the show,' said the BSC, upholding the complaint. 'The panel considered the depiction of the firearm had been realistic and demonstrated how effective use of a gun could be made in controlling situations.'

A spokesman for ITV1 said stiffly, 'The whole sketch was a broad farce, with over-the-top gusto in the best tradition of knockabout comedy. The gun was a toy and clearly not real.'

It was an uncomfortable reference back to one of their less successful projects, but the boys, as ever, moved on. Plans were advancing for a new prime-time show – not a second series of *Slap Bang*, as had been erroneously reported some months earlier – and the timing couldn't have been better as far as Ant and Dec were concerned. *Pop Idol* had, of course, been a huge success, but the two were still aware of the need to front a prime-time show that revolved around them, rather than one in which they merely played a part. So, when they were asked to front a documentary about the making of *Pop Idol*, they showed some reluctance to get on board. In public they said they loved the idea, but privately they were more circumspect. Ant was spotted having a drink with some friends in London's Sanderson Hotel, during which he shared his misgivings. 'He didn't seem very keen,' said a fellow drinker. 'When asked if they were going to do it, Ant just said, "I don't know, it depends if we want to be seen as *Pop Idol* people."' Their agent pooh-poohed this, saying they would love to do the show. Clearly, everyone involved realised *Pop Idol* had become very big indeed.

9

Back to the Future

The nation really was caught up in what was happening in their new obsession. And *Pop Idol* fever only intensified as Darius was voted off the show, leaving Will and Gareth to go head to head. Gareth had been the favourite to win, not least because he won over the hearts of the country by managing to overcome a severe stutter, but Will put on such a polished performance that it seemed he was moving ahead of his rival. 'Will's performance astonished everyone last night,' said an insider on the show.

'All week it was too close to call between Darius and Will, who were trailing Gareth in second place. But so impressed were the public with Will's singing that he shot way ahead of Darius when the polls closed. Now there's a real feeling that next Saturday Will could achieve what many people thought to be impossible only a few hours earlier and actually go on to win the top prize.'

The contestants themselves were wilting under the strain, with Will admitting, 'I feel like screaming. It was just mad. This was the worst week as far as nerves go.'

Ant and Dec joined in the fun, revealing that Robbie Williams was backing Will. 'He voted for Will a couple of weeks back and he's planning to do so again,' said Dec.

On the eve of the final they went further, admitting that they had been rooting for fellow Geordie Aaron Bayley. 'It would have been great if Aaron had gone further,' said Ant. 'He's a great lad with this amazing voice.'

'We struck up a rapport with him from the word go on the show, perhaps more than with the others,' Dec chipped in. 'He's a Geordie, man. We have a kinship. There will be an outright winner but Aaron, as with all the ten finalists, is a winner in his own right. We had a great laugh with him. He'll go far. He's just a canny, down-to-earth lad.'

Whatever their thoughts about who was going to win, Ant and Dec professed themselves amazed at quite how big the show had become. Not only was it garnering an audience of millions, something increasingly rare in these multi-channel days, but it was even getting millions ringing in to vote. It was the kind of programme that the whole family could watch, and they were doing. 'We're being totally truthful here,' said Dec. 'When we agreed to do it, we didn't have a clue it would turn into this phenomenon, with almost six million viewers voting. It just grew, grew, grew. Suddenly everyone was talking about it. All the family wanted to know the gossip, too.'

'It was incredible watching these kids coming though the

audition process,' added Ant, 'in front of that panel of judges and then going on to perform like that on live TV. Every time you picked up a paper it was all about *Pop Idol*. At the beginning we didn't know how the public would take to it. It seemed like a good idea to us, but what do we know? Suddenly everyone was gripped by it, and the talk down the pub was all *Pop Idol*. Even Simon Cowell helped it on its way – but don't tell him I said that!'

The pair were their usual modest selves about their own contribution to the success of the show, claiming it was the contestants, not the presenters, who were the stars.

The big night came and, as the world now knows, Will won. Viewers phoned in in their millions, with 8.7 million getting through, making it Britain's biggest-ever phone poll. So great was the demand on the nation's phone lines that the system went into meltdown, while viewing figures had now risen to 15 million. Will was in tears. 'When they said the percentages, I just thought I was second,' he said afterwards. 'I had lost by this much. I thought, Oh well, that's not bad. When they said I'd won, I stepped backwards. I couldn't believe it.'

Poor Gareth appeared to be in shock. He had been widely expected to win, and looked so distraught that even Simon Cowell dropped his Mr Nasty act, putting an arm around Gareth's shoulders and whispering, 'You're still a star – and I am still giving you a record contract. This isn't an end, it's a beginning.'

Gareth himself, after the initial shock, was magnanimous in the extreme. 'If there is one person who deserves this, it is Will,' he said. 'We have become really good friends and he is an awesome guy. Of course, I am disappointed, but I've really enjoyed the whole experience. I am experiencing all sorts of emotions – I'm genuinely happy for Will – but obviously I wanted to win!'

Will was equally generous about his rival. 'When they said I'd won, there was this feeling ... of being really isolated. And suddenly there was this whole audience here and I felt like I had woken up again. I am absolutely ecstatic. There was no loser on *Pop Idol* tonight. I think there were two winners.'

Ant and Dec were amused by his reaction. 'Your face!' Ant told him. 'I thought you were going to keel over.'

At the after-show party Ant and Dec proved themselves to be true sports: they sang 'Let's Get Ready to Rhumble', a brave thing for two grown men to do. It was a riotous night. 'At 2.30am the bar stopped serving drinks, but we refused to go home,' said Kate Thornton, who had presented ITV2's weekly *Pop Idol Extra*. 'It was like one of those parties you never want to leave.' It had been a glorious occasion for all involved.

As it happens, Will was right: there were two winners (or three if you count Darius Danesh, or even more if you count Rik Waller and countless others who made a name through the show). Given that Gareth had been widely expected to win, recording contracts were already in the bag, not least because money can't buy the kind of publicity *Pop Idol* had generated, and Gareth was guaranteed to be the subject of major media interest for some time to come. He made better heartthrob material than Will, too, for it turned out that Will was gay and thus unable to allow all but the most optimistic (and unrealistic) teenage girl fans to imagine that he might one day be theirs. The result could hardly have been more cheering: both Will and Gareth are now stars.

The fuss surrounding the show hadn't done any harm to its presenters, either. Ant and Dec had presided over something that had turned out to be a phenomenon, uniting the country around the television set in a way that hadn't been seen for well over a decade (something that Eric and Ernie, incidentally, had also once done with unerring results). It had increased their already high profile and was almost certainly a component in their winning television personalities of the year in February's Variety Club's fiftieth Showbusiness Awards – not bad going, given that they were still only 26.

It was decided that the one-off special about the show would go ahead – and indeed it would be presented by Ant and Dec. They, meanwhile, said they loved the whole experience so much that they would be buying tickets to the forthcoming *Pop Idol* tour. But they also needed a rest. *Pop Idol* had turned into such an all-consuming experience that it had been exhausting in itself, and that was without taking into account the rest of their work schedule. It is said that the best actors are those who make acting look easy, and so it is with Ant and Dec. The two remain the personification of laid-back charm, and yet their workload rivalled that of Chris Evans. To stay at the top in the entertainment industry is no mean feat, requiring extremely hard work and an ability for reinvention, but the two weren't going to let go of what they had now.

Not that there seemed much danger of that happening. They were developing a new prime-time slot which they remained very coy about, and that World Cup song was on the horizon. 'We don't know what the song will be, but, if we like it, yes, we'll do it,' said Dec.

'If it gets us free flights to Japan and Korea, we'll do it,' added Ant.

But they did need a break and were planning on spending some time back home. 'Time to spend with the family, friends, partners, definitely,' said Ant. 'Time back in Newcastle and somewhere hot to chill out. It's been non-stop for months.' And, in truth, it had been non-stop for years, and was going to continue to be so.

As to whether they were going to go somewhere hot together, they kept shtum – despite that vow a few years earlier to holiday separately, old habits are hard to break and the two, with their girlfriends, had still taken some vacations together. (Dec indignantly pointed out that it had made sense: he and Clare had booked a villa with three bedrooms, so why shouldn't Ant and Lisa go along too?)

But the two were getting increasingly excited about another project they had been working on, one that had been simmering away in the background for some months and was now ready to be unveiled to the world. It was a project very dear to their hearts, for it involved their beloved Newcastle and what was probably the most famous television series to be set in the North-East. And who better to recreate what had now become a television legend? Yes, the two boys were going back to the future. They were going to star in a remake of *The Likely Lads*.

The world of television was awash with rumours. The news was spreading fast: Britain's current most popular Geordies, Ant and Dec, were making plans to pay homage to the most popular Geordies of 30 years earlier, Rodney Bewes and James Bolam, in a remake of a classic episode of *The Likely Lads*. Opinion was sharply divided on the issue: on the one hand, Ant and Dec were clearly the obvious choice to play a pair of working-class friends based in Newcastle, but, on the other, was this wise?

Classic television series from the past are often best left just there: witness Reeves and Mortimer, said the doubters, who had recently tried to do exactly the same thing with *Randall and Hopkirk Deceased*. It hadn't been a patch on the original. Were Ant and Dec in danger of messing about with people's memories of the older series and damaging themselves in the process?

One person who was in favour of the new show was Rodney Bewes, the star of the original. He called the old show a gentle comedy about a gentle world, pointing out that there was no sex, swearing or drunkenness in the programme. It was certainly a snapshot of a long-lost Britain: pre-decimalisation, with only the test card to watch on daytime television and with a certain gentility that seems to have been lost since then. The episode in question was to be 'No Hiding Place', in which the boys desperately try to avoid hearing the results of the England versus Bulgaria football match, until they see the highlights on *Match of the Day*. That in itself was a sign of the changing times – these days they would probably have watched the game live on a hand-held portable television – if they weren't watching it on Sky Sports in a pub.

The idea had originated about 18 months earlier. Ant and Dec had appeared on a *This Is Your Life* devoted to Denise Welch and, while there, bumped into the original Geordie duo. The newcomers revealed that they were great fans of the original series, at which point someone had the bright idea of doing a remake. Rodney Bewes agreed to appear in a cameo role, as a one-legged newspaper seller whom the boys try to avoid as they don't want to see the match results on his newsstand. Ant and Dec themselves were thrilled with the idea. 'Ant and I really bonded over the *Likely Lads* repeats,' said Dec. 'I suppose we are lads and we are likely. I have so much respect for the original series and of course they're two lads from Newcastle and so are we. We were born in 1975 and we grew up with all the repeats.'

The writers of *The Likely Lads* were Ian La Frenais and Dick Clement, who were also responsible for *Auf Wiedersehen, Pet*. They had been based in the United States for decades, but returned to these shores for a brief visit, partly because of Ant and Dec's project and partly to launch a third series of *Auf Wiedersehen, Pet*, a mere 12 years after the last one. These long gaps were something of a feature of their writing career. *The Likely Lads* had first gone out in three series in the early 1960s, but it was another decade before they became firmly established in the public consciousness, with two series of *Whatever Happened to the Likely Lads*, and it was this later material that Ant and Dec were reprising.

La Frenais and Clement had met four decades earlier and formed a partnership that was, in its way, to be as enduring as Ant and Dec's. They had the same habit of speaking in tandem, too. When they first met, through a mutual friend at the London School of Economics, Clement was a BBC trainee and La Frenais was unemployed after a stint selling cigarettes for Gallaghers. 'He was having his gap year,' explained Clement.

'They didn't call it a gap year then,' said La Frenais.

'What did they call it?'

'Being out of work.'

The two first worked together on material for a pub cabaret, which was in turn to become a sketch that Clement was asked to direct as part of his training for the BBC. This was the first manifestation of *The Likely Lads*, and the BBC was soon expressing an interest in a series, which was to be the first British television comedy to be set outside London. The two realised immediately the kind of opportunity they had in their hands. 'It's like suddenly somebody chucked you the ball and you found yourself in a small field and you decided you'd better run with it,' said Clement. 'We just said, "If we blow this, we'll never have another chance."' Not only did they not blow it, but it also was the start of a very illustrious career. The two were also responsible for, among much else, *Porridge* and the screenplay for *The Commitments*.

And now Ant and Dec were to reprise the famous roles. But, as ever where Ant and Dec were concerned, this was only one of several projects in the pipeline. They were still working on a top-secret idea for that prime-time Saturday night slot, along with dealing with the continuing interest in *Pop Idol* – the series might have finished, but the national obsession with it certainly hadn't, and it went on to win a Bafta for the best entertainment programme.

And then there was that year's Brit Awards. Ant and Dec weren't presenting them, which was being seen as a snub in some quarters, and indeed had initially been overshadowed by this year's host, Frank Skinner, who had been paid £50,000 to host the awards, considerably more than the Geordie duo. In the event, his performance was widely acknowledged not to have been a success. Skinner himself acknowledged this to be the case, brusquely snapping, 'Fuck off', when asked if he'd host the awards again.

Ant and Dec were sympathetic, revealing that, despite the way they had appeared on the night, the experience hadn't been a happy one. 'It was one of the most horrible things we have ever had to do,' said Dec. 'It really was an endurance for us. The music industry is possibly one of the most difficult audiences. It was very weird. We weren't at all upset at not being asked to do anything for this year's ceremony. When we had finished last year, everyone said how well we'd done but we were just relieved it was over. I thought Frank was quite good actually – he had a hard job.'

As for what that new prime-time show would be, the boys were enjoying keeping everyone guessing. 'We're doing a new, ground-breaking Saturday evening show this spring, which involves celebrities, but it's devised by myself and Ant,' said Dec. 'It will be light entertainment, but it will be something that's never been done before.' The boys clearly had high hopes: they had been looking for some years now for the perfect prime-time vehicle and it seemed that they might finally have found it.

But almost immediately it sailed into choppy waters. At this stage the show had the working title of *Now That's What I Call Saturday*, and the ground-breaking idea turned out to be as follows: contestants on the show would win everything shown during the commercial breaks, be it loo paper or a sports car. 'One contestant will win everything shown in the ad break – and that could include a packet of washing powder or a luxury holiday,' said an ITV insider.

There was just one small problem: no one was sure whether it was actually legal to run a competition along those lines and so the Independent Television Commission was called in to rule on whether it was acceptable television. 'Nothing like this has ever been done before, so we need to make sure the ITC are happy,' said the ITV source. It was certainly a clever idea and not just because it made for popular viewing – it would also make ITV very happy indeed by giving it a chance to raise the cost of its slots.

During prime-time television a 30-second slot usually cost about £60,000, but that could go up to £300,000 during big events such as football matches. Funnily enough, ITV had worked out that one as well and rewarded the boys with a £2-million contract to present the show, the equivalent of earning £1,600 an hour. Whatever the ITC's ruling, it seemed certain something would go ahead.

Before the show was due to air, though, that episode of *The Likely Lads* had to be completed, and the duo returned to Newcastle, where filming began. Ant was to take James Bolam's role, the layabout Terry Collier, while Dec was to step into Rodney Bewes's shoes to play the hard-working Bob Ferris. It was the first time either had taken on any major acting role since *Byker Grove* and there was even talk of making a whole series if the one-off episode was a success.

Both were clearly thrilled. 'We're so excited to be working with Rodney Bewes – it's a dream come true. The episode we are remaking is one of our favourites. Whenever anybody asked us what kind of comedy we would like to do, we'd always say, "Something like *The Likely Lads*." To be actually doing it is amazing.' said Dec.

'*The Likely Lads* was always there when we were growing up and we have been fans all of our lives,' said Ant. 'In Newcastle, everyone knew it, loved the two fellas and the series. It was the first show we'd seen on television that featured our city. Everything else was shot in London. But we could watch the show and then go out and see the locations in our own backyard. When Dec and I moved to London and shared a flat we'd have *Likely Lads* nights watching loads of tapes of old episodes. When the chance came along for us to play them, it seemed too good to be true.'

The people of Newcastle were just as pleased as the stars themselves. For their first scene, Ant and Dec had to leap from a Vauxhall Vectra and run towards a run-down block of flats. In doing so, they caught the attention of a group of schoolgirls at a nearby comprehensive, who promptly surrounded them, holding up filming. Ant and Dec responded with their customary charm: they didn't tell the girls to move off, but instead chatted and signed autographs. Their audience lapped it up. As for the show itself, everyone involved wanted to keep it as close as possible to the original. 'We stayed close to the original script because most of it is still really funny today,' said Ant. 'But we took out the references to Enoch Powell because I'm not sure people still talk about him any more.'

Filming complete, the two turned their attention to the World Cup song. It was to be called 'We're on the Ball', a reworking of an old Arsenal song, and was due to be released when the tournament began on 27 May. Ironically, another single to be released on that day was a reworking of the Doors' 'Light My Fire', sung by none other than Will Young. 'This is going to be a massive battle, with the popularity of Will going up against that of the presenters who helped make him,' said an industry insider. 'Everyone is going to want to have a copy of the World Cup song, but Will has a huge fan base and his last song smashed all sorts of records.'

But Ant and Dec also had a huge fan base. 'We chose Ant and Dec because they are quite simply the hottest entertainers around,' said a spokesman for Sony, the record label releasing the single. 'We are certain it will become a classic football song. It is perfect for radio and will have everyone dancing at their barbecues.'

The lyrics were much as you'd expect, kicking off with 'They thought it's all over but it's only just begun/The cup of eastern promise in the Land of the Rising Sun.' All right, so it didn't quite scan, but who cares? 'It's a light-hearted song, but we're trying to stir the emotions,' said Ant. 'It has to be catchy, it has to be fun. You want the crowd singing it on the terraces, it's a tool to stir the emotions.'

Further crowd-stirring lyrics included: 'Send an SOS, a country's in need, Sven's the man, he's got a plan, we've found a super Swede.'

And why, they were asked, were the England players not enlisted to help out with the vocals? 'Because they're crap,' said Dec.

To accompany the song, the two had recorded a video in which they impersonated Sven-Goran Eriksson, David Beckham and David Seaman. This had a plot in which they stow away on the trip to Korea and Japan by disguising themselves as Sven and his assistant Tord Grip. At the launch of the song, the boys were asked about Sven, at that point undergoing a little local difficulty as his fling with fellow Swede Ulrika Jonsson had just come to light. 'Sven's done a brilliant job for England,' Ant said stoutly. 'As a football fan I'm not bothered about his personal life. He's the England manager and that's all I care about.'

And what of the upcoming chart battle with Will Young? Here the boys displayed more than a little steel. 'Will's a great guy and we're mates, but he's sold 1.2 million records already and that makes us all the more determined to kick his skinny little arse,' said an uncharacteristically defiant

Those they have loved …
Above left: Dec with former girlfriend and fellow TV star Clare Buckfield.

Above right: Ant with long-term girlfriend Lisa Armstrong. Could there be wedding bells soon?

Below: The couples were often seen out together.

The duo are more popular and in-demand than ever.
Above left: As Starsky and Hutch for their TV show *Ant and Dec's Saturday Night Takeaway.*

Above right: With their miniature counterparts, Little Ant and Dec.

Below left: Taking on the roles made famous by James Bolam and Rodney Bewes, in their version of *The Likely Lads.*

Below right: Ant and Dec during the recording of their interview with the Prince of Wales. The Prince invited them to Highgrove to discuss his Prince's Trust charity.

The faces that woke up Saturday morning television.
Above: With *SM:tv* co-presenter Cat Deeley.

Below: The three presenters made kids and adults alike laugh, with their impersonations of the Corrs.

Above: Ready for action – about to present the Brit Awards.

Below: The Geordie pair provide the voices for children's TV favourites Engie Benjy and Jollop. They even learned German to avoid their voices having to be dubbed for the show's launch in Germany.

Above: With *Pop Idol* judges Simon Cowell, Pete Waterman, Nicki Chapman and Neil Fox.

Below: With the first *Pop Idol* finalists, Gareth Gates and Will Young.

Getting the recognition they rightly deserve for their talent and dedication.
Above: With their Best Comedy Entertainment Personality Awards at the annual British Comedy Awards.

Below: Ant and Dec received the award for Best Comedy Duo at the *Loaded* LAFTAS Comedy Awards.

Above left: This painting was an amusing take on John Everett Millais's painting *The Princes Edward and Richard in the Tower*. The artwork was commissioned to mark the British Comedy awards in 2003 and sold for charity.

Above right: Pulling pints at The Lodge, their favourite Tyneside bar, into which they have ploughed substantial amounts of money.

Below left: Out on the town in North-West London.

Below right: The pair on holiday in Mallorca.

In the latest series of *Saturday Night Takeaway*, the pair introduced a new feature to find out which of them is the greatest. 'Ant versus Dec' saw them go head to head in a range of challenges.

Above: In one of their tasks, they had to train as motorcycle stunt riders. As Dec completed his test jump, he suffered a painful crash landing which caused him to spend the rest of the series with his arm in a sling, *below left*.

Below right: In another of their challenges, Ant and Dec tried their hand at escapology. During the series they also attempted dog training, darts, ventriloquism and song writing.

Dec. 'We love our song and people sing to the tune on the terraces already. We hope it can be as big as "Three Lions".'

Nor was theirs the only song to be released in connection with the World Cup. Fat Les had recorded a tune called 'Who Invented Fish and Chips' and Bell & Spurling were re-releasing 'Sven's Song', with a new B side about England captain David Beckham entitled 'Golden Balls'. There was also a rumour that Bubble and Dean from *Big Brother 2* were thinking of putting something together. Ant and Dec were unperturbed. 'We wouldn't have done the song if it wasn't the official one,' said Ant loftily. 'It's a great honour and we're delighted to be involved. We couldn't turn down the opportunity, despite saying we'd never get back on stage. It's very exciting. Sven and Tord love the video. We were going to get the players to sing, but they were too crap and too busy earning pots of cash.'

Even before its official release, the country took the song to its heart. At the end of April, still a month before it would be available in the shops, it was downloaded more than 10,000 times when Virgin Mobile put it online as a ringtone. 'We knew it would be popular, but we never expected this kind of response,' said a slightly shell-shocked spokesman for the company. 'The ringtone was available from Friday morning and within a few hours it had been downloaded thousands of times. It could be the most popular football tune of all time.'

Ant and Dec certainly hoped so, and were merciless to poor Will when the three of them turned up in the same bar in Montreux, where they were all plugging *Pop Idol*.

'Ours is a great song and it's going to go straight to the top,' Ant teased him. 'We know you're a big celebrity now. But the singing boys are back and we're going to give you a run for your money.' Will was clearly not sure what to make of it all.

And it wasn't just the song the boys were busy with. Filming of their *Likely Lads* episode had been completed some months earlier and now, with the programme about to be aired, the two were having to take on the doubters. Dec was insistent that the show was quite as relevant in 2002 as it had been in 1973, citing one scene in which Bob mocks Terry for his failed marriage to a German. 'The failure of my marriage only goes to prove my point – them and us don't mix,' says Terry. 'England should take heed of my failed entry into Europe. God didn't make this country an island by accident, you know.'

'When I first read that exchange about foreigners, I thought, that could have been written now,' he said. 'It's perfect. When you look at Dick and Ian's writing, there's very little concept. *The Likely Lads* is just two best friends sitting in a pub and arguing. Similarly, *Auf Wiedersehen, Pet* is just six builders who have to move away from home to find work. The way Dick and Ian write relationships makes these series work and endure. The basic quality of friendship never changes.'

The boys were also accused of cynically using the show on the back of the massive popularity of *Pop Idol*. 'This is not just a cynical ploy to grab ratings,' said a slightly irritated Ant. 'Of course, people are going to say, "I preferred the original and Ant and Dec aren't as good as James Bolam and Rodney Bewes." But the reason we want to do it is because we're massive fans and we think it still stands up. We want to bring this great writing to a new generation. It a "hats off" to *The Likely Lads*.'

It was a perfectly reasonable argument and one that was supported by Rob Clark, the show's executive producer. 'If you can still do great plays over and over again with different actors, why can't two performers do a great TV show again?' he asked. 'The issues in *The Likely Lads* are where to get a pint, where to get a shag and where to get a job, in that order, and those haven't changed in the last 30 years. Bob and Terry are characters who can live in any time. Why should they always be fossilised in flared jeans and brown suits? If they're great characters, they're universal. That's why it's OK to reinvent them now.'

Dick Clement, unsurprisingly, felt the same way. 'There have always been people who have the kind of relationship Bob and Terry have,' he said. 'They are like the ant and the grasshopper. Bob is always desperately striving to better himself while Terry calls him a class traitor as a way of distracting us from his own lack of achievement. It's one of those symbiotic relationships. In spite of the fact they row all the time, there's this enormous and deep friendship between them. People can relate to that.' Ant and Dec certainly could, although in their case, of course, they were both high achievers and they didn't row.

Unfortunately, given the clear love of the show demonstrated by everyone involved, *A Tribute to the Likely*

Lads, as it was billed, was something of a disappointment when it finally came on air. For a start, it was trounced in the ratings by *Test the Nation* over on the BBC, and, secondly, the critics hated it. Made by Ginger Television production company – once, but no longer, owned by Chris Evans – the programme was deemed to have none of the fizz of the original, and was subjected to a blistering attack by the brilliant television critic Charlie Catchpole in the *Daily Express*.

'Ant and Dec starred in a remake of the classic "No Hiding Place" episode of *Whatever Happened to the Likely Lads*,' he wrote. 'What a brilliant idea. But why stop there? Why not make a new version of the famous Germans episode of *Fawlty Towers*, starring Matthew Kelly as Basil and Ruby Wax as Sybil? Or update *Steptoe and Son*, with Bruce Forsyth as Albert and Keith Chegwin as Harold? There's only one question to ask about Ant and Dec taking over James Bolam and Rodney Bewes's fondly remembered roles as Terry Collier and Bob Ferris, and that is, "Why?"' There was a good deal more in this vein and other critics agreed. It had been a brave undertaking on the part of Ant and Dec to recreate a part of television history – but one that simply hadn't worked.

10

Making Waves

FORTUNATELY, AFTER the disappointment of *A Tribute to the Likely Lads*, Ant and Dec had so much else going on in their lives that they didn't have time to brood. Work was continuing on the new prime-time television show, although there was some embarrassment when they were refused entry to a party at which they were supposed to be meeting production staff on the show – in other words, their own party. There were red faces all round. 'Their names were not down on the guest list because it was assumed everyone would know who Ant and Dec were,' said an insider on the show. 'The lads were a bit embarrassed when they had to start coming out with the don't-you-know-who-I-am? routine. But even that didn't work.' The manager of the restaurant who turned them away was even more embarrassed the next day when his faux pas was pointed out to him: there were apologies and offers of meals on the house all round.

Rather more successful was the duo's attendance at David and Victoria Beckham's Japanese-themed party to wish the England team good luck in the Far East. The couple had erected a huge marquee in the grounds of their house, turning it into a spectacular event for the great and good. 'You walked in through a hallway decked out as an enchanted forest, where there were gymnasts dressed as trees who would suddenly move,' said Jonathan Shalit, Charlotte Church's former manager. 'Then you were into the main marquee, where there was a huge gazebo. David and Victoria were in the middle, sharing a table with Sir Elton John and his partner David Furnish and Joan Collins and her husband Percy Gibson. They looked amazing.'

Other guests included Cilla Black, Graham Norton, Sven-Goran Eriksson and Nancy Dell'Olio, Gary Lineker, Sir Richard Branson and others too numerous to mention. Among those others were Ant and Dec, who had been asked to perform a special function: along with Graham Norton, they ran an auction that raised more than £200,000 for charity. This was quite clearly an indication that they were now mixing with showbiz royalty as equals, and yet still the two came over as genuinely star-struck. 'At Posh and Beck's party, I was conscious of not standing on David's toe while talking to him,' confided Dec. 'I would be the most hated man in England. But I spent most of the party open-mouthed. Joan Collins … everyone was there.'

It also gave them the chance to meet Sven-Goran Eriksson for the first time. 'We take the piss out of him in our video, so I didn't have the bottle to go up to Sven,' said

Ant. 'Eventually he came up and said, "Good humour, boys." We were so excited to get his seal of approval. You can't get better than that.'

Nor was that their only football- and charity-related activity that May: they also took part in the Music Industry Soccer Six football match, held to raise funds for 95.8 Capital FM's Help a London Child charity.

As the World Cup loomed ever nearer, so everyone's attention began to turn to that other up-and-coming battle: whose football anthem would get to the top of the charts? Ant and Dec were joint favourites, with the bookies putting them at 6–5 along with 'Three Lions', which was being re-released by the Lightning Seeds, but they had an increasing amount of competition.

DJ Otzi's reworked 'Hey Baby' and England Boys' 'Go England' were both ranked at 6–1, followed by Bell & Spurling's 'Sven's Song' and Dario G's 'Carnival' at 10–1. Nor was that all. The ITV theme from *Madama Butterfly* by the Opera Babes and 'We've Got the World Cup in Our Hands' by People United were also in with a chance at 16–1, while outsiders included Fat Les, Bubble & Deano, Mr Smash and Friends, Terry Venables and New Order. The World Cup was proving something of an inspiration among the musical community, so Ant and Dec were going to have a fight on their hands.

But, if the boys were nervous, they were putting a very brave face on it. After all, they were old hands when it came to having a singing career – and football just happened to be their great shared passion. 'We knew the disadvantages,' said

Ant. 'We didn't really need to do it because we don't release records any more. But if I'd turned it down and once World Cup fever had kicked in and somebody else recorded it, I'd have been kicking myself for the rest of my life.'

'We couldn't turn it down, not being football fans,' said Dec.

What made the pair happier still was that Newcastle had qualified for the Champions League. 'We're over the moon,' said Ant. 'It's more than we could ever have hoped for this season.'

'I would have been happy to scrape into the UEFA Cup,' said Dec.

One interviewer really put the pair on the spot. Which would they prefer, he asked, England to win the World Cup or Newcastle to win one trophy? They weren't allowed both. There was a tiny pause. 'I think,' said Dec carefully, 'you go with your club, let's be honest.'

'And we haven't won anything in so long,' said Ant. (Here it was Newcastle he was speaking about, not Ant and Dec.) 'Not in my lifetime, anyway. But after finishing fourth, I'm right behind everyone backing Bobby Robson for a knighthood. He's brilliant.'

'We were getting a bit worried because Newcastle's bad run in London tallied with when we left home,' added Dec. 'When we realised, we were like, "Ah, shit!" But we went to the Arsenal game which we won before Christmas, so it's OK now.'

The pair weren't so sanguine on the subject of Frank Skinner. Despite their support for him in the wake of the lukewarm reception to the Brit Awards, Skinner felt no need to repay the compliment and branded the song rubbish. It stung. 'The first time I heard "Three Lions" I didn't think it was all that good,' said Dec stiffly. 'But when I got into World Cup fever it became a classic and I think ours will, too. I think it's a bit strong to say it's garbage. It's a football record, it's not supposed to be anything other than that. I'm surprised and disappointed in Frank.'

In the event it was actually Will Young who had the last laugh. Ant and Dec did record the best-selling of the football anthems, but it only got to number three. It was Will who held them off the top spot and reached number one.

Dec had had his sensationalist moment, courtesy of Tina Benson: now it was Ant's turn. And who should turn out to be his partner in crime, according to some newspapers? Why, none other than Cat Deeley. Perhaps it was inevitable – in one of his more laddish moments, Ant had cheerily and ungallantly remarked, 'I'd shag her', and now some papers were insinuating that he was doing just that.

It all came about because of an evening Ant, Cat and, yes, Dec spent at a West End club called Teatro. Fellow guests saw the two chatting together, put two and two together and ended up with about 196. There were mutterings that kissing and cuddling had gone on, that Cat had been looking tearful and that Ant was doing everything in his power – in a very real way – to cheer her up. 'They looked very comfortable in each other's company and didn't leave each other's side all night,' gossiped one onlooker. 'Ant did kiss Cat but it was in more of a brotherly way than anything else. It looked like he was trying to cheer her up. She did look upset.' Some reports went a great deal further than that.

When the allegations surfaced, the boys reacted with a combination of hilarity and incredulity. In an interview, the two were asked what Cat was up to now. 'She's doing *CD:UK* and she's got a travel show,' said Ant. 'I'll phone her and she'll be like, "Hi, I've just got back from the Far East" and I'll be like, "Hi, I've just got back from Sainsbury's."'

'We met up with her just the other week, when her and Ant were having sex in the corner of Teatro,' added Dec.

'We do like to do it out in the open,' said Ant. 'There's no point in hiding these things.'

So what was the real truth of the matter? 'There's nowt to tell!' cried Ant. 'We'd been out for something to eat and we went into Teatro and had a drink. Suddenly 30 tabloid journalists descended upon Teatro because they had some awards thing next door.'

'We were a bit merry,' Dec went on. 'I went to the bog and, when I came back, Ant and Cat went, "Let's go." The next morning the papers were saying, "Cat and Ant were kissing in the corner!" I phoned him up and I was like, "What the fuck did you get up to when I was in the bog?"'

Continued Ant, 'It was just one of those nights when you get really drunk and you're like, "You're great!" "No, you are!" "No, you! Give me a hug!" There was nothing to it.'

Someone had clearly got hold of the wrong end of the stick – and it brought back some awkward memories for Dec. Six months had passed since he'd featured in Tina's kiss-and-sell and, given that he was now able to laugh about it, the wounds were clearly healing. 'Erm, it wasn't very nice,' he admitted. 'It's just one of those things, really. It happened. I haven't really talked about it too much and I'm not going to. It just kind of happened and it was there and it has gone now. It all sounded much more interesting than it actually was. That was it, really. There's nothing to really talk about.'

Did he not realise at the time this might not have been a brilliant idea? 'Of course I did,' said Dec. 'It just kind of … it kind of came out and it all sounded much more fun than it actually was. Most people rang up and were like, "What was all that about?" I think they just took it on face value for what it actually was – nothing much.' And what of his mother, the formidable Mrs Donnelly? How did she react? 'Even she treated it as, "Well, it's a load of rubbish." Everybody just kind of went, "What newspaper was it? [It was the *Sunday People*.] Oh right, let's not worry about it too much."'

Anyway, they had better things to think about. The new show, now called *Saturday Night Takeaway*, was due to go on air, and it is a measure of just how big they'd become in the industry that they also felt able to make some acerbic remarks about the outcome of *Pop Idol*. It had been observed in some quarters that Gareth, the runner-up, was in many ways receiving more kudos than Will, the winner. The boys were clearly on Will's side, and had openly criticised the decision to release Gareth's debut single just a few weeks after Will's.

'I've got nothing against Gareth, the beef I've got is that we stood up there for 21 weeks and banged on about – and were led to believe – that there would be only one winner of *Pop Idol*,' Dec said bluntly. 'That was the show we sold to 30 million people or whatever and I don't believe that there was one winner. And I don't believe the guy who won it has been treated like a winner. It's made a bit of a mockery of it.'

Ant took a more conciliatory approach. 'I can see both sides,' he said. 'I spoke to a couple of people from 19 [*Pop Idol*'s management company] and they said, "You do understand Gareth was such a star we would be foolish to let him go."'

'I think they're absolutely right,' admitted Dec.

'He is a star, and so is Zoë and a lot of people will buy Darius's record,' said Ant the peacemaker. 'Who are we to say they can't have a record deal? What we're saying is that there should have been a greater passage of time between single releases.'

'Three weeks after the winner released a single, the runner-up did one and I don't think that's fair,' said Dec. 'Once *Pop Idol* was finished we and the TV show had no influence over what happened. It was all down to the record company and their management. I still stand by what I said, but it's gone now and there's no point moaning about it. I just think it could have been handled a bit better.' And would it put them off doing a second series? 'No way. We loved it,' said Dec.

A second series was indeed in the pipeline, but before that the two had *Saturday Night Takeaway* to launch. The format had been refined and redefined until everyone was happy with it, with the result that it seemed that, at long last, Ant and Dec were to have a prime-time show that was a real success. They were clearly determined that this programme was going to be the one to do it for them and sure that they had learned from the past. 'We are very thick-skinned – you have to be in this industry,' said Dec. 'Television is a fickle world. But we are getting more and more confident.'

'Yeah,' said Ant. '*Pop Idol* was brilliant for us. It made us older and wiser. Saturday night family TV entertainment is a hard one to crack. But it's where we want to be. We are workaholics.'

'We did make mistakes in the past,' said Dec. 'Although we were proud of *Slap Bang*, our old show, it was a mistake to go straight from Saturday morning to Saturday night TV. *Pop Idol* has allowed us to adapt, evolve.'

The new show was much as had been originally envisioned. 'The idea is that you randomly pick any advert from big shows from the past seven days – whether it's *The Forsyte Saga*, *Heartbeat* or *Coronation Street* – and you win everything that's advertised in all the breaks,' said Ant. 'So you could literally be going home with three cars, a new kitchen, sofas, holidays, soft drinks etc. But if you gamble and lose you could be walking home with bog rolls.'

'The show is an hour long and it's not just a gameshow – there will be loads of other things going on as well,' added Dec.

Further explanations of how it would actually work

were forthcoming. 'We'll get three contestants from the audience and whittle them down to one,' said Dec. 'That person will then play for the products advertised in a break during the programme.'

'That final contestant will get a series of questions,' said Ant. 'For every one they get right, they win the contents of an advert – but they don't know what they've won. Then they can gamble it all on one question. If they get it right, they win the entire prize package. If not, they only get the cheapest item advertised.'

One guest on the first night's show was none other than Gareth Gates. The boys had made it quite clear that it wasn't him they were criticising in the wake of *Pop Idol*; it was his record company. Gareth good-naturedly agreed to get into Puff Daddy mode and sing with the boys, as well as performing his new single, 'Anyone of Us (Stupid Mistake)'. And there were certainly plenty of ideas surrounding the launch. Will McVay, a student at Durham University, was one person who discovered this: he went to a free showing of *Star Wars: Episode II – Attack of the Clones* and got the shock of his life when those human versions of R2-D2 and C-3PO, namely Ant and Dec, appeared on the screen instead. They proceeded to read out four names, including Will's, and berated the four for being at the cinema rather than staying at home to watch the new show. Will was then informed that, if he got home before it ended, there would be £3,000 waiting for him. He did – and won the money.

But heaven forfend that the boys should at this stage quite suddenly let it all turn their heads. They were simply far too canny for that: they had their priorities spot on and for both of them the other came first. 'First and foremost we are best friends,' said Ant. 'Everything else is secondary. We don't take anything for granted. The day you do is the day you may as well retire. How lucky are we to sit down with ITV and say, "This is what we want to do."'

And their relationships were still rolling on smoothly in the background. Dec and Clare had made up their differences, while Ant and Lisa were closer than ever. Both Ant and Dec had begun to talk about the possibility of marriage, although neither was yet ready for it, while they all acknowledged that it was fortunate that the two girls got on with each other. Given the closeness of the boys' relationship, anything else could have caused quite a problem. 'We are both very happy,' said Ant. 'The girls are our fiercest critics. They tell us to shut up about work, tell us to stop telling shite jokes! Which is great! And I know it sounds all very perfect, but the girls get on really well. We never forced them but, over the years, they have become close. They have even been on holiday together!'

And that famed parsimony was still intact. 'We've got a house each and a car,' said Ant. 'But no Ferrari, just an Audi. We don't purposefully not spend money. Perhaps more CDs and treats for our mams, but that's about it.'

In fact, their caution had nothing to do with meanness and everything to do with planning ahead. Asked why they stashed away their cash, Dec replied, 'Because then we can use it when no one likes us.'

There didn't seem to be much chance of that. As ITV

prepared to launch the new show, they were given a further fillip by the news that Siemens mobile was to sponsor the show for a hefty £600,000. This was a real vote of confidence: it was a lot of money to spend on something that was going to be very high profile, and if it flopped it would make its sponsor look bad, too.

And so the show kicked off – initially, it must be said, to mixed reviews. There was a bit of eyebrow-raising in some quarters about the fact that advertising and editorial content were to be so closely associated with each other within the format, although it was pointed out that the contestants' winnings would be based on ads screened at other times during the week, not the ones screened during the show itself. But must people found it harmless. 'Ant and Dec's *Saturday Night Takeaway* resembles *SM:tv* meets *Jim'll Fix It* meets *The Price Is Right*,' said *Campaign*, the magazine for the advertising industry. 'Sounds like a terrible recipe, but the truth is that Ant and Dec, those inoffensive Reeves and Mortimer-lite pranksters, held together the show well and produced an enjoyable hour in the 7.15pm *Blind Date* slot.'

The show soon began to find its feet. 'The Saturday night prime-time slot has long been weak, but this offering has the potential to make the grade with its fast-paced mix of fun and big prizes,' said another review. 'The first 45 minutes are taken up with a whirlwind of entertainment ideas, some of which work and some of which don't. The poorest element of the show is "Make Ant Laugh", which falls flat because the acts who perform before Ant are so bad you end up laughing out of sympathy. Most bizarre of all is the fact that Jeremy Beadle is stranded in an island prison, joined by a different contestant for a week at a time to complete a tough challenge – like learning the Chinese national anthem. Eat your heart out, *Big Brother*.'

It wasn't initially clear whether the show was going to be a success. Ratings fell slightly after the first programme went out, but that is almost inevitable when a new prime-time show is launched, so no one worried unduly. Wisely, Ant and Dec continued to appear in spoofs of other programmes, among them *Coronation Street*, in which they appeared as Ken and Deirdre (Ant as Deirdre, Dec as Ken) and, more recently, *Starsky and Hutch*, in which they played on the confusion so many viewers have with working out which is which by getting the identities of the 1970s cop duo mixed up.

Viewers and critics were quite definitely coming round. 'I hate to say it, but I am beginning to warm to Ant and Dec,' said another review, which also gave a clue as to why there was so much confusion over the identity of the two. 'At the heart of the show, holding it all together, are the two hosts. It is an interesting partnership. Their comic personas are virtually interchangeable, with neither taking the inevitable subordinate role of straight man. It is this equality and mutual dependence that give Ant and Dec's act its strength and explains why light-entertainment execs are falling over each other to employ the pair. Being irredeemably cynical, I like to think that, away from the cameras, Ant and Dec loathe the sight of each other.' Fat chance. The two grew closer as each day went by.

They were also meeting up with old friends on the show, among them Donna Air, formerly in *Byker Grove*. And, to everyone's surprise, they were even managing to shed the slightly naff image of yesteryear: in a survey of a thousand 18- to 30-year-olds, the two were actually named as one (*sic*) of Britain's coolest celebrities, coming second only to David Beckham. On top of that, the Ant and Dec golden touch continued to rub off on other people: the actual idea about winning the contents of the advertisements came from Denise Harrop, a studio assistant at LWT. She had put the idea into a suggestion box and now not only was the show airing in Britain but it also looked as if the format was going to be sold abroad, which was making a lot of money for her. 'Everyone is thrilled to bits for her,' said an ITV executive. 'She is a great girl. It proves what can happen if you have an idea and are brave enough to volunteer it in front of others. She can't believe her lucky stars.' Neither could Ant and Dec. They had pulled it off and the only way to go was up.

Their next venture was to be yet another massive success, for just as it can be hard to jump off a losing streak, so the same can be said of when you're winning. If you get a reputation for having a Midas touch, that reputation will often become self-fulfilling. Accordingly, even if Ant and Dec weren't themselves alone responsible for the success of their next undertaking, it is still a measure of their standing in the showbusiness world that it was they, and only they, who were considered to be right for the job.

The job in question was to present *I'm a Celebrity, Get Me out of Here!* and, as they had done with Cat Deeley, they were to have a female sidekick in the form of Louise Loughman, although in this case the workload was split. They would be presenting the main show on ITV1 whereas Louise would be presenting the ancillary offering on ITV2. And the premise for the show was this: a group of celebrities was to be taken to what the publicity people describing the show called a jungle deep inside Australia, actually about 50 kilometres inland from the town of Tully on the coast of northern Queensland, where they would undergo a series of endurance tests in order to win food for the group. Viewers back home would choose who had to undergo what, and these same viewers would also vote contestants off the show, starting with the least popular.

Louise Loughman was ecstatic, almost more because she was going to meet Ant and Dec than because she was going to be on the show. 'This is the first time I've worked with Ant and Dec and I am over the moon,' she said. 'They're great guys and anything associated with them is such a huge deal. This is my first job in Britain [Louise is Irish] and what a great series to get my big break on. Not only am I working with ITV, but to find I'd be working with Ant and Dec was a massive bonus. I've been a complete and utter fan of the guys for a long time. And my mum loves them too. She's asked me to get their autographs for her.' It seemed a fair bet all three presenters would get on.

The celebrities in question for the first series were self-proclaimed battleaxe Christine Hamilton, ex-boxer and DJ Nigel Benn, Rhona Cameron, famous for being a lesbian and a comedienne in that order, the model Nell McAndrew (who had previously gone on record as saying she thought Dec was the sexiest man on television), the actor and singer Darren Day, society girl Tara Palmer-Tomkinson, veteran DJ Tony Blackburn and Uri Geller, who, to be honest, defies most descriptions.

No one really knew what to make of the new show. The celebrities were described as Z-list, which wasn't actually true, and there was much jeering about how the producers hadn't managed to produce a real celebrity such as, to pick a name at random, Madonna. One report announced, 'The most likeable people on it aren't the contestants, they're chirpy chappies Ant and Dec, who will be presenting the live eviction shows every night.' There was bafflement as to why some of the participants wanted to appear and a good deal of cynical muttering that everyone involved really wanted to do a Jack Dee. The comic and actor had become a national hero after appearing on *Celebrity Big Brother*, and, given that this new show was in essence a celebrity version of *Survivor*, it was widely felt that everyone involved wanted a bit of the Jack Dee action. And then, of course, there was the money. The last surviving celebrity was to pick a charity to benefit at the end of the show, but everyone involved was being paid to do it as well.

The participants were all interviewed as they prepared for their ordeal, and all came out with very much what you would have expected. Christine Hamilton announced that she enjoyed a challenge. Tony Blackburn admitted that he had always wanted to go to Australia. Nell McAndrew confessed that she would probably cry if she saw a snake or a spider. Darren Day professed a desire to be Rambo. Nigel Benn said he was going to cut his hair so that nothing insect-like could live in it. Rhona Cameron fretted about the potential lack of sleep. Tara Palmer-Tomkinson was adamant that this was a chance to show that she wasn't a snob. And Uri Geller? 'I will try to put everyone in a positive frame of mind, but I will not use my psychic powers because it is not fair,' he said. 'I would be cheating and have an advantage.'

On arriving in Australia the celebrities were herded off into the bush. Ant and Dec, meanwhile, were herded off to the four-star Horizon Resort at Mission Beach, a spectacular resort in a spectacular setting. There they brooded on what lay ahead. Asked what they thought was the scariest thing in the Australian jungle, both chimed: 'Christine Hamilton!'

'The woman is rampant, absolutely rampant,' continued Ant. 'Now she's started cuddling me and stuff. I really don't think Christine will hack it. How's she going to live without alcohol?'

That might have been a bit rich coming from the boys, but neither was in a mood for introspection: they were thoroughly enjoying dissecting the poor celebrities on their way out to the bush. Tony Blackburn got a very definite thumbs up. 'I just go, "Aaaah" when his name's mentioned,' said Ant.

'If anyone is nasty to him, it'll be like kicking a puppy,' said Dec.

They were pretty nice about most of the contestants,

complimenting Nell and standing up for Darren. 'The public have got a strong perception of him, and I don't think they could be more wrong,' protested Dec. 'Everyone thinks he's a love rat, but he's a very funny, decent guy.' They were diplomatic about Tara. 'The public have a pretty strong idea of what Tara's like, too,' said Ant. 'And I don't think they're far off, to be honest! She's scatty but fun.' As for Uri Geller: 'He's obviously a very serene, spiritual person who's going to talk to the universe and listen to the trees,' said Dec. 'But by the end of Day Two is he going to be crying and begging for food?'

And so the series began. Poor Tara Palmer-Tomkinson was the first to be chosen by the sadistic viewers back home for one of the endurance tests. Tara had to face one of the so-called Bushtucker Trials, after she confessed to a fear of snakes and recoiled from a leech: she was showered with eight buckets of maggots, bugs and scorpions. She acquitted herself extremely bravely. 'I am going to die. I am shaking. I am so scared,' she told Ant and Dec. '[But] I am going to do this. There are people on the other side of the world having their legs blown off.' And do it she did, winning food for herself and the rest of them, food that was badly needed, given that the celebrities had already scoffed three days' rations in one go.

It is hard to escape the conclusion that the endurance tests were unnecessarily cruel. Nigel Benn, known for a snake phobia, was forced to delve into a glass box full of snakes, in the course of which he was bitten by a python. He was so terrified he was unable to continue with the ordeal. Then Rhona Cameron was buried alive and the vegetarian Uri Geller was told he had to eat insects.

No matter that it was Ant and Dec who were soothing the celebs as they faced their various trials, it all made for pretty repellent viewing, as even the two presenters admitted when a clearly terrified Rhona demanded to be let out. 'This was the most uncomfortable trial yet,' they told the audience. 'Rhona was not happy. It was excruciating listening to her get wound up.' But it pulled in the ratings all the same.

11

The Midas Touch

WHAT WAS rather more interesting about the show, and if truth be told, this had nothing to do with Ant and Dec, was the way the various celebrities reacted to each other. Tara had a row with Rhona, after which Tara had a row with Darren, after which she disclosed that she was only angsty around him because she fancied him. 'I tell you why I am very uptight,' she announced to Darren and the viewers after the two shared a snog with each other and the watching millions. 'It's because I think you are so fucking sexy. It's deprivation. When you can't have something you want. To be honest, when it comes to you, I am wound up. I'm very highly sexed – I'm like all day long, love.'

'Tara, can I ask you something?' said Darren. 'Why didn't you tell me that four years ago?'

Not to be outdone, Rhona shoved herself back into the forefront of the conversation again, calling Darren a dickhead, Tony slow and Tara childlike, before going on to inform Tara that she was chosen for the first trial because the public hated her so much. Clearly not a devotee of the 'less is more' school of thought, she then informed a startled Darren, 'I couldn't control my passion and my desire to love women.'

It might have been tacky, but the viewers loved it and Rhona seemed almost keen to provoke ever more rows. After a spat with Nigel Benn, she snarled, 'Why don't you go and read your Bible? In fact, why don't you fuck off and leave. That would be nice.'

'If you were a man, I'd knock you sparko,' retorted the boxer.

'You bore me shitless,' our heroine returned. 'You should read a dictionary rather than a Bible.'

Darren joined in the fray. 'I live near her,' he said. 'I have actually seen her in a shop near me and, if I ever see her again, I will not talk to her. That's how I feel. I never want to speak to her again as long as I live.'

And so it went on, with the celebrities alternatively bickering, flirting, threatening to storm out and, in the case of Tony and Nell, saying remarkably little. Uri Geller was the first to be voted off the show – 'Somewhere inside my heart I knew I would be the first,' he revealed. 'Inside my mind, it said, "Uri, you are out today"' – followed by Nigel. Tara and Darren had a spectacular row over whether or not she tried to seduce him and managed to upset everyone else so much that Tony, until now the personification of mildness, was moved to remark, 'She's a stupid little rich girl. Bugger off and give us all a break. There comes a time and that's it.'

Ant and Dec observed all this with their usual hilarity, although they did manage to appear sympathetic during some of the more gruesome of the Bushtucker Trials. And even they weren't entirely immune to the discomforts of the jungle, getting the shock of their lives when they came across a snake in their hotel's reception area. But the nightly exposure they were receiving certainly wasn't doing them any harm: it emerged that they were now able to charge about £30,000 in appearance fees, which put them at the top of the A-list. Their fabled parsimony continued, but it was clear the two were now becoming seriously rich.

Back in the jungle, Darren became the third to be voted out. 'I'll be honest with you, of course it's a bit gutting to have the least amount of votes, but I've got to tell you – I'm a bit relieved to be out of there,' he told Ant and Dec. 'In all honesty, it's been a lot tougher than I thought it would be.' He was also rather harsh on Tara for propositioning him. 'There was a time when I would have risen, but I am very, very happy,' he pontificated. 'I have been a naughty boy with girls in the past, but I am very, very happy in a relationship now and I think, quite honestly, I found it quite offensive. Darren Day is no longer an easy lay.'

That was telling them. Nell was the next to leave, followed by Rhona, then Christine, leaving just Tony and Tara. Meanwhile, tensions were beginning to rise at the hotel: the evicted contestants might have been living in the lap of luxury, but the absence of anything to do was clearly getting to all concerned, with Nigel and Darren nearly coming to blows after the latter pushed the former into the swimming pool. Nor was that Darren's only misdemeanour: he continued to rant about Tara, accusing her of trying to break up his relationship with his girlfriend.

At long last everyone was put out of their misery: Tony Blackburn won the show and was crowned King of the Jungle, with the largest chunk of the show's cash going to his nominated charity, the National Autistic Society. He wasn't the only person to have benefited from what had become a national obsession. 'How will they cope when the spotlight is off? Well, they will just have to get on with their lives!' said Uri Geller. 'Seriously, I believe the boys' career will soar after this. I've watched their assured professional manner gain an extra level of confidence in the past few days. They've coped brilliantly with the nerve-shredding demands of live TV on the edge of civilisation.' He was right. For Ant and Dec, the future was brighter than ever.

I'm a Celebrity, Get Me out of Here! had been a phenomenal success. More than 12 million viewers in the UK had tuned in to see the finale, more than a fifth of the population, a fact which reflected as well on the presenters as it did on everyone else involved in the show. With spectacular timing, just as the show came to an end another Ant and Dec-presented show also gained yet more kudos: *Pop Idol* was named best reality show of the year at the TV Quick Awards.

Like *Pop Idol*, the waves caused by *I'm a Celebrity* … continued to reverberate well after the show was actually over. Given its enormous, and to some extent, unexpected success, LWT wisely decided to milk it for all it was worth, and staged a live reunion of the eight contestants, fronted, of course, by Ant and Dec. Tony Blackburn, who was perhaps the show's greatest beneficiary, promised there would be no rows. 'Now I'm King of the Jungle, they will obey every order I give them and behave like good children in kindergarten,' he said. 'I think people will be civil to each other for the hour because they can just get in a car and go home this time.'

Everyone was remarkably well behaved. The eight were reunited in front of a studio audience and much kissing and making up ensued. Tara and Darren had a reconciliation of sorts, with Darren again mentioning a propositioning note Tara had given him and Tara, rather surprisingly, owning up to her behaviour. 'I was absolutely smitten, I hold my hand up, I was right there,' she said. 'It's very sad what happened, because we had a lot of fun in the first week.'

Darren relented, paying tribute to his girlfriend, Adele Vellacott. 'I thought my lady handled the whole situation with grace and dignity,' he intoned. The two duly embraced and shoved their problems behind them.

Nigel Benn also had an apology to make: 'To my Christian brothers and sisters [and the public] for acting the complete jerk out there.' Not content with that, he added, 'If I was Rhona, I would have knocked me out.'

And dear old Tony Blackburn came across as the thoroughly nice man he is. Rhona clarified her description of him as 'slightly slower' by saying, 'I meant dreamy.' If Tony had been offended, he certainly wasn't showing it, claiming to be 'too slow' to have worked out what she meant. What did he make of his fellow contestants? 'They are all very nice, but put them together and it's a nightmare,' he said. 'It was like a Jerry Springer show gone out of control.' And what of the fact that he had seemed to develop a strange obsession with collecting logs during his time in the outback? 'I'm still collecting logs,' he said. 'I've had a fire going since I came back, 24 hours a day, and I sleep in the fireplace.' Oh, and did he still think Tara was a spoiled little rich girl? 'Yes – no, she's not, she's lovely, we had a lovely last day together,' said our Tone.

There was one last Bushtucker Trial to be performed: it involved plunging one's hands into a 'hell hole' filled with cockroaches, mealworms, tiger salamanders and marine toads to retrieve orange stars and so raise £1,000 for every star retrieved each for charity: viewers were given the chance to vote on who should undergo the trial. The unlucky loser was – well, there were two of them, actually, given that Ant and Dec were chosen, but the two carried it off with aplomb, raising £8,000 in total.

Such was the success of the show and its two presenters that life for the duo seemed to go up a gear, if that were possible. Everyone, absolutely everyone, was clamouring for a slice of Ant and Dec, and they were happy to oblige, especially where their native Newcastle was concerned. They agreed to support the *Newcastle Chronicle*'s Young Achiever Awards, as well as turning on the city's Christmas lights. Awards were flooding in thick and fast and some of them were pretty unlikely: they won the Disney Channel Kids Award for the best

TV star, while Dec actually got one all on his own – he came top of *Chat* magazine's poll of Short 'n' Sexy Celebrities. Number two on the poll was a Mr Tom Cruise.

The really serious prizes came next, when Ant and Dec won three awards at the National Television Awards: best entertainment performers, best entertainment show (for *Pop Idol*) and a Special Recognition Award, which in the past had gone to the likes of John Thaw and Des O'Connor. Both were quite clearly stunned. 'Is it after nine o'clock? Shit,' said Ant. 'That's possibly the biggest surprise I've had in my life. I think everybody sat in the Albert Hall is as surprised as us.'

'I just feel really unworthy of it now,' said Dec. 'We're both 27 years old and to receive something like this is really quite unbelievable.'

Celebrations carried on throughout the night. The two, along with Clare and Lisa, went first to London's fashionable Met Bar and then back to Ant's house, where they caroused the night away. 'I was floating on air and just wanted to get back home to carry on drinking,' Ant admitted afterwards. 'We came back to mine and it was me, Dec and our girlfriends and we drank anything we could get our hands on. By six there was nothing left. We drank the fridge dry.'

'I had the worst hangover in the morning,' added Dec. 'When I went to bed, I dreamed it had all been a dream. But when I came downstairs I saw the awards on the kitchen table and just started laughing. I couldn't stop. We still can't believe what's happened. I was at a sandwich bar this week and all the women came out of the back and congratulated me. We even got stopped in the street with people saying, "Well done." It's really nice.'

The full extent of the popular affection in which they were now held came from the most unlikely of quarters: British *Vogue*. The magazine ran an issue devoted to British television and among the many stars featured in the issue were Ant and Dec. In a tribute to the great Morecambe and Wise, the two posed in a bed together, just as Eric and Ernie used to do in their act, and got away with it, something that it was unlikely any other two male television stars in the country would have been able to do. 'People said, "You can't do two blokes in a bed these days – things were different then,"' said Ant. 'But it was just a bit of fun and it worked well. We were very happy with it.'

They were very happy with the way their careers were going, too. A second series of *Saturday Night Takeaway* was now in preparation. 'There'll be a few changes to the show, but you'll have to wait and see what they are,' said a happy Dec. 'I can't wait for the show to start, so Saturday nights are an event again for us.'

And the boys were being handsomely rewarded for their efforts: they signed a new £1.5-million contract with ITV, while ITV Director of Channels David Liddiment added, 'Ant and Dec are special. They bring something unique to everything they do.' The pair were now among the very highest-paid television earners, in the same league as Cilla Black and Anne Robinson.

It was almost inevitable that the two should be given

the ultimate honour (bar a knighthood) awarded to entertainers: they became the latest to be immortalised in wax at Madame Tussaud's. 'They were absolutely brilliant to work with and the whole process was great fun,' said Jim Kempton, who sculpted the duo. 'It was slightly chaotic because they had to pose together and they kept giggling and laughing and telling jokes to the crew. I kept having to tell them off for moving and playing the fool, but it was all good-natured and they did stand still when I told them to. They were a little bit shy to start with. I think they were rather daunted about having all their measurements taken and being handled by so many different artists.'

The two were actually quite taken aback when they saw the end result. 'We never let the stars see their doubles until they get unveiled officially to the press and public,' said a spokeswoman for Madame Tussaud's. 'We like to keep them in suspense. When they first saw them, they were amazed at the detail and likeness and said it was quite spooky. It must be a weird feeling seeing and being able to walk around an exact 3D replica of yourself.'

As Christmas approached, Ant and Dec headed back to Newcastle, as they did every year, to spend the festive season with friends and family, where they came out with some gems about how to run a successful party. 'You need aunties and uncles, with one who gets pissed and makes a fool of himself telling terrible jokes,' instructed Ant. 'And you need a couple who break up and get back together. It's a good talking point.'

'Guests are important,' said Dec. 'A couple of those sexy Page Three lassies would be good – and you need people to make you laugh. Eddie Izzard is good – and Ricky Tomlinson as Jim Royle, so he can shout, "My arse!"'

'Footballers make good guests,' said Ant. 'When you're not dancing, you might as well be talking about something you like. I'd invite Alan Shearer, Bobby Robson and Des Lynam. The worry is that the footballers might get off with the Page Three girls.'

'You need a good spread,' said Dec. 'Sausages on sticks, Cheesy Wotsits, dry white wine for the ladies and compilation albums with tracks like "Agadoo".'

'We play a game called Post It Notes when we've had a few,' said Ant. 'Everyone has the name of a famous person on a note stuck to their forehead and they have to ask you questions and guess who it is. It's great.' However many awards they might have won, it was clear the boys hadn't lost their common touch.

By the beginning of 2003, when they were getting ready to launch the second series of *Saturday Night Takeaway*, they were, if anything, more down-to-earth than ever. Neither had forgotten the hard times, nor had any intention of allowing himself to be carried away by their success. 'People forget that, while we've had a fantastic couple of years, not everything we touch turns to gold,' said Dec. 'We've done a lot of shit stuff, too. Have you heard our single "Tonight I'm Free"?'

They also recalled the period when their record company dropped them. 'It's at times like those that you find who your real friends are,' said Ant. 'The phone stopped ringing and there were no more invitations to parties. It was a real eye-opener.'

And what would have happened if they hadn't made it in showbusiness? 'Ant says I would have been a mobile phone salesman,' said Dec. 'Or he would have ended up in jail or an off licence or in jail for robbing an off licence.'

Romantically, however, the pair's fortunes were slightly different. Lisa had by now moved in with Ant, who was extolling the virtues of domesticity. 'I'm loving it – it's nice to be together all of the time,' he said, before going on to admit that he was beginning to think about children.

Dec himself talked about how happy the two of them were together. 'He is so besotted with her,' he said in an interview with the *Daily Express*'s *Saturday* magazine. 'The most romantic thing Ant's done is to take Lisa to Paris. One weekend, he said, "Pack your bags, we're going away!" When they got to Eurostar at Waterloo, Lisa said, "But I haven't got my passport." Ant produced it from his pocket and said, "Yes you do, my lady." He'd had it sent from her mum's.

'In fact, Lisa is one lucky lady, because Ant, unlike me, is a very good cook. Although I can't resist telling you that the first roast dinner was a disaster. The meat looked fabulous from the outside, but, when he cut into it, it was raw. He thought his mum had told him to cook it for 25 minutes. He failed to hear her say per pound. Doh! Ant never lets anything faze him, although one thing which really riles him is watching TV soaps, although Lisa loves them. When they're on, he'll leave the room. He sees watching a soap as a complete waste of half an hour – half an hour he'll never get back.'

Dec himself, however, wasn't in the same situation. He and Clare were back together again, and he admitted that marriage was an issue, but from the way he talked about it, it didn't seem as if he was in any mad rush to get to the altar. 'After all these years, you've either got to join the navy or jump ship,' he commented and, while he might have been joking, it was clear that he wasn't yet ready to settle down. That episode with the lap dancer wasn't that far behind him and the very fact that he and Clare kept splitting up hinted that all wasn't entirely on an even keel. The very fact that they had been together on and off for the best part of a decade yet were not engaged or living together spoke volumes.

And anyway, they had a new series of *Saturday Night Takeaway* to think about. The events of the past year were beginning to sink in: after all, so much had happened that the boys had barely had a chance to digest their good fortune. That Special Recognition Award had touched both of them deeply, not least because it was final proof of just how much they were loved both by their peers and the public. 'Our reaction was exactly as you saw it on the night – complete disbelief,' said Ant. 'First I thought it was for somebody else, then I thought it was a wind-up, then I was just in shock.'

'It's only now that we realise what an amazing night that was,' added Dec. Nor was that all. In a poll conducted by Madame Tussaud's, Ant and Dec were voted the favourite TV personalities of 2002.

Behind that boyish façade, the ambition, if anything, intensified. Having got to the top, Ant and Dec weren't going to let it go again, and both admitted to being highly driven. Asked if they had thought about what they'd do if *SM:tv* didn't work out, Dec said, 'Never. Because if you talk about failure you're inviting it in.'

'But I also know it could end tomorrow,' said Ant. 'We had an argument with our girlfriends about this last year. We'd been at some awards do and we'd won something and before the night was even over I'd put my award away and we were going, "The pressure's really on to win it again next year." The girls got annoyed and told us to get pissed and just enjoy the night and they were right. We're always worrying about the next show, the next thing.'

That was understandable – after all, when you're at the top, the only place to go is down – but it must be said that Ant and Dec themselves were making sure that they continued to be liked and respected within the industry. Everyone who has worked with them ever since they started out, aged 12, has talked about their professionalism. The two are well aware that their behaviour makes a difference to how they are seen in the outside world. 'I think we're good to work with,' said Ant. 'We're conscious of it because we've seen other people behaving terribly. You don't hear those stories about us, like "Oh, they're a right pair of pricks – they've changed." We were brought up to be well mannered, and I don't think this business can knock that out of you.'

And the professionalism extended to every part of their lives. Nothing was left to chance. The two knew they didn't just have to act professionally, they also had to look the part and so admitted to a fitness regime slightly at odds with their boyish appearance and happy-go-lucky attitude to life. In short, just like the Tom Cruises of this world, they worked out – although they did put it in typically blokeish fashion. Asked if they looked after their appearances, Ant said, 'We do, aye, because we drink so much and we have to try to work it off. We go to this great bloke called David Marshall [actually one of the most celebrated of the celebrity personal trainers] and, I have to say, he's bloody brilliant. We went through a stage where we just ballooned because we were living alone with money in the bank and we were down the pub all the time or eating takeaways.'

'David's taught us how to exercise properly so we get the maximum results with the minimum work, which, of course, suits us very nicely,' Dec chipped in.

And so the new series of *Saturday Night Takeaway* prepared to launch. The boys believed that part of the secret of its success was that it was live, which meant that not only was it nerve-racking: it was also spontaneous. And, although they didn't say so, it was also proof of their professionalism: many a seasoned entertainer refuses point-blank to do live television because the possibility of mishap is so great. The boys, however, were unfazed. 'Live television is the best,' said Ant. 'It really gets the adrenaline going. As soon as you see the titles come on the nerves start going and you just get on with it. We did two series of *Friends Like These* on the BBC, which was a pre-recorded show, and it was a great show to do, but it was tough because it takes so long. If a director can do something again, they will do, but when it's live, you can't. It's gone and if you make a mistake you just have to muddle through and get on with it. We love that early Saturday evening slot, because it's the slot we grew up loving. We love that style of show, like *Noel's House Party*, as it has that live element and a family audience.'

The new series was to be much like the previous one, although new items had been added, including a five-minute slot called 'Unplanned', which would actually be entirely unscripted. The idea was that the producers would throw something at the boys without telling them what it was in advance. 'We might be presented with something or there might be a guest,' said Ant. 'We just have to get on and do it. It will be funny if it all goes a bit pear-shaped, which I'm sure it will.'

The new series kicked off with an absolute masterstroke, which also revealed that the boys had lost none of their acting ability. The two flew to America and donned a heavy disguise for a new slot called 'Ant and Dec Undercover' – and auditioned in front of Simon Cowell for the US version of *Pop Idol*. Performing a rendition of fellow judge Paula Abdul's hit 'Opposites Attract', the two, posing as Jimmy and Scott Osterman, brothers from Denver, were awful beyond belief and got even worse when they started to dance. Cowell looked on in horror, preparing a blistering put-down, until the boys revealed that all was not as it seemed ... 'Oh my God, I don't fucking believe it,' said an absolutely flabbergasted Cowell.

Ant and Dec were jubilant. 'Simon said afterwards, he thought Hey, this guy looks a bit like Ant but never thought it would be us, until we started dancing like loons and then I think he sussed it,' said Ant.

'He didn't realise it was us,' said Dec. 'I thought later he would say he'd known all along, but he just kept saying, "You got me. You actually got me."'

The disguise had certainly been clever, having something of a Bill and Ted nature about it. 'We thought we looked ridiculous until we saw some of the other people there to audition,' said Ant. And it turned out that only the producers of the show had been in on the secret, and that it had almost come unstuck when a researcher on the show chose only Dec, and not the two of them, to appear before Cowell, Paula Abdul and the third judge, Randy Jackson. But Dec managed to salvage the situation.

'I was trying not to talk too much or make eye contact with Simon,' he said. 'They wouldn't let me and Ant go in together, so I had to pretend to be so nervous that I couldn't speak or sing. Paula took pity on us and asked if I'd like to bring my brother in with me.' Ant duly got in, and the boys together dedicated their song to Randy. Jackson gracefully thanked them. 'No, Randy's our dog,' said Dec. 'He choked to death on a rabbit.'

The slot was to prove massively popular and the two even managed to pull off posing as women: later in the series Ant and Dec pretended to be Ron and Yvonne, a managing director and his secretary. They even fooled their old boss at *SM:tv*. On another occasion they were Bernice and Patti, two bosomy, middle-aged fortune tellers – and again they pulled it off without being found out.

The two clearly enjoyed their sessions in drag. 'Trying to put on tights with false nails was the hardest thing in the world,' confided Ant.

'I never thought I'd be upset about snapping a nail,' said Dec. 'The prosthetics took four hours to apply and three quarters of an hour to remove and they look brilliant. When I was dressed as a woman, I ran into our old *SM:tv* producer in the corridor and couldn't resist winding him up. I asked him, "Do you know me?" He had no idea what was going on. I said, "Are you sure you don't know me?" He thought I was some mad woman.'

Not that they confined themselves to merely attempting to fool the public. They continued to mimic other celebrities and did it with such good cheer that no one seemed to mind, not even Mr Nasty, who came in for some more gentle ribbing. 'One of our favourite things is dressing up as famous people, so there'll be plenty more of that,' said Dec. 'Doing the judges during *Pop Idol* was hilarious. Simon Cowell's whole trouser thing was a comedy gift from the gods. Luckily, he got the joke. But I don't think Dr Fox liked our impression of him very much.'

They certainly knew which buttons to hit. One episode brought warmth to the hearts of men of a certain age all over the country: they got Legs & Co, the famed dancers on *Top of the Pops*, to reunite for the first time in 21 years. The viewers loved it. They warmed to the real people on the show, too: one contestant in one of the quizzes was an 18-

year-old student nurse called Laura Heraghty. She had been down to her final £5 before joining the audience of *Saturday Night Takeaway*: after being randomly selected to take part, she left with three cars, two luxury holidays, £1,000 in cash – and some loo rolls and wood polish. The audience was beside itself with delight.

And the boys were capable of laughing at themselves: when they went out shopping together and returned to find that Dec's BMW had been clamped, they didn't fly into a rage – rather, they spotted nearby photographers, took it well and hailed a taxi. Nothing seemed to get to them – on screen or off.

1 2

Just Regular Guys

THE SECOND series of *Saturday Night Takeaway* was clearly as successful as the first, now regularly pulling in over eight million viewers. The same was expected of the boys' next venture: a second series of *I'm a Celebrity, Get Me out of Here!* Some nay-sayers were moaning that it wouldn't work, and that reality TV had had its day, but Ant and Dec were having none of it. 'There's a lot of snobbery about this, but the good shows will stay around,' said Ant firmly. 'I think it's a fantastic format. We had great fun doing it, and still get stopped by people saying they loved it. I think we've learned from *Celebrity Big Brother* that it's all about the characters. You can't just get ten stars and put them in a room and expect a fantastic show. It's about choosing the right characters which they did really well on series one of *I'm a Celebrity* ... There was friction, there was passion – it was everything you wanted from a soap and I didn't see that as much on *Celebrity Big Brother*.'

'Both series will be very interesting to see again,' said Dec. 'As a viewer, I'd like to watch another series of *Pop Idol* and *I'm a Celebrity...* I'd feel cheated if I didn't see them again.'

And yes, there was to be another series of *Pop Idol*, too. Ant and Dec continued a passionate defence of reality television – unsurprisingly, given that they appeared on so much of it – but with hindsight it is clear they knew what they were talking about. 'Everyone says the reality TV bubble has burst but I don't think that's true,' said Dec. '*Pop Idol* is the benchmark talent show – I think it's the best of that genre. I think the good shows will stick around and they'll get rid of a lot of the bad shows.'

'It's like any genre of television – you get good dramas and bad dramas, good comedy and bad comedy and it's exactly the same with this genre,' said Ant. 'Unfortunately, there have been a lot of bad reality TV shows around and people get sick of them. But the good ones will stand the test of time.'

'The success of *Pop Idol 2* will depend on the people who audition and the talent we find,' said Dec. 'If we find another Will or another Gareth or another Zoë, the show will work again because they're very talented people. A girl won *American Idol* and I'd love to see a big female presence in the second series to give the boys a run for their money.'

That would have been a big enough workload for most people, but Ant and Dec are workaholics – and haunted by a fear of failure. The early setbacks had taken their toll, and so, not content with fronting three hit series, the boys continued to look for other projects, not least because they wanted to do more acting. '*The Likely Lads* whetted our appetite to do more,' said Ant. 'We're planning a comedy drama for the next couple of years. We've been having discussions for ages. Our ultimate aim is to do a sitcom but they're so hard to get right. I think you've got to take your time and get the right characters and the right storylines. We would never rush into it but it's something we'd love to do.'

The duo also had the big screen in their sights. 'It's being written as we speak,' said Ant. 'We've been through the development process and we should be getting scripts and first drafts in the next couple of months.'

'It's such a long process – we've been talking about it for a year already,' said Dec. 'We're taking our time and trying to do it as quietly as possible. We don't want to balls it up.'

'You've got to devote a lot of time to a film,' said Ant. 'Last year was very busy for us and we think this year will be the same. We'd have to devote some months to it and we haven't got that kind of time at the moment, which is a shame, but I'm sure we will in the future. It's a dream come true to make a film.' Given all that they were planning, you could be forgiven for thinking that their dream was world domination. They'd achieved just about everything else.

Meanwhile *Saturday Night Takeaway* continued, with much hilarity over the various stunts pulled. The two appeared on *GMTV* as randy old pensioners in love with two young women: the presenter, Lorraine Kelly, was completely taken in. 'It was a hilarious wind-up,' she said. 'Ant and Dec are so good.'

The next victims were the regulars of *Emmerdale*: the duo dressed up as two young female West Indian fans, Patti and Bernice, who had walk-on parts. Then, as the cast attempted to film the scene, Ant and Dec repeatedly ruined the takes by making mobile phone calls and having loud conversations, before revealing that all was not as it seemed. 'It was probably when Ant fell off his chair that people began to twig that things weren't quite right,' said Dec.

Everyone involved, especially Elizabeth Estensen and Emily Symons, who play Diane and Louise, took it very well. 'I was in fits of giggles,' said Emily. 'Liz even whispered, "They're men."'

'The cast had no idea but found it very funny when they realised the joke was on them,' said a spokesman for ITV.

Another enormously popular slot was when two eight-year-olds, James Pallister and Dylan McKenna-Redshaw, were billed as Little Ant and Dec. The two, quite as cherubic as their adult counterparts, were delighting the audience by asking adults questions that adults found difficult to answer. Everyone involved took it well: when Kylie Minogue agreed to be interviewed by the two, she managed to answer questions about the world's most famous bottom with a relatively straight face. The audience was enchanted, as were the adult Ant and Dec.

But this was only the beginning of what was to turn out to be their most successful year to date. Both were now topping the A-list: they were rich, successful, probably the most sought-after television presenters in the country and had that rarest of qualities: they appealed to every generation. For Ant and Dec, nothing was succeeding like success.

As *Saturday Night Takeaway* continued to get the nation tuning in on Saturday evenings, the two found the time to combine business with pleasure, so to speak: they spent £175,000 on a 50 per cent share in a bar back in Newcastle. Originally called Jonny Ringo's, it was renamed The Lodge, and was located at the entrance to the city's Quayside. 'Everybody knows the nightlife in Newcastle is second to none,' said Dec.

'Dec's so excited he might even get a round in,' said Ant.

The purchase summed the boys up perfectly: canny businessmen who hadn't lost touch with their background and still came across as just regular guys.

All their other myriad interests needed tending to as well. Preparations had begun for the second series of *I'm a Celebrity ...*, and the producers found themselves with an enviable problem on their hands: an awful lot of celebrities wanted to go on the show. 'To be honest, there are too many,' said producer Alex Gardner. The previous show had done wonders for the participants: it had, for example, revived Tony Blackburn's career, turned Tara Palmer-Tomkinson's reputation around and made Christine Hamilton more likeable. These were all very good reasons for going on the show, and speculation as to who would brave the horrors of the jungle began to intensify in the press.

Two people whose reputations didn't need a helping hand were, of course, the show's presenters. *Saturday Night*

Takeaway wasn't just pulling in the viewers, it was charming the critics as well. 'Both old-fashioned and terribly post-modern, Ant and Dec's *Saturday Night Takeaway* is a show that really is a show; it sends you out with a kind of glow. And you say, as you go on your way, that's entertainment,' wrote one rather poetic critic, before going on to trash Chris Evans's latest offering, *Boys and Girls*.

Nor was it just the critics who were charmed. The pair appeared in that year's Pride of Britain Awards and engaged in an impromptu ballet dance for five-year-old Hollie Ashe, who saved her father, Jason, when he fell into a diabetic coma. In return they received a gap-toothed smile that lit up the whole room. 'She spent the whole night talking about her new friends Ant and Dec,' said Hollie's mother, Nadine, afterwards. 'She thought they were hilarious. With famous people, you always worry that they won't be as impressive in the flesh. But I can't speak too highly of Ant and Dec. Hollie won't shut up about them either – and she can't wait to get home and tell all her friends about them.'

Ben Housson, ten, was similarly taken with the pair. 'Ant and Dec and the man who sang to me were my favourites,' he revealed – the man being none other than Sir Paul McCartney.

Also gaining in popularity by the day were James Pallister and Dylan McKenna-Redshaw, aka Little Ant and Dec. They were getting away with far more than an adult could, on one occasion giving George Clooney a bottle of hair dye. 'You're going grey, so hopefully that will make you look a bit younger,' said Little Dec, prompting Clooney to reply, 'That hurts a little, y'know. I thought we were pals.' After the two had left the room, he turned to the camera and added, 'Selling me down the river – the little bastards!'

That wasn't all: after asking after Clooney's pot-bellied pig, Max – George revealed it was housetrained, but wouldn't say if it slept on his bed – Little Dec also enquired, 'You directed a film and you gave yourself a part. Isn't that a bit greedy?'

'It was a little greedy,' said Clooney. 'I'm ashamed – thanks.'

On other shows James and Dylan informed Chris Tarrant he had 'a great face for radio', had a pillow fight with Will Young and remarked to Jennifer Lopez that she had 'the best seat in the house'.

Behind the scenes, the two were quite as adorable as the real Ant and Dec had been as youngsters. After having an underwear fight with Kylie Minogue, a contretemps most adult men in the country would have paid good money to be involved with, they professed insouciance. 'Girls are evil,' said Dylan. 'We had to have an underwear fight with Kylie and it was horrible. If she tried to kiss me, I'd kick her off Tyne Bridge. Hugh Grant agrees with us. He told us, "Girls will destroy you."'

'Girls come up and ask for our autographs,' said James, 'sometimes we sign for them, but most of the time we run away. The worst time was when Christine Hamilton kissed me – I got Hamilitis and had to wash it off in the shower.'

Meanwhile, over on the BBC, what you might call the curse of Ant and Dec was still wreaking vengeance. Not only had they demolished the competition on Saturday morning, but they were now proving that they, and only they, could present *Friends Like These*. Finally, falling ratings prompted the BBC to wield the axe. 'Everyone felt it had reached the end of its life,' said a glum BBC spokesman. Ant and Dec were magnanimous and managed not to crow about their triumph, just the latest of many.

The line-up for the new series of *I'm a Celebrity ...* was beginning to take shape and it was even starrier than the previous one. Most reality TV shows tend to attract a lower calibre of guest as they go on (think *Big Brother*) but the opposite appeared to be happening here. The former *EastEnders* star Danniella Westbrook had agreed to appear on the programme, along with the dancer Wayne Sleep, weather girl Sian Lloyd, footballer John Fashanu and ex-*Coronation Street* star Chris Bisson. Also in the jungle were cricketer Phil Tufnell, singer and presenter Toyah Wilcox and Linda Barker from *Changing Rooms*. The chef Anthony Worrall Thompson and Catalina Guirado completed the line-up. Ant and Dec, of course, were presenting the main programme, while the producers had decided to emulate *Big Brother* and run 24-hour coverage of the festivities on ITV2, in a programme presented by Mark Durden-Smith and, on a more ad hoc basis, Tara Palmer-Tomkinson.

And so the circus flew off to Australia and the usual shenanigans began. The celebrities were allowed to take in a couple of creature comforts each: Linda Barker opted for a pillow case with a picture of her husband and daughter printed on it and a set of yoga cards. Anthony Worrall

Thompson and Danniella Westbrook both chose a journal and a pen. Toyah Wilcox carried with her a hot water bottle and tweezers; Wayne Sleep needed tap-dancing shoes and a roll-up wooden tap mat; Phil Tufnell made do with just a pillow and Chris Bisson went for an inflatable two-seater chair and a water gun. John Fashanu had tweezers and a battery razor; Catalina Guirado went for tweezers and a compact and Sian Lloyd took in a cuddly tiger and Elizabeth Arden Eight Hour Cream. Just about everyone tried to smuggle more in, however, and the guards collected a haul of crisps, chocolate, make-up, pens, notebooks, cigarettes, a fishing net, plasters, a potato peeler, a torch and a bottle of tomato ketchup, among much else.

The Bushtucker Trials were as unpleasant as ever, but, again, it was the dynamic between the celebrities that became the focal part of the show. First to crack was Danniella Westbrook, who burst into tears just 48 hours into the programme. 'There are lots of different personalities in here and it's hard,' she wept to the Bush Telegraph. 'I've just bitten my tongue as I don't want to create any hard feeling. There is one person really bugging me. I can't cope with it. If it gets any worse, it's gonna kick off. This is the first time I've been away from my family. It's the first time I've been apart from Kevin since we got married. I'd never do it again, not for any job in the world. I know my friends are supporting me and wanting me to do it, but I can't see me hacking it. I can't do it.' She finished off by demanding to see a psychiatrist.

As the nation tuned in, Lisa and Clare gave a rare joint

interview about their respective boyfriends, kicking off by announcing that the two wouldn't have stood a chance if it had been they who had to brave the terrors of the jungle. 'They wouldn't be any good because Ant's terrified of spiders, and he can't be out in the sun because he's got really pale and sensitive skin,' said Lisa.

'And Dec hates rats and snakes,' said Clare. 'He's cringing when the contestants go through the Bushtucker Trials. I think he'd hate to have to do it.'

The two girls had obviously become close. They talked together in much the same way Ant and Dec did themselves, complimenting each other in the course of the conversation. 'The boys work together and are best mates, so it would be terrible if we didn't like each other,' said Clare.

'Can you imagine? We all spend so much time together, it would be impossible if we weren't mates,' said Lisa. 'We look at them and think, Wow, you've done amazingly well, and we're really proud of them. They've won 17 awards and, looking back at their PJ and Duncan days, you would never have thought they'd be at this level now.'

'What they do is just a job,' said Clare. 'They don't live a celebrity lifestyle. When they go back to Newcastle, they go to the same pubs, and they still have the same friends. They're the same working-class boys they always were.'

'Girls do flirt and sometimes they try to budge us out of the way,' said Lisa. 'But the lads make a point of introducing us as their girlfriends.'

'And I think if you're secure enough in your relationship, you don't mind that sort of stuff. And we are,' added Clare.

It was easy to see how the couples were compatible. Both girls were firmly of the opinion that they should not lean too heavily on their famous partners and were adamant that they would pay their own way. 'People say to us, "Oh, you should have this and that,"' said Clare. 'But why should we? It's not our money and we haven't earned it. I have my own flat and I pay the mortgage.'

'I do get nice Christmas and birthday presents, but I've never thought, Ant is very successful, so now I can just swan around,' said Lisa. 'I went to college to train as a make-up artist and I work really hard. Even now, I never tell anyone who my boyfriend is because I want them to book me because I'm good at my job, not because of Ant.' It was a commendable attitude and one that her boyfriend clearly approved of.

Back in the jungle, the success of *I'm a Celebrity ...* was so great that the showbiz powers that be in the United States were beginning to sit up and take notice. The format of the show had already been sold to ABC, but there was also the possibility that *Saturday Night Takeaway* would make it across the pond, presented by Ant and Dec. 'It couldn't be done without them,' said a spokesman for Granada.

The boys themselves were cautious not to commit to anything. 'They can't think about it at the moment,' said their spokesman. 'It is a choice between a couple of networks, but they have to wait until they get back from Australia. They are both very flattered, of course, but I know they would never go and live there permanently. They are far too attached to this country.'

The antics in the jungle continued. Catalina Guirado was chosen for the next Bushtucker Trial: she was forced to swim past two slumbering crocodiles as Ant and Dec yelled from the safety of the shore that, if either attacked her, they would be shot with tranquilliser darts. The tension was relieved slightly when it emerged that the two crocs were, in fact, two latex models – although, in fairness, Cat didn't know that. Danniella Westbrook began to confide in her fellow celebs about her cocaine addiction: 'My doctor wrote me off,' she said. 'I kept passing out and stuff and I thought I was pregnant but I wasn't. If your mind doesn't go first, your body will and they said, "Your liver and everything has given up on you."' Mercifully, she managed to kick the habit, and was downright sporting about her Bushtucker Trial: she had to walk under five containers of creepy-crawlies and was showered with their contents.

It certainly wasn't a programme for the nervous. John Fashanu was known to be terrified of heights, and so what was his challenge? To hold on to something called the Bridge of Doom, a wobbly walkway high above the jungle floor, as all the handrails were cut down, and then finally the bridge itself. Dressed in a safety harness, John had to climb back up it. As if that were not enough, he then had to plunge into a nest of vipers – and that despite also having a fear of snakes.

The viewers loved it. The programme was getting around ten million viewers a night and Anthony Worrall Thompson nearly achieved the status of national hero when he led a revolt over the tiny amounts of food the participants received. For his pains, he was promptly nominated to undergo a Bushtucker Trial, which at least made a nice change for John Fashanu, who had by now been asked to take part in four of them.

The first celebrity to leave was Sian Lloyd, who claimed to be relieved to be out. 'I was so, so bored,' she told Ant and Dec. 'Hours and hours with no telly, no books and no music. I really wasn't myself at all. The boredom was ten times worse than what I'd expected and the lack of food – because we all suffered from lack of food. The hours just dragged, dragged, dragged on and on and I was going crazy with boredom.'

She was followed fairly shortly afterwards by Danniella, who hadn't been voted out but walked off because she'd had enough. She missed her family, and she was worried her recovery from cocaine addiction was being compromised, she explained. 'I was living hour to hour in a world of hurt, and thought, I've got to go to an AA meeting and centre myself,' she said. 'I had an AA book with me but couldn't get centred. I need the support group I have got at home and, if I don't have my recovery, I do not have a life. I'm relieved to be out, to see my husband and phone my kids. I have never spent a night without Kevin. First I lay down and cried my eyes out – and then it got worse. I'll never do another job to take me away from my family without contact.'

Chris Bisson was voted off next, followed by Catalina. Back at the camp, there was more drama: Anthony strained his back climbing up a waterfall and Wayne hurt himself after attempting to use his bed as a trampoline. Linda Barker, meanwhile, had to do her first Bushtucker Trial:

she had to scale a flimsy ladder and stick her hands in globes full of revolting insects, an ordeal she underwent with much good humour.

Toyah Wilcox became the fourth star to be voted off the show, followed by Anthony. 'I'm no softy, but it was tough,' he said. 'Everything you're used to is taken away. Everything, the sanitation, the washing. It's the boredom more than anything else, not knowing what to do with yourself. But it was a great experience. I would never have missed it, for sure, although it was punishing, very punishing.'

Ant and Dec confirmed the hardships the celebrities faced. 'On the telly, you'll see everyone comes up and says how nice we smell,' said Dec. 'Well, that's because they all smell really bad in there, right now. They all stink.'

'That's right,' said Ant. 'And Tuffers is the worst. He came up for his trial the other day and he really honked.' They weren't exaggerating – at times they had to wear face masks when talking to the celebs.

The two announced that they were thoroughly enjoying the show. 'I loved all the camp mutiny stuff,' said Ant. 'It was hilarious. Anthony has been brilliant. They need someone in there to stir it all up a bit. I love his stories.'

Dec felt the best bit was when Wayne broke his bed. 'The thing that makes it the best moment for me was that everybody crowded around asking what had happened,' he said. 'Fash told them Wayne had broken the bed by bouncing on it and he said, "No I didn't." I was screaming at the screen, "Yes you did!" He seemed to have forgotten that 32 cameras had recorded him doing it.'

Wayne was voted off next. He looked a little disappointed, but took it well. 'If I am honest, I didn't expect to get this far,' he said. 'I am a dancer, while the others are footballers, sportsmen, media people or presenters. I felt like an outsider.'

The trials got ever more repellent. Linda Barker was the next to leave and finally Phil Tufnell beat John Fashanu to become King of the Jungle. 'It's been emotional,' he said. 'I've had a great time, I'm sorry to see the little jungle go. I've got quite attached to it. I think I've learned a lot, but what it is I can't quite put my finger on yet.' Greeted by his girlfriend, Dawn Brown, he hugged her and confided, 'I missed you, babes.'

'I've noticed,' said Dawn rather coolly.

Phil and Linda had become increasingly flirty in the latter stage of the jungle: neither Dawn nor Linda's husband, Chris, looked overly impressed.

Ant and Dec professed themselves delighted. 'I think Phil deserved to win – he was funny,' said Ant. 'He had a bit of a lull in the second week, but he said he wanted to come to the camp to have a kip and relax – and that is what he did! The success of the show is staggering. Everyone says reality shows are over, but this just proves that, when they are well done, they are gripping.'

'Phil went in there not looking to win or to up his profile,' said Dec. 'He did pull my heartstrings when he kept going on about his girlfriend Dawn or "my Dawnie".'

The duo, like much of the country, admitted to a crush on Linda Barker. 'She was the camp sex kitten,' said Dec.

'We had a real schoolboy crush on her.'

'We would get over to the set at 4.30am and she'd be getting out of bed and she still looked good,' said Ant. 'She would always give us a kiss and a squeeze.'

Indeed, it was Linda who became the *de facto* winner of the show. Like Tony Blackburn before her, her profile and reputation received a massive boost from the programme, which she used to the full in gaining lucrative work on the outside, not least in the many commercials she was signed up to do.

As for Ant and Dec, the show had been very hard work. They had to get up at about 2am every morning, as the show was broadcast live, starting at 6am Australian time. But it had been worth it. 'We've had a right laugh,' said Ant. 'Last time it was quite a hard slog because it was the first series and everybody was finding their feet. But this time it's been great.'

'There were 350 people working 24 hours a day, on shifts,' said Dec. 'Doing a live broadcast and beaming it to the other side of the world was amazing.'

There was a lot more that was amazing, too, not least because, as with the first series, the undoubted stars of the show had been Ant and Dec. One psychologist had even written that you could tell the two were suffering when they watched the celebs having to undergo the Bushtucker Trials, thus highlighting yet again their warmth, good nature and concern for their fellow man. The future was looking brighter still for Ant and Dec.

13

The Beat Goes On

As WITH the previous inhabitants of the *I'm a Celebrity ...* jungle, this year's crew reconvened to face a grilling from a celebrity audience, one which indeed contained last year's contestants. Public fascination with the programme showed no sign of waning – and nor did public fascination with Ant and Dec. Just about the only person who seemed to have any negative thoughts about them at all was John Fashanu, who, safely back in the UK, couldn't resist having a dig.

'I remember Ant and Dec enjoying watching me suffer during the Bushtucker Trial with the eels,' he said. 'They are mates of mine but I looked at them and thought, You bastards. And when the rope bridge collapsed I was screaming for my life, I was petrified, and one of them was shouting out, "Keep low." I thought, I'll get you two.' For what it is worth, he was almost certainly wrong. There were times during the Bushtucker Trials when Ant and Dec looked as if they were suffering almost as much as the contestants. At any rate, it was all in a good cause: the show raised £1 million for charity.

Meanwhile the Fox network in the US was still trying to get hold of *Saturday Night Takeaway*, and it didn't just want the format of the show – it wanted Ant and Dec. This posed a couple of problems: the time involved if the two had to go to America for filming, and the question of whether US audiences would be able to understand Ant and Dec's Geordie accents.

'Fox want to buy the format and we would have done the deal already, except that they want Ant and Dec to do it,' said Paul Jackson, Granada's Head of Entertainment. 'That's difficult because of the time pressure here. We believe there is some time in the diary to do *Takeaway* in the US. The show is great and broadcasters around the world are trying to buy it.' As for the accent issue, he was sanguine. 'The thing is, they're actors, so they would be able to soften their accent,' he said.

Scarcely pausing for breath, Ant and Dec promptly leaped back into their other presenting shoes, as hosts of *Pop Idol 2*. Like *I'm a Celebrity ...*, the success of the first series had been such that the second, if anything, was garnering even more attention. An unbelievable 20,000 young and not-so-young hopefuls had auditioned to get on the show, but the final selection was whittled down to just 100.

The same judges – Simon Cowell, Pete Waterman, Neil

Fox and Nicki Chapman – were on board and everyone was enthusiastic about the prospects for the show. 'It's much more unpredictable than last time,' said Simon Cowell. 'People who don't look like a pop idol are going to play a bigger part this year. Last year I thought Gareth would win it and he came pretty close. This year it's much more open. There are eight or ten who could win it.' In fact, Cowell had been as big a winner as anyone on the first series. In the time since the previous series he had taken the idea to the States with the show *American Idol*, and had been such a success that he was now the third highest-paid presenter on American television. The experience had done nothing to tone down his ego.

And Cowell was certainly living up to his reputation for bumptiousness, boasting that he was more popular with women than Ant and Dec. 'More girls come up to me than to them,' he boasted. 'It's only natural. They're good boys – they actually really are. And I'm a bad boy.'

Ant took a rather more realistic view of Cowell. 'He's like a panto villain – he walks in and all the kids go: "Booo!" And, of course, he loves it,' he said.

Dec was pithier still. 'He's the campest ladies' man I've ever met,' he said.

Once filming started, the usual rows and controversies began. Early on a contestant called Daniel Webster managed to upset all the judges by revealing that he knew a great deal about their personal lives, telling them in detail where they all lived, before going on to tell Nicki that he knew what she'd been singing at dinner the previous night.

It was 'Tainted Love', which, for good measure, he then sang in the audition. The judges were not impressed. 'Simon Cowell told him he was one of the worst singers he had heard in his life,' said a source on the show.

Fiona McLean tried different tactics but fared no better: she appeared wearing see-through clothing, announcing, 'This is for you, Simon!' It didn't wash. Then there was Morwena Marshall, also skimpily attired, who did some sort of bizarre exercise routine designed to show off her curves. She didn't get through, either, although the boys were a bit naughty at her expense. Nicki Chapman branded them 'mischievous fairies', adding, 'She told them she warmed up with scales and exercises, so they got this poor girl to do some yoga moves while the camera homed in on her obvious assets. I don't think she realised what was going on.'

Ant and Dec took it all in their stride, chatting merrily about the foibles of the various contestants. 'These two sisters turned up a bit worse for wear,' Ant revealed. 'The first one didn't get through and her sister could hear her arguing outside, so she went in and there was a big row.'

'We've had tears of relief, joy and happiness,' added Dec. 'But Simon's got worse since he's been to the USA. He's been a nightmare!'

As the show began to air, the all-important ratings held up: an average of five million viewers tuned in, the audience peaking at 6.3 million. And, despite the fact that it was obviously a good format, this was due in no small part to Ant and Dec themselves, who continued to make mischief where the contestants were concerned. They were merciless to Andrew Creelmen, who was dressed as an Elvis lookalike, teasing him so much that he finally blew his top – to Simon Cowell.

'Ant and Dec were winding me up before I went in, asking me what I was going to say to Simon,' Andrew recalled. 'I think they knew he wouldn't like my Elvis costume. When I walked in, the judges looked at me as if I was stupid and before I'd even started singing Simon asked me why I was there. I thought that was really rude, so I said, "Why don't you shut up and listen." That obviously got me off on the wrong foot because he interrupted halfway through my song and told me to shut up and leave the room. I tried to argue, but I think I upset him even more. I asked if he was wearing his trousers so high he couldn't hear my amazing voice. He told me other people were waiting to audition and I was wasting his time. I was waiting outside for ages in case he came out to tell me he'd made a terrible mistake. Unfortunately he didn't. I blew it.' But at least he'd had the chance to do what the nation was yearning to do – tell Simon off.

Given all that was going on in their professional lives, it is hardly surprising that Ant and Dec won yet another award, as top TV personalities of the year at the GQ Men of the Year Awards. Following that, they won Best Entertainment Show for *Saturday Night Takeaway* at the TV Quick Awards and at the same awards ceremony *I'm a Celebrity* ... was named Best Reality TV Show. Ant and Dec's bankability soared with each award that was theirs: by now no one at all could question the fact that they were the two most successful television presenters in the country – as long as they worked as a team, of course.

And so *Pop Idol 2* continued, producing this time a woman who would seem an unlikely contestant, Michelle McManus. Michelle, from Baillieston, Glasgow, had two things going against her: she was very large and she was a woman. Conventional wisdom had it that a woman wouldn't be able to be a pop idol, because the female fans would want a fanciable man to win, but since the previous winner was, in fact, gay – why not? And even Simon Cowell was on Michelle's side. 'You came out for the first time tonight believing you can win this competition, and that is what we're looking for – belief,' he said as she made it to the final 12. 'I think you have that belief and you know that you are potentially a great singer.'

It was around this time that a subtle shift was occurring in the way that Ant and Dec were regarded in the industry. Although they had long been seen as seasoned television professionals, the fact that they look and behave on screen like teenagers rather than young men meant that they were valued more as performers than as ideas men. But that was beginning to change. While their on-screen charm was clearly a crucial element of their success, their off-screen savvy was not to be underestimated either, and the industry was beginning to recognise that. They won yet another award, but this one was different from the rest in that it came from the very serious *Broadcast*, probably the most important magazine in the television industry.

Ant and Dec came top of a survey of the industry's most bankable talent, beating the likes of Jonathan Ross, James Nesbitt and Graham Norton to pole position, and the survey in question was of directors, station bosses and the heads of light entertainment – in other words, the people who actually mattered. 'Ant and Dec's names came up again and again – I'd say everyone had them on their list and, if not on top, then somewhere very near,' said a spokesman for *Broadcast*. This was serious stuff, for, if the most important people in the industry all rated Ant and Dec more highly than anyone else, then their already golden status was confirmed.

The two were also doing a fair bit for charity. In the summer they hosted an event for the Wish upon a Star appeal in London's Battersea, which paid for 100 terminally ill children to go to Lapland. They also remained keen to support the folks back home, and so did various events for Newcastle-based charities, not least the Young Achiever Awards scheme, which honours children who have achieved great things against the odds. They were also involved with the Northern Children's Book Festival Gala Day, in which they held a free radio workshop for the over-tens. Other charity work included support for the Foundation for Children with Leukaemia and Northern Stage's appeal to raise over £7 million to turn the Newcastle Playhouse into a European Centre for Performing Arts. The two clearly had a strong social conscience and were determined to repay some of their good fortune.

Pop Idol 2 was nearing its finale and the two gamely

played it up for all it was worth. After Sam Nixon and Susanne Manning took the final two slots in the top 12, Ant and Dec speculated happily about who would actually win. 'It could be a dark horse like Mark, it could be the bookies' favourite, Roxanne,' said Dec. 'It will be a roller-coaster ten weeks and the winner could just come out of the blue. Susanne showed she's really Miss Sexy Voice last night, so who knows?'

'It always gets good when it comes down to this stage,' said Ant. 'It just kicks up a level. Sam went through on a wild card. He's got a real fan base already.'

'It's a siege mentality,' said Dec. 'We feel like England before the Turkey game every Saturday. It's like a panto with Simon Cowell as chief dame.'

Perhaps Cowell's crack about attracting the girls had irritated the boys more than they let on, but Simon himself certainly took it in good heart. 'I think they're brilliant,' he said. 'To me, that's what the show is all about – them taking the piss. They're so funny.' And how did he feel about them describing him as camp? 'Coming from them, that's a bit rich,' said Cowell. 'They're the campest duo on TV.'

Also the most popular. The National Television Awards took place in October that year and, yet again, Ant and Dec swept the board. They arrived at the ceremony with Little Ant and Dec and managed three awards: they were named Most Popular Entertainment Presenters for the third year running, *Saturday Night Takeaway* was Most Popular Entertainment Show for the second year running and *I'm a Celebrity* ... won Most Popular Reality Programme. 'We had so much to live up to after last year,' said an ecstatic Dec. 'And we're chuffed *Takeaway* won – it was our baby, our programme.' Clearly, when you're hot, you're hot.

It was sweet of the boys to bring their junior namesakes along, and Little Ant and Dec also had a thoroughly enjoyable evening. 'We thought we'd bring them along,' said Dec. 'They were just as much part of our show as us.'

Deborah McKenna, mother of Dylan – Little Dec – was clearly pleased. 'They had a brilliant time and they really enjoyed themselves,' she said. 'It just went so quickly. I think they pretty much met everybody who was anybody. Everyone was coming up and talking to them and saying hello. They were with Ant and Dec most of the night and me and James's mum, Lesley, were sitting behind them. We had a great time, too.'

It was nearly time for the finale of *Pop Idol 2*, but before it happened the boys even managed to be part of yet another success, taking cameo roles as themselves in the Richard Curtis film *Love Actually*. It wasn't merely a canny move: it was a sign that their own filmic ambitions were as strong as ever. Although they said nothing publicly at that stage, there was still some intensive work going on in the background and they certainly endeared themselves to everyone else involved in the making of the film.

'Ant and Dec were completely charming,' said Bill Nighy, who played a pop star past his prime who guests on shows hosted by Michael Parkinson and Ant and Dec. 'On the evening of the shoot, they were at least as concerned with how Newcastle were doing as they were with their performance. People kept running up to them and saying, "2-0." But they, and Michael Parkinson, were great sports. I virtually exposed myself to Michael, but he took it quite well under the circumstances. He was extremely keen and touchingly nervous about whether he got his lines right.'

The boys also proved themselves to be very good sports, not least as the film teased them mercilessly about the fact that they might be the most popular television presenters in the country, but no one had the faintest idea which was which. At one point in the scene, Bill Nighy turns to Dec when asked a question and refers to him as 'AntorDec'. It got one of the biggest laughs in the film.

And, yet again, the nation was transfixed as *Pop Idol 2* put its finalists on stage. They were Brian Ormond, Kim Gee, Marc Dillon, Michelle McManus, Andy Scott-Lee, Mark Rhodes, Susanne Manning, Chris Hide, Sam Nixon, Kirsty Crawford, Leon McPherson and Roxanne Cooper. But, as the nation held its breath, Ant and Dec came out with a bombshell: this series of *Pop Idol* would be their last. It was not, after all, their baby, and the two now wanted to concentrate more on *Saturday Night Takeaway*, not least because it was looking increasingly likely that a deal would be struck in the States.

'The boys have both enjoyed the success of *Pop Idol*, but now they are very keen to concentrate on shows which don't just involve turning up and reading an autocue,' said an ITV source. 'It [*Saturday Night Takeaway*] is the series that means most to them because the whole show is about them entertaining the public – not other people. They are really excited about taking the show to the US and if it works out they are likely to spend six months of the year over there and six months over here.'

Nor was that all. 'For a long time now, they have talked about wanting to get back into drama, but they've been so busy with project after project and simply haven't had the time,' the source continued. 'Now they feel the moment is right to scale back on certain areas so they can move on to tackle fresh TV challenges. And that means no more *Pop Idol*. Ant and Dec have a very good relationship with ITV1, but that's not to say every other channel wouldn't jump at the chance to work with them. It wouldn't be a good move on ITV's part to insist the boys stick with *Pop Idol* because they simply don't want to – and there's always the chance they will walk.'

It was pretty clear who was calling the shots now, but, cautious and modest as ever, the boys played down their future movements. 'We have been asked by the Fox Network in America to do a pilot of *Saturday Night Takeaway* and we'll be filming that before Christmas,' said Dec, playing it down for all he was worth. 'I think the plan is to get an American audience in for the show, but we're filming it in the UK. Then we're just going to see how it goes, see whether Fox like it and whether we like it. There's nothing firmed up at the moment or any plans for us to move to America.'

Ant was adamant that taking the United States by storm had never been the masterplan. 'We are signed to ITV until next year and we're doing two more series of *Saturday Night*

Takeaway with them,' he said. 'We haven't got huge amounts of time to do other things, but we'll have to wait and see what opportunities come up. The first one will be in the spring and the second in the autumn and we're really looking forward to it. It certainly is our favourite project out of the things we do, because it is the most fun. We really love it.' They did, however, agree to host *World Idol*, which was to be shown in two parts, with the performances on Christmas Eve and the results announced a week later, on New Year's Eve.

But while their professional lives were leaping from one pinnacle of success to another, the private lives, or rather Dec's private life, was rather more rocky. He and Clare had been together on and off for ten years now, give or take the odd break, and after such a long time together it was clear they had to decide whether they were to stay together forever or to part. They decided to part and the news finally broke in November 2003.

'The fact is that Dec and Clare are giving each other a wee bit of space at the moment,' said Dec's manager, Paul Worsley, as he confirmed that the couple had split. 'But they remain firm friends and they always will be. I want to set the record straight that that's the situation and make it clear there's absolutely nobody else involved. To be honest, they are absolutely fine. Clare came to Ant's twenty-eighth birthday party the other day and they will continue to remain friends.'

Naturally, there was a good deal of speculation that there was rather more to it than that. Dec's fling with Tina Benson had been forgotten by no one, but there had been rumours about Clare, too. During one of the couple's various breaks from each other, she was said to have had a fling with Darren Day – the same Darren Day who had appeared in the first series of *I'm a Celebrity ...*, back in 1996.

The two had been appearing in *Summer Holiday* in Blackpool and had seemed to be getting on as well offstage as they were on, which would have been fine if it weren't for the fact that Day had been dating Anna Friel at the time. Everyone denied everything, although Clare did say, 'Yes, we have been holding hands – though we are just good friends.'

Dec would seem to have recovered quickly. Now that the secret was out, everyone suddenly realised that his companion at the National Television Awards had been his agent, Alison Astall, who, like Clare, was petite, pretty and blonde. 'Dec works closely with Alison and there is nothing more to it than that,' said his spokesman firmly. Others weren't so sure.

Dec finally confessed he and Clare had parted. 'I'm afraid the rumours are true, we have split,' he said. 'We need some space right now. We broke up once before and got back together once before. But I don't know if it is for good this time. It's hard – but I'm not feeling too bad today.'

Dec's mother made a rare public pronouncement about the situation, pointing out that his workload was enough to finish off any relationship. 'He may well be away for six months of the year but that is just what he has to do for work, it is the price he has to pay,' she said. 'It is a very amicable split. They will stay friends, that is the main thing.'

Rumours continued to circulate about Alison. She was spotted leaving Dec's house early one morning and the two were seen shopping together, setting tongues wagging still further. 'They are always going shopping or doing the sort of stuff together couples usually do,' said a source, who knew them both. 'He was so incredibly close to Clare, they'd known each other since they were children, and now she's gone there's a void in his life. He's found himself relying on Alison more and more. She's been his Girl Friday at work for four years now. She virtually runs his life. Now they're constantly talking and going out together – she has really stepped in where Clare left off. They're very close, but who knows how it will develop in the weeks and months ahead. He's very vulnerable at the moment.'

Tina Benson, never one to lose an opportunity to get into the papers, was happy to talk about her role in the break-up. 'It seems my name came up every time Clare and Dec had an argument,' she boasted, before going into yet more lurid details of the night in question. She also claimed she and Dec had stayed in touch longer than he had admitted, before adding, 'Anyway, I think I have done him a favour. He and Clare were together out of habit. Now Dec will be able to live the life he really wants.'

That life would probably include the avoidance of lap dancers who sell their stories to the papers, but it certainly looked as if his relationship with Clare was well past its sell-by date. Dec himself admitted as much, when he confessed the sexual side of the relationship had all but disappeared. 'To be honest, I'm too busy for romance,' he said. 'I haven't had any action for ages. It's quite depressing thinking you're too hectic working for nookie. Clare's a bit like my sister, really. When you have been seeing someone for so long, she's more like my best friend than anything else. She's been with me throughout everything, but we both know things have to move on. It's very sad that Clare and I have split. Right now we are taking time out and I will be working as normal. We really hope to hit the States.'

Anyway, the most important person in Dec's life was still right by his side. Ant was still there, looking after his friend.

14

As Good As It Gets

PERSONAL TRAUMAS aside, it had been quite a year for Ant and Dec and the nation's eyes were still firmly fixed on them as 2003 drew to a close. And, while they might have decided not to continue with *Pop Idol*, the current series was still running and attracting massive attention from the public. The finalists had been whittled down to four: Chris Hide, Mark Rhodes, Michelle McManus and Sam Nixon, with Chris the favourite – and so, of course, it was he who was voted out of the show as the finale neared. There were actually gasps from the audience as the decision was announced and it all made riveting television.

Then, a week later, Sam left, a result that had even Ladbrokes gasping for breath, as they had originally given odds on Mark winning of 50–1 and Michelle 33–1. 'Both were outsiders from the beginning, so it's a massive shock for us,' said Ladbrokes spokesman Warren Lush. 'We didn't take either of them seriously at first. We didn't think they would get to the top three, never mind the final. If Michelle wins, we will have to pay out a six-figure sum. It's going to be much closer than we had anticipated. We are amazed.'

And indeed that six-figure sum duly had to be paid out when Michelle triumphed. Appropriately, given the atmosphere of drama surrounding the show, Pete Waterman walked off in disgust, while Simon Cowell, who had supported Michelle, gloated over the result. Michelle herself broke down in tears when the results were announced, saying, 'I just want to say thanks – and to everyone who said I couldn't do it, I've done it.'

One of those people, of course, was Pete, who earlier in the series had told Michelle that, although she might have been a great singer, a pop idol she wasn't. Now that she had a £2-million record contract and was to be represented by 19 Management, Michelle quite rightly felt she could rise above it. 'It doesn't bother me what Pete thinks,' she said. 'I will always respect Pete because he has been so successful. He has made a lot of money out of doing what he does. But this is my night and, if he wants to storm away and make an issue of it, it may be that he has other people to go to at the end of the day, but I am not going to think about it. I just won *Pop Idol*, I couldn't give two hoots what Pete Waterman thinks now.' In hindsight however, it seems Pete might have beeen right.

Now that Ant and Dec were leaving the series, alongside Simon Cowell, who had made it known that he wanted to concentrate on *American Idol*, it did seem that the show had run its course. *World Idol* was screened over the Christmas period, but was widely held to be something of a disappointment, pulling in just 4.5 million viewers on Christmas night itself, against 14 million for *EastEnders*. Simon Cowell, as usual, created ructions: he nearly walked off the show, saying, 'There's such a gulf between these singers, it's like comparing donkeys to racehorses.'

The contestants had their own nits to pick. The eventual winner was Kurt Nilsen from Norway. 'If this competition had been on radio, you'd walk it,' Cowell told him. 'The problem is you are ugly.'

Kurt then complained bitterly about Will Young, who had only come fifth. 'This is totally amazing. I love you guys,' Kurt began. But then the bitching kicked in: 'Will Young is an arsehole,' he went on. 'He didn't want to shake my hand and say hello.'

The friendly rivalry between Cowell and Ant and Dec continued. At the beginning of the New Year, S4C's children's magazine programme *Uned 5* dished out its own awards: Cowell was voted Baddie of the Year. 'I'd like to thank all the viewers for voting me Best Baddie – the fact that I don't have to share this award with someone else like Ant and Dec makes it even more special,' he said. In fact, Ant and Dec had their own award, for being Best English Presenters, while *Pop Idol* won Best English Programme. The series might have been coming to an end, but it had been an absolute boon for everyone involved.

And with *Pop Idol* out of the way, it was time to prepare

for the third series of *I'm a Celebrity* ... The line-up was announced in January: it was to be singer Peter Andre, Alex 'wife of George' Best, former royal reporter Jennie Bond, disgraced peer Lord Brocket, athlete Diane Modahl, TV presenter and ex-Atomic Kitten Kerry McFadden, Page Three girl Jordan, ex-football star Neil Ruddock, DJ Mike Read and, most controversially, John Lydon, aka Johnny Rotten of the Sex Pistols. ITV was clearly torn by its coup: on the one hand, Lydon could be relied upon to cause a bit of drama, but on the other, he wasn't known for holding his tongue.

'His most famous album might be *Never Mind the Bollocks*, but he has been told to mind the bollocks and every other swear word as well,' said an ITV source. 'Barring any last-minute problems, he is in the show – and we are very pleased at that. But there's a feeling he could find the whole experience no fun at all and may turn the air blue. He's done it on prime-time TV shows in the past when he's unhappy and there's no reason why it couldn't happen this time. There may be a time delay on the live parts – and it could end up as a series of bleeps if he can't control himself.' This, of course, is known as having your cake and eating it, too. To choose a man who is well known for his foul language to appear on your TV programme and then worry that he will use foul language is disingenuous in the extreme. ITV bosses knew perfectly well that Lydon's presence would add yet another frisson to the show: would he or wouldn't he swear? You'd have to tune in to see.

The show was to follow the same format as before: the

main edition would be presented by Ant and Dec at 9pm on ITV1, while additional footage would go out on ITV2, again hosted by Tara Palmer-Tomkinson and Mark Durden-Smith. The proceedings were briefly marred by a row, when the other contestants discovered that Jordan was being paid £100,000 to appear on the show, twice as much as everyone else, but eventually the new lot assembled in the jungle. Jordan was becoming a centre of attention herself. Not only were viewers promised the possibility of John Lydon swearing live on air, but there was also the constant possibility that Jordan would take her top off.

So keen were the producers to provoke some kind of controversy that they cut the amount of space in the camp to about half what it had been the previous year. This meant no one had room to escape anyone else. 'The contestants will be totally in each other's pockets,' said producer Alex Gardiner. 'Last time they were able to use much more space, which meant, if they wanted, it was possible for them to spend time relatively alone. This year that just won't be possible. Tempers are far more likely to fray when the beds are so much closer together. The new layout will encourage them to congregate round the campfire. We really want them to sit together, chat together and fall in love in the camp's perimeters.'

He was certainly being honest and the contestants seemed equally keen to stir things up. Lord Brocket was to become the show's lech and started as he meant to go on: 'If Jordan does sun bake in the nude, she won't just have bugs all over her – she'll have everyone in the campsite. All the women are very nice, especially Alex Best.'

Jordan herself, while maintaining she would stay faithful to her boyfriend, Scott Sullivan, was greatly relieved to hear that Alex was also planning on doing some topless sunbathing. 'Alex said she'll get her top off, so I won't be the only one,' she said.

And so the series kicked off. Two things immediately became apparent: that the Bushtucker Trials were going to be even more grotesque than usual and that Peter Andre had the hots for Jordan. John Lydon didn't seem to be taking too kindly to all of this, not least because it meant he wasn't the only focus of attention. He seemed to develop an immediate antagonism to Jordan, telling her, 'Take your implants out of my face.'

He did, however, manage his own trial with some degree of grace: after being dressed in protective clothing, he was smothered with treacle and bird seed and sent into an ostrich enclosure. After commenting that they were 'fat budgies', Lydon discovered where the eggs he had to find were hidden: 'Did you have to bury them so deep?' he asked. 'I've never known such spite. They are ground in. What a set-up! What a death trap! It's fantastic!' He emerged, covered in beak marks, having won six out of a potential ten dinners for the team.

His presence – indeed the combination of contestants – was certainly boosting the ratings: almost 11 million viewers tuned in for the show, 200,000 more than for the previous series. And so they saw Jordan and Neil wearing helmets into which were poured all manner of creepy-crawly, Jennie Bond buried in a coffin with 30 rats running all over her and Jordan and Peter flirting more ostentatiously by the day. Jordan also began to talk about a book she was planning to write, which would reveal all. It promised to be gripping stuff. 'If someone upsets me I believe you can get them back one way or another,' she said darkly. 'We'll see who has a smile on their face.' The face in question was thought to be that of Victoria Beckham, who had once famously burst into a rendition of 'Who let the dogs out?' when Jordan walked into the room.

John Lydon remained unimpressed, calling Jordan a 'Page Three blow-up balloon'. There was more. 'I just don't like lazy people, I just don't like carrying dead weight,' he raged. 'I don't. That's coming across now, really, really strongly. It's a good-for-nothing waste of time at the moment. Make her get up and do something. Give her a poke up the arse like she deserves. It's not right, she's dragging it all down to silliness. Much more of that, and I'm walking, I'm telling you. I'm not here to support that kind of crap, I'm here to have a laugh with some good people. She can't even bloody wash a teacup without the effort of it all. And it eats and it's non-stop and it don't cook bugger all.'

First to be voted off the show was Mike Read, who complained about, of all things, being forced to leave before doing a Bushtucker Trial. 'Since the first day I haven't had to encounter a spider or snake and I thought, Wonderful, nobody wants to persecute me,' he told Ant and Dec. 'But it gives you something to do. If you go and do something like that, people think, Wow. Look at that. That's fantastic. But if you don't get to do a Bushtucker Trial you probably look like a lazy slob enjoying yourself and not doing anything.'

Back in the jungle, Neil Ruddock had to walk a tightrope to win the group some food, while Alex Best was made to crawl through tanks filled with the local flora and fauna. She wasn't able to brave the final tank, though, which was filled with snakes, and then had to endure being soaped down by Lord Brocket after the whole thing was over. The viewers turned on in their droves.

Diane was the next person to leave the jungle, an event that was overshadowed by John Lydon letting loose with all the words the producers were worried about him using, particularly the one that most producers do get rather sensitive about. Dec hastily apologised on air, but it provoked some quite genuine outrage in some areas. 'I think it was a pretty foregone conclusion that, after the last series, they [the producers] were going to pick a much more volatile group, because the others got on far too well in the last series,' said John Milton-Whatmore, chairman of Mediawatch UK, the country's leading broadcasting standards watchdog.

'It was only a matter of time before one of the incumbents of the present series went off the rails and Rotten is in there for this sort of purpose. The producers are anxious to get good ratings and they are not going to get them by everyone getting on well. Johnny Rotten's behaviour has been quite consistent over the years. He is a radical, controversial person, who has in the past sought to be sensational. It was only a matter of time before he came up with an expletive like this.' He had summed the situation up in a nutshell. The producers might have dreaded that outburst, but they themselves knew that something like that could happen. That said, they did realise it must not happen again and so built in a seven-second time delay to bleep out any future offending phrases.

Neil was the next person to be booted off the show, but his departure was rather overshadowed by the fact that Jordan and Peter were now well on the way to becoming an item. They shared an intimate moment with the 11 million viewers when they finally had an intimate kiss: poor Scott, Jordan's now ex-boyfriend, was said to be flying to Australia to confront the guilty pair, but there was no escaping it – he had been very publicly dumped.

It was all too much for one of the contestants. John Lydon, like the professional that he is, managed to cause yet another furore when he walked off the show, announcing that he didn't want to become another Des O'Connor. He also managed a last blast at Jordan. 'That's Silicon Valley, the crap-end version of it,' he said. 'That's one really lazy, spoiled sod. Who raises these people?'

The next upset came courtesy of Lord Brocket, who until now had been the favourite to win the show. In a conversation with Jordan, Lord B started bitching about Jennie Bond, calling her an 'old slag' who was 'arrogant' and 'dogmatic'. This proved to be a mistake and Ladbrokes, a keen observer of the show, promptly slashed Kerry's odds of winning from 4–5 to 2–1. 'Punters are smitten with the former Atomic Kitten,' said spokesman Warren Lush.

'While her former bandmates have split and their stardom is fading, Kerry is on the up and is odds-on favourite to become the very first Queen of the Jungle. Viewers are attracted by the fact that she appears to be a normal, down-to-earth girl. Lord Brocket's fortunes have changed dramatically in the last 24 hours. He was hot favourite to win after John Lydon left but his odds drifted when he revealed his bitchiness and contempt for Jennie Bond. This could prove to be his downfall.'

Alex Best, who seemed to have maintained a near-monastic silence during her time in the jungle, was the next to leave. Back at the camp, tensions were mounting: Jordan and Peter were having a lovers' tiff over whether their relationship was real or simply put on for the cameras (Jordan had actually confided to Neil that she would like to get her hands on Dec), while everyone was getting upset about Lord Brocket's behaviour. Kerry in particular was miffed when the two were sent on a joint challenge and he took no notice of her suggestions. 'I thought there was no "i" in team,' she protested, showing herself to be no stranger to the self-help section of the library.

Everyone cheered up again when Jordan and Kerry admired each other's embonpoints before sharing a kiss between themselves, the camp and the millions of rapt viewers back home, after which Jordan began playing Peter and Lord B off against each other. The viewers loved it and so did Ant and Dec, who gave every appearance of enjoying themselves enormously. 'It's a real joy to go into work,' said

Dec. 'We have to get to the camp at about 3am but straight away we ask for the Peter Andre footage and he cheers us up. He always provides us with a little gem like, "I was brought up to eat food."'

'I love them all,' said Ant. 'My only let-down has been Jordan. She said she'd strip naked. I'm going to go in the camp tomorrow and tell her she's on a deadline and she should get on with it during the live show.' The two did claim to be shocked at John Lydon, however. 'I was quite surprised he did it, because he's a 48-year-old guy,' said Ant. 'But he's been worth his weight in gold.'

The two claimed some credit for the success of the show, saying it was they who picked the original celebrities. 'We go to the pub with friends and say, "Who would you like to see in the jungle?"' said Dec. 'It starts off with people like Victoria Beckham and then we realise she's never going to do it, so we get more realistic. We had a big, long list when we went to Granada – and Frank Carson was one of the people on it. We really wanted him to be on it.' In fact, Carson was deemed too old to take part by his doctors and Mike Read replaced him at the last minute.

The duo professed concern about the relationship between Jordan and Peter. 'There's no chance of it working outside of the jungle,' said Dec firmly. 'The thing is, if they are attracted to each other, it's like a holiday romance. It's all because of the surroundings – and then you go back home and think, What the hell have I done?, and it's never the same.'

'I think she was playing along with him to start with

and she was enjoying the ride,' said Ant. 'I think she liked him chasing her and instead of running she stopped for a couple of days and let herself be caught. But now she's run off.'

With five celebrities still in the running, the two gave an assessment of the people left in the camp. Of Lord Brocket, Dec remarked, 'We were pleasantly surprised by him, considering his fear of heights in the Ladder Lottery Bushtucker Trial.' Of Jordan, Ant said, 'I think the show's been good for her. People have seen her in another way. But she hasn't done a Tara [Palmer-Tomkinson].' Of Peter, Dec said, 'I'm going to write to whoever it is and get Insania released. Peter was one of the original names on our list. He's a gem.' Of Jennie, Ant said, 'Jennie was great in her challenge. We giggled at how she was so British about it all. We poke fun at all the celebs, not just her.' And Kerry? 'I was worried about her after the first Bushtucker Trial,' said Dec. 'I took her aside and said, "Keep your chin up." She's great.'

The next surprise evacuee was Jordan, who was a little vague about whether she and Peter would have a relationship when both were on the outside. The remaining foursome then had to climb a muddy hill while being drenched with jets of water, after which Lord Brocket was booted out. Various more grotesque challenges followed, after which Peter left the jungle, to be followed by Jennie. Kerry had indeed become the first Queen of the Jungle. 'I cannot believe I am sat here,' she said as she was crowned. 'I am gobsmacked.' Of the other two, Peter seemed rather keen to have a chat with Jordan, while Jennie declared, 'It was such fun, with moments of utter horror. Never to be repeated, but it was such fun.'

Jennie also took to the two hosts immediately. 'I hadn't ever met them, funnily enough,' she said. 'The show was the first time and I was terrified I was going to get it wrong and call Ant Dec and vice versa. I did my homework and I sorted it out. I hear there was a survey while we were out there that most of the population can't tell them apart.

'Literally all you see [of them] is when they come in or when you do a Bushtucker Trial and you talk to them "as live", so there is no room for chit-chat. But I thought they were charming. Particularly little Dec. I followed them for a number of years. I wasn't sure of their appeal or their charm until this series and looking back and listening to my husband and my daughter who were watching. They said that Ant and Dec were absolutely brilliant in this series.

'It's a very, very good partnership – you felt that when you are working with them. When I looked back on the tapes and saw Dec's imitation of the Queen, and sort of me imitating the Queen – very, very funny. They seem to have a real, ready wit and working with them they made you feel very comfortable and they were just easy to get along with. They have obviously got some kind of magic ingredient. But I'm not quite sure what it is.

'I seemed to have more of an immediate affinity with Dec. He has got a lovely twinkle in his eyes and he is a cute-looking little guy. And I just seemed to talk to him more than Ant for some reason, but I mean they were both charming and very funny. On the Hill of Hell, when we were covered in 3,000 tons of water and mud, they were having terrible difficulties keeping a straight face. It was fun.'

It was also a massive success. Again over £1 million had been raised for charity and again the viewing figures were spectacular: 16 million people tuned in to see the last episode of the show. And it later turned out that Jordan did try to get together with Dec, saying, 'You're single now, Dec – how about it?'

'We just had a bit of a laugh,' Dec said hastily. 'She's a nice girl. I know that Jordan plays the game. She knows the power she has over men and plays on it.'

Dec was adamant that he wasn't getting it together with anyone, and that included Alison Astall. 'I just want a bit of time to myself and I'm concentrating on work,' he said. 'I am very single. I've just come out of an 11-year relationship and I am not ready to jump into something else with someone else. I am too busy to go out on the pull, it's all early nights in front of the telly at the moment.' And he denied an involvement with television presenter Sarah Cawood, also the subject of much rumour.

Ant, more firmly than ever with Lisa, was on the verge of getting engaged. He was also amazed at the amount of coverage Dec's split with Clare had garnered. 'I'm quite happy with Lisa,' he said. 'I'm not tempted to be single again and go out on the pull with Dec. Lisa and I have talked about getting married, but there's no plans to do it yet. The surprising thing about what happened with Dec is that we've never had that sort of interest in our private lives before. We don't hang out at celeb haunts, we normally just do our jobs and go home and watch telly. So it was quite surprising people were so interested.'

It wasn't really that surprising. In March 2004 Ant and Dec were jointly named Britain's favourite TV personality and, when you are that popular with the public, people are going to be interested in your private life as well. Even so, a poll at the same time revealed that 70 per cent of the viewing public still didn't know which was which, something the boys were at last coming to terms with. 'We thought the percentage would be higher,' said a rueful Ant. 'I mean – folk call me Antandec when I'm on my own in Boots.' But when you're fast turning into a national institution you can afford to laugh.

15

Boys No More

THE BOYS were as fresh faced as ever, but time was beginning to take its toll. A new series of *Saturday Night Takeaway* was in production, and, slightly to their shock, Ant and Dec were asked to film a new opening for the programme – because they looked too old for the one that kicked off previous series. The new sequence involved leaping across rooftops in a satire of Jump Britain on Channel 4, and went down very well with the audience, but it was a testament to the passing of time. 'It was quite a shock for us when the producers told us they needed to re-shoot the introduction because they said we'd last shot the scenes three years ago and they told us we looked a lot more grown up now,' said Dec. 'This is my 30th year and it just made me realise we're getting older!'

They were indeed, and by this time, the two had also spent well over half their lives as major television stars. But their work ethic remained as strong as ever, as did their ability to don a disguise and completely fool the cast of another television show. On this occasion the show was *Coronation Street*, when the duo dressed up as a pair of female Japanese reporters.

Amazingly, no one cottoned on. The cast of Corrie were told that the two were to report on news that the soap had been sold to Japan and so, after four hours in make-up, out came Keiko (Ant) and Yuki (Dec), pretending to be obsessed with Todd Grimshaw, the sexually confused character played by Bruno Langley, who had recently experienced the show's first ever gay kiss. And indeed, after being on the receiving end of much attention from the Oriental duo, Todd ended up with a kiss on the lips from Keiko. 'I just didn't know what was going on,' said a slightly bemused Langley afterwards. 'The whole experience was just so out of the blue.'

It all added to the fun of the nations, something that was tacitly acknowledged in April 2004, when the boys went off with two awards at the prestigious Golden Rose awards in Lucerne, Switzerland. They won both Best Game Show Host and Best Variety Programme for *Saturday Night Takeaway* at the Rose d'Or television festival, something that assured not only their own standing, but the future of the programme. 'Picking up not one but two awards is very special for us,' they said. 'We love making *Saturday Night Takeaway*, so it's brilliant that it's been recognised at such an important and prestigious event, especially when we were up against some of the world's finest television talent. We really appreciate what an honour this is and look forward to making more *Saturday Night Takeaway* in the future.'

But behind all the excitement, Dec was very much feeling the absence of Clare. The rumours about a relationship with his agent looked increasingly implausible, and there were reports that he had been visiting Clare on the set of *Steel River Blues* in Leeds. 'Dec has made the trip up to Leeds a few times to come and see me,' she confided to a friend. 'We have always remained extremely close and always talked on the phone. But he has been calling me a lot more recently. And he has said he's really keen to get back together. At the moment it's a matter of taking one step at a time.'

Clare was certainly as upset as Dec, even if not as sure about a reunion. 'I'd just come out of my relationship with Dec when we started filming *Steel River Blues*, so the timing was good,' she said. 'I could pour myself into my work. It's sad when something like that happens, but I was surprised about how big a story it was. I wouldn't have imagined it would be front page news. There were photographers following me and people on my doorstep all the time, but my way of dealing with it was not to say anything in public. The most important thing for me was to keep talking to Dec. Whatever happened, we had grown up together and nothing is going to change that. We were together a very long time. I did think it would end up in marriage, but that didn't happen, obviously. It was horrible, painful and difficult but that time is over and we're doing different things. We've moved on.'

And professionally, the boys were leaping to new heights, although it did take its toll. 'We still get nervous before every show,' admitted Ant during an interview in front of 200 people, for which the boys had travelled back to the North East at the opening of an extension at Newcastle Airport. 'Especially when doing the undercover bits on Takeaway. It takes so long to put all the make-up on, four or five hours, so the last thing we want is to go up to someone and they say, "Hi Ant." That has happened once and it will never be shown.'

They didn't need to worry: their massive popularity showed no sign of flagging and in September 2004, the duo were named TV Personalities of the Year at the annual GQ Men of the Year awards. They also appeared on *Parkinson*, on which, yet again, they denied reports that they wanted to work separately. And indeed, why break up such a winning combination? 'Everything we're planning for the future is with the two of us involved,' said Ant. 'We love working together and we're pleased with the shows we do. We have made a pact that if one of us wants to do something and the other one doesn't fancy it, we're not going to get cross and have a row.'

But no one, least of all ITV, wanted to see them split. The pair had just signed a three year contract with the broadcaster, said to be worth £3 million each, much to the relief of ITV given that the BBC was said to be nosing around again. 'ITV would be absolutely sunk without them,' said one BBC executive. Between them and Simon Cowell they are the core of ITV's plan.' ITV was well aware of this. 'Ant and Dec are an enormous asset to ITV,' said Nigel Pickard, director of programmes. 'They have a unique appeal to our audience and are loved by everyone from kids to grannies. They are immensely talented presenters who really do get better with every series. They're also incredibly nice guys.'

They were also increasingly financially astute guys. As aware as they always have been that their days as on screen talent may be finite, the two were continuing to develop their roles as programme makers as well presenters and had by now formed a new company, Gallowgate Productions, named after an area of Newcastle and one end of St James's Park. They were also now named as executive producers on the latest series of *Saturday Night Takeaway*, which was pulling in eight million viewers, equating to 39 per cent of the audience, a role the boys clearly took very seriously. 'The real big learning curve for us was *SM:tv*,' said Dec. 'We really got involved in that, came up with this idea for a Saturday morning show, got it commissioned, then it was, 'Hurray, we've got the fifty two-week commission for a Saturday morning. Shit. What do we put in it?'

It was a rare sighting of Ant and Dec as businessmen, but they soon revealed quite how involved they now were behind the scenes. Indeed, they were talking about their work more in terms of marketing that performing, an approach that ensures a long term future in television. They revealed that initially *SM:tv* had been envisaged as having only a thirteen-week run and that it was Nigel Pickard who insisted the show be put on for a year. 'He wanted to build the brand and we were lucky he gave us time,' said Dec.

Ant was more forthright still. 'You go through an awful 17 per cent share for three months and no awareness of it, because everyone just switched on BBC1. It was trying to turn that round. We never said, 'We'll be more shocking, or we'll be more real and then we'll get the viewers,' we just kept going and people found us. If we'd only had a commission of thirty two or twenty six [weeks] we probably wouldn't have got a second series, to be honest. It was as soon as [*Live and Kicking*] came off air for the summer, we picked up. Once you see those share points grow, everyone gets a bit more confidence in what they're doing and believes it a bit more.'

Indeed, the two were positively nostalgic for the work involved in the show, 'and feeling it could be done,' said Ant. 'That was the big thing – being down the pub on a Thursday night and talking about items and ideas and, like, we talked about Challenge Ant, which was an item where the kids challenge me. We went into rehearsal on the Wednesday and it worked up, and we thought, 'Oh, we'll try that next month' and it really worked and it stayed there even after we left. Seeing it up on screen and thinking, 'Shit, that's our idea..."

They also understood that the format and positioning were exactly right in terms of developing ideas and a presence on the screen. 'We loved the process and it was a very forgiving playground,' said Dec. 'Saturday morning, you've got three hours of live telly and it's really forgiving.

If you do a crap sketch, the audience will let you off because half of them are hungover and half of them are kids and they didn't understand it anyway.'

History proved quite what a success they made of it, but the boys were far too canny to allow the business side of their lives to spoil their image as real life likely lads. On the one hand, there were talks in the background about their production company coming up with a sitcom – a long term dream of the boys that has yet to come to fruition – and yet in public, they remained as boisterous as ever. The latest to fall for their escapades was Geri Halliwell, who was fooled into thinking the pair were her chauffeur and a policeman. Dec was the driver of the car, who was desperate to go to the loo, and Ant was the policemen, who arrested him, and would only let him go if la Halliwell sang 'Happy Birthday' down the radio to a colleague. The former Spice Girl duly obliged.

And their status as the undisputed kings of TV was bolstered yet again that autumn, when they won two gongs at the National Television Awards for Best Entertainment Presenters and Best Entertainment Show for *Saturday Night Takeaway*. This brought their total from this particular awards ceremony to seven, equalling Michael Barrymore, who had previously held the all time record. But there was little time to celebrate; such was the success of *I'm A Celebrity...* that by November, the duo were already making plans to return to the Australian jungle.

1 6

Another Rumble In The jungle

ANT AND DEC were ready to preside of more antics in the jungle and again it became apparent quite how seriously they took everything they were involved in. When the show airs, the two come across as a soothing presence holding it all together: sometimes reassuring a distraught participant, sometimes gleefully siding with the audience. It looks effortless, spontaneous and spur of the moment. In reality, it is nothing of the sort - it involved hard work, planning and an understanding of how to make the programme work. Indeed, the two were canny enough to put their experience on *Pop Idol* to good use.

This experience was first applied to the early scripts. '[They] weren't happening for us,' said Dec. 'It was all taking itself a bit seriously like it was an important social experiment and we were like, no, it's ridiculous.' 'And it was great because we'd come off Pop Idol and we'd learned that language of someone being voted out and almost knowing the right phrases and the right terminology,' said Ant.

Dec took over again. 'Things like looking at *Big Brother* and, 'Big Brother house, this is Davina,' and on *Pop Idol*, 'You're safe, you're not safe,' and we got out there and there was nothing,' he said. 'We sat there and said, 'What's the language of the show? How does the show sound?' They were very much, because it was the factual department, they wanted us to go in and refer to the VTs and say to Christine, 'You said this about Rhona, why did you say that?' And we said, 'We don't want to be all Paxman about it, we just want to go in and tell them who's been voted out and get out of there. We were like, what if we start outside every morning and we say, 'It can only be I'm A Celebrity, Get Me Out Of Here!' What we do is to react to the telly, really. I see our job as being one of the viewers.'

And that sums up quite why the two have become so astronomically successful. Unlike other presenters, they have never lost touch with where they have come from and, indeed, the British public. Obviously they are talented and professional, but they are also down to earth, and that remains as crucial to their success as any other quality.

Indeed, *I'm A Celebrity...* was becoming more popular than ever, but shortly before the latest proceedings were due to commence, a row ensued that very nearly overshadowed everything else. Paul Gascoigne had been due to take part in the programme, and at the very last minute was dropped from the show, seemingly because the producers felt he was too famous. This might well have been a blessing in disguise for the troubled star, now only a shadow of his former self, but Gascoigne and his agent were furious. 'I've really been fucked about,' he said.

'They pestered me for weeks and I kept saying, "No, no, no," because I didn't fancy it. But because they were so persistent and it was a big challenge I finally agreed to meet them last week and told them I was prepared to do it. I know the British public wanted me to go in the jungle. Then this week I got a letter from the show saying they didn't want me anymore. Perhaps they felt I was too famous for *I'm A Celebrity*. I can't understand it. Now they've got Joe Pasquale and someone from the Three Degrees. My agent is not happy one fucking bit.'

It was a surprising decision, but the show's producers had by now come up with the line-up they wanted. This time round the participants were to be as follows: the model Sophie Anderton, Janet Street-Porter, Sheila Ferguson of the Three Degrees and the comedian Joe Pasquale. Also on board were Princess Diana's erstwhile butler Paul Burrell, Nancy Sorrell, nightclub boss Fran Cosgrave, Brian Harvey, Antonio 'Huggy Bear' Farga, who was brought in at the last minute after the model Emma B pulled outs, and Natalie Appleton, who, at this stage at least, was the favourite to win the show.

As before, there was a huge amount of publicity and excitement generated by the proceedings. Contestants were interviewed and gave their own take on what was to happen, as ever, mixing the bizarre with the mundane. The down to earth Sheila Ferguson commented, 'I'm going to miss my Jacuzzi, champagne, caviar, texting on my mobile, my cooking, McDonalds and KFC,' before expressing the desire that appearing on the show would help her to move on from being associated with the Three Degrees. Nancy Sorrell was more puzzling. 'I want to design my own range of underwear so, when I'm out there, I'll design it with some twigs and leaves and then model it,' she said. 'I'm having a serious waxing session. I've got to get my back done. I'm seriously hairy.'

Everyone was nervous. 'What happens if you're stuck out there for at least a week and they don't like you?' demanded Joe Pasquale. 'I'm not bothered about my liking people, I'm worried they won't like me. I might turn into a freak who wants to strangle everybody with a vine leaf.' Not everyone was prepared: it emerged that Antonio Fargas had never actually seen the show. 'Normally I don't like reality shows, but I thought it was a nice opportunity to share something with the British public,' he said. 'I think my greatest problem will be getting bored with it all and saying, 'I hope I get voted off so I can go home."

The contestants were also living up to their image. Paul Burrell commented, 'I don't think there's a cat in hell's chance of me winning. I've had an education in the best: how to be the best, how to behave, how to dress, how to be polite, how to manage yourself in situations and how to entertain at the highest possible level. You couldn't get a better pedigree. It's not about a certain lady, it's about my knowledge.' Sophie Anderton, who had very publicly battled drink and drug addiction in the past, was determined to stay clean. 'I don't want to relapse,' she said. 'Drinking now makes me feel physically sick. I know what it all leads to.'

And some of the stars were clearly going to find it an ordeal. 'I am a sadistic, masochistic freak, because I hate all the things you do out there in the jungle,' said Natalie Appleton. 'Absolutely nothing has prepared me for this. I got on a rowing machine the other day for 15 minutes, and woke up in agony the next morning. I am unfit, I have phobias and compulsive disorders and I hate flying.'

Brian Harvey was no better. 'I can't swim and I fell into the canal several times when I was younger,' he said. 'When we used to go swimming with the school, I'd just not turn up that day. I hated it. If I get a task involving water, I won't be able to do it.' The former East 17 singer did, however, have a very good reason to go: reviving his career, as Peter Andre had done after his appearance in the show earlier in the year. 'I decided to take part because I can't get a record deal and after seventeen million people a day have watched you, the record companies are more interested,' he said. 'All I'm going to do is be me. If people like me, they like me. If they don't, then fuck them.'

And some, uncharacteristically, even showed a degree of self-knowledge. 'When I told Elton that I was going,' said Janet Street Porter, 'he just pissed himself laughing and said, "I feel sorry for the other people. I don't care who they are, I feel the utmost sympathy."'

The series kicked off in spectacular style. The producers had been wracking their brains to find someway of starting the proceedings that stood out from the last and they certainly did that: four of the contestants, Paul Burrell, Nancy Sorrell, Fran Cosgrove and Joe Pasquale were parachuted into the camp from a plane 12,000 feet up. Paul was clearly terrified: 'No, no, no!' he cried as he leapt out, although he and the others all landed safely (actually, Paul missed the landing site but was brought in soon afterwards.) Nancy was thrilled by what she had done. 'I really loved every second of it,' she said. 'After jumping off a plane millions of feet up, I think I can do anything. Well, not really, but it's given me so much confidence.'

Meanwhile, the other contestants arrived by more sedate means: helicopter and horseback, with Brian Harvey very bravely taking his place. His grandmother, who had brought him up, had died shortly beforehand and the singer was clearly utterly grief-stricken but went on. 'My nan's death came as a great shock,' he said. 'I'm not doing this because I'm looking for the sympathy vote. My nan was really excited about me doing the show and I really do think her and my granddad wouldn't have wanted me to miss this amazing experience.'

And so they were off once more. Just as in the previous series, right from the start there were surprises about who was popular and who was not, with the previous favourite to win, Natalie, appearing to unravel almost as soon as she set foot in the jungle. There were many tears before bedtime, as she sobbed that she wanted to go home, something that cut no ice at all with the viewers, who voted for her to do the second Bush Tucker trial. In the first Fran had been showered with the usual creepy crawlies: now Natalie, who was terrified of heights, was told she had to wheel a shopping trolley above a cable 200 feet high.

This did not go down well. 'I said I couldn't do this,' she told Ant and Dec. 'It's something up high. How am I going to do this? I was preparing to eat pus and bugs. My knees have gone like jelly. I couldn't go on my hotel balcony. Do you realise this is really serious for me? I'm doing this for my kids. This is my ultimate fear.' Nonetheless, Natalie decided to have a go, although once up, she whimpered, 'I'm not happy. Help me. Help me.' But with the duo guiding her on, she managed to collect seven stars – before being given oxygen by the camp medic.

Janet Street-Porter, however, was acting true to form. From the start, she had been billed as the controversial contestant, and she lost no time in making her views known: Natalie was lashed out at for crying, Brian for smoking, Sheila and Antonio for talking too much and Paul for being brainwashed. When Paul remarked that he 'knew his place,' Janet could barely contain herself. 'What a mindset that takes … the monarchy is past its sell-by date and in spite of how they treated you, you'll stick up for them.'

In this particular case, karma came round quickly. The very next day Janet was picked for the next Bush Tucker trial, in which she had to search in a tank full of snakes for the gold stars. She certainly proved quite what a toughie she really is: despite being bitten by three snakes, she still managed to get nine stars. 'People say snakes are not venomous but when they bite you, it's not very nice,' she confided to Ant and Dec. 'They are so quick.' She had also made it up with at least some of her fellow camp mates. 'I can live on rice and beans, but other people, especially Brian, can't. I've got to do it for Brian.'

Indeed, Janet was turning out as one of the show's success stories. She might have been difficult to deal with, but she made for very good television, something the boys recognised. 'I love Janet, she's hilarious,' said Dec. 'In her own world, she's just a moany cow. She's a bit Johnny Rotten, so I think she's great.' 'I don't dislike her, but there's something about her,' added Ant. 'She makes us laugh and she's very opinionated. If you argue with her, she says her piece and then leaves it in the air. She's good on the show.'

But opinionated contestants were not enough: the producers needed to keep thinking up new ideas to make the programme lively and innovative. This they now did to spectacular effect: the comedian Vic Reeves, who is married to Nancy Sorrell, was suddenly and unexpectedly ushered into the jungle, where he and his wife, as the only married couple present, were given the use of the tree house. The producers might well have been hoping that this would result in some on air shenanigans – in the event they were disappointed. But Vic's arrival ensured yet more coverage. This series was shaping up to be quite as successful as the last.

As before, the boys offered good natured commentary on the proceedings as events unfolded. Of Nancy, Ant said, 'I think she's a real team player and gets on with everyone, particularly Sophie. Now Vic's come in, if they become a married couple, that's going to cause a bit of conflict.' 'I think Nancy's been brilliant,' said Dec. 'Not just because she's dead game, but she had this huge secret hanging around her. It was obviously playing on her mind, but she kept it quiet and dealt with it.'

Of Natalie and her histrionics, which some people suggested were being put on, Ant said, 'In the Grand Calamity trial, she was petrified. She's got a bit quiet now, I'd like to see her around a bit more.' 'I thought Natalie on the way in was hilarious,' said Dec. 'When she said, 'I touched a tree' – that was brilliant. I've heard people say she was faking it, but you can't fake being scared of touching a tree, surely?'

On Joe, the eventual winner, Ant and Dec were their usual canny selves. 'Joe seems to be doing really well,' said Dec. 'I get lots of texts from friends and family saying they love him. It'll be interesting to see what the dynamic is now another comedian has come in.' 'I like squeaky Joe,' said Ant. 'I'd seen him do stuff in the past – and he is what he is on the telly. I think it's always nice when you see somebody as they are.'

And of the newcomer, Vic, the two were clearly fans. 'I love Vic Reeves,' said Ant. 'I'm at the right age – I was a drunken student when he started off and I'm sure spouted all his catchphrases. He can blow hot and cold. He can be up and down, passionate and quiet.' 'I feel a bit sorry for him,' said Dec. 'He's got a difficult job being like the new kid at school. I know how he feels when he says he feels like he gate crashed a party.'

Meanwhile the contestants themselves continued to provide the high drama that was expected of them and in the end it was Brian who finally blew his top and walked out. He had been in the jungle for five days, clearly in a state of grief, and the row, when it came, was based on a seemingly trivial incident – as domestic upheavals so often are. It came when he loudly and deliberately, broke wind.

Janet was standing nearby, de-boning a fish. 'Now don't do that when we are cooking,' she said. 'It's so inappropriate.'

Brian almost immediately went ballistic. 'Oh come off it ma,' he said. 'You are on the fucking other side. Stop having a go at me for farting, man. For fuck's sake.'

'I'm trying to cook dinner,' said Janet.

'You're fucking over there and I'm over here,' Brian replied. 'Don't keep fucking having a go at me about farting.' Janet tried to calm him down, to no avail. 'No, no, no, no!' Brian went on. 'Don't keep fucking telling me what to do. If I want to fart, I'll fart. I'm nowhere near the fucking food. I'm sick of people having a go at me.' Janet was clearly getting a little annoyed. 'Do you think farting on television looks intelligent?' she asked. 'I'm farting cause I need to fart, cause all I've eaten is fucking beans,' snarled Brian, before momentarily calming down.

But it was not to last. After apologising, Brian seemed to brood for a few minutes, before standing up, tearing off his microphone and saying, 'I'm outta here, right fucking now. I'm fucking tired and hungry. Fuck the dinner. Enjoy it. I'm a celebrity – get me fucking out of here – now! I've had enough of this bollocks,' he continued to a bemused Paul. 'I'm outta here – it's getting silly when you crack a little joke,' he told Natalie and Nancy. 'I'm just really looking forward to getting outta here now,' he went on as he entered the Bush Telegraph. 'Still, what an ending. I've done my peace making on the way out. I don't mind ending it on a fart.' It was hardly Shakespeare, but it made for good television.

Indeed, walking out soon became the new staying in. On day nine, Natalie also left the show after the public voted for her to take her fifth Bushtucker Trial, she had clearly had enough. 'I'm going home, I've come to the end of my road, I physically can not give any more, I've got nothing left,' she said. 'I feel like I'm Dorothy saying goodbye to the Lion, the Tin Man and the Scarecrow and I'm tapping my shoes together. There's no place like home, there's no place like home, there's no place like home.'

'I was neither mentally or physically prepared for the show – it was very surreal,' she told Ant and Dec later on. 'At the hotel I ordered room service and put half my sandwich in the fridge. I just can't deal with being out.' Asked who she wanted to win, Natalie wouldn't say. 'I want everyone to have a fair chance of winning and I think everyone has an equal chance of winning,' she said. 'I love every single one of them. I have no regrets about being a contestant because I met every single one of them. I have learned to appreciate food.'

And she was philosophical about the whole experience. 'I did my best and I know it was still not good enough,' she said. 'I didn't come here to win. I came here to see how I could do and I have done my fair share of going through it. I'm tired and don't have the energy left. I got this far and it was the end of my dream. I take my hat off to the people who have done the show before and gone the distance because it's tough. I'm not as tough as I thought. I've done what I came to do. I've been through the mill, doing more trials than I expected. It has been one heck of a journey. I'm not going to be so anal in the future and hope this experience will alleviate some of the worries I have had down the years.' And as far as the trials were concerned, she had a point. Apart from the high wire act, Natalie had also been forced to deal with giant eels, fly pupae and eat rotten fruit, in the course of which she managed to obtain remarkably few stars. She can hardly be blamed for tiring of it all at the end.

Her departure provoked mixed reactions in the group. Joe was disappointed that she'd quit, but the hungrier of the participants were relieved. 'She made the right decision,' said Sheila. 'We'd have had just one star and no food again,' and then proved she could put her money where her mouth is by undergoing the trial herself. Dressed in a spectacular designer swimsuit, which she later wistfully revealed was ruined, she waded into a rat infested swamp to retrieve the stars. She did well: despite having to slide around under a wooden grid which held both stars and rats, she managed to win six meals, giving up only when a crocodile joined her in the water.

It was also on day nine that the first eviction came and it

was a surprise when it happened: Nancy was chosen to go. Everyone, her included, was taken aback, not least because she had not been forced to do a Bushtucker Trial. But the problem soon became clear: the arrival of her husband Vic was seen by neither the audience or the other participants as fair game. 'I think the public hated me for that and that's why I went out, the fact I knew he was coming,' she said. 'I think people may have wanted to split us up a little bit. Maybe people were a little bit jealous, I didn't care because he helped me a lot.' And of the big question - did they or didn't they – the answer was firmly no. 'We didn't have a bit of whoopy – there was none of that,' she said. 'We cuddled – nothing else. We wouldn't have had a bit of how's your father in front of millions of people.'

She was almost certainly right in that a couple being in situ did seem to have caused some resentment. Vic was the next to be evicted: 'Thank you, yes!' he cried. 'I had a great time but I'm so pleased to be out. The most difficult part was when Nancy went. I got very miserable and I was going to make a run for it tonight.' And of the couple issue, he confessed, 'Perhaps they thought we were a bit too close.'

Next out was Sheila, who confirmed quite what hard work it was in the camp. Asked whether she'd enjoyed it, she replied, 'No! It really was tougher than I'd expected. Every trial was like three trials in one and it took a lot of endurance to get through them.' She was also clearly relieved that Natalie had gone. 'Natalie deciding to leave helped the others to get on the mend foodwise,' she said. 'I couldn't have gone on, it was exhausting.' It didn't take long for tensions to spill out, either. Shown a video in which Sophie called her patronising, Sheila pulled no punches. 'She is a little spoilt brat,' she said. 'She is a rotten spoilt bitch and I can't stand her. She can't talk about anyone but herself.'

Back in the jungle itself, Sophie was feeling fretful. 'I haven't felt like I have this week since I was doing drugs,' she confided. 'I actually feel like I'm going mad in here. I can't do anything because every time I get up I feel dizzy. I'm worried that something is going to bite me and worried where I have to put my feet – I'm going proper barking insane.' Fran became a particular confidant. 'You are the only one keeping me sane in here,' she told him. 'I'm the only young girl left in here so I'm the Princess of the Jungle.' Fran was sympathetic. 'She's tired and she's a model,' he teased. 'She's missing her boyfriend and she's a model.'

Meanwhile, a rather strange friendship was developing: one between Janet and Paul. Indeed, Janet was positively revelling in his company. 'Burrell baiting just keeps me on top form with the repartee,' she said. 'Not being at home and not having my friends and my boyfriend to moan at, I've got Paul here. It's perfect because he does so many things that I find incredible. It's like having your own little pet.' Paul himself was taking it in good part: when he began a rendition of 'I've Got You Under My Skin', Janet hit him with a dishcloth. 'You haven't released an album with Woolworths or something, have you?' she asked. 'Oh please. I'm embarrassed. It makes me puke.'

Paul himself was wearing a t-shirt with cut-outs that Sophie had customised for him and what he referred to as 'my boutique bandana.' 'That's the first and probably only time I will have a supermodel rip my clothes off,' he said. Janet took a different approach. 'If anyone came up to me in a club wearing that outfit I would simply make my excuses and leave,' she said, as Paul embarked on 'Anything Goes'. 'You will be in *Attitude*. You'll be a gay icon.'

The next contestant to face eviction was Sophie Anderton. 'I'm so happy, I'm so happy,' she said as she cavorted with the remaining quartet, 'I'm so happy I get to see my boyfriend.' By the time she got to the Bush Telegraph for a chat with Ant and Dec, Sophie, in fact, came across as a very good sport, laughing as some of the show's highlights were played back to her. 'I'm in civilisation, I'm very happy,' she said, revealing that she had at first treated being there as a military exercise. It was an argument with Natalie that had calmed her down.

'As I got to know people a lot better and thanks to Nat and our big argument – I didn't realise I was being so unemotional,' she said. 'I was trying to be so perfect. Once I relaxed, the last week has been really good fun.' Indeed, she said that she was pleased Natalie had called her a prima donna. 'In the beginning I didn't realise, I was just so focused on getting through,' she said. 'Once I relaxed and once that was made apparent to me I was mortified by that.' She was even magnanimous when told that Sheila had called her a 'spoilt bitch.' 'That's fine, I don't have to see her again,' she said. 'I admitted that [being spoilt] myself, I was spoilt when I came in here, but I lasted 15 days so obviously I did something right.' With that she was reunited with her boyfriend Mark Alexiou, with a joyous reunion in front of the cameras.

There were now only five contestants left and the next to go was Antonio. He accepted his fate with grace. 'I've had my bags packed for a while,' he said. 'I think you have the right people left in. But it has been a great, great experience for me. Be unpredictable, have fun,' he advised Fran, before shedding a few tears when Ant and Dec went over the jungle footage with him. 'They're real, they're real,' he said.

Fittingly, given his most famous role, he later told the duo he had been the Daddy Bear of the camp, and expressed sadness at being evicted. 'I've never been evicted from a home, from a club maybe, but this had become my home. We had become a family and real issues came up.' He was open to admitting that Sophie had got on his nerves, and that he had tried to be a counsellor to her. 'Obviously, everyone knows she's going through a lot,' he said. 'She needs to be taken car of, so I tried to help.' Back in the jungle, Janet was determined to go for it. 'I'm thrilled to still be here,' she said. 'I really want to be the winner.'

Alas, it was not to be: Janet turned out to be next for the chop. She was typically forthright on her departure, too. On seeing the line-up, 'I thought, how can I talk to these load of deadbeats,' she told Ant and Dec. 'But that was cruel. Once I got to know them we established a rapport. But they're not going to be my best friends.'

It had always been a funny combination of people, and she and Paul managed one final bust-up before Janet left when she accused him of betraying Princess Diana by writing a book about her. Burrell responded by calling her a snarling Rottweiler – and then talking about Diana some more. 'She was at times selfish,' he said. 'In place of that, she included my family. They were a surrogate family to hers and were included in events like theme parks. She tried to compensate for taking me away too many special times from my family.'

As for Janet, she seemed to be genuinely glad to be out. 'I knew it would be me, I'm happy I've done it,' she said when Ant and Dec presented her with the news. 'In a perverse, sick kind of way, I actually enjoyed it. The bloody children can run the camp now,' she added later, going on to say that she wanted Joe to win. 'He's really interesting, he does adapt,' she said. 'He's an incredibly hard worker out of all the people there.' And Paul? 'He's wallowing in the past,' said Janet. 'He has a sentimental view of the monarchy. He ought to get a grip. He's a thoroughly decent bloke, but he's got to move on.'

In the event, it was Paul who was the runner up, while Joe was the overall winner. 'Don't cry mate. Well done Buzz,' he said to Paul (Buzz, as in Lightyear, was Burrell's nickname), before accepting a glass of champagne and being crowned with fern and leaves by Tara Palmer-Tomkinson. 'I saw you guys,' he said to Ant and Dec, 'at a party and I said if they ask me to do it I will tell them to stick it up their arse. But it's been an experience and I have made ten friends – twelve with the emus.'

Indeed, Joe was overcome with the attention he now received. 'I've been in the business for twenty years, then I come on this show, sit on my arse, eat crap and jump out of an aeroplane – and now everybody wants to talk about me. It's amazing. You could say this show gave me the best and worst experiences of my life. I honestly thought that someone would give us a Spam sandwich after a couple of days, but they didn't, so we all ended up starving.'

Paul, whose dancing, singing and squealing had made him an immense hit with the viewers, was feeling emotional. 'What an incredible journey,' he said after bursting into tears. 'I can't stop shaking. It's restored my faith in the British public.' And Fran, in third place, gratefully accepted a pint of Guinness. 'It was the best experience of my life,' he said. Janet, meanwhile, managed to have the last word. 'I'm Queen of the Jungle. I don't need a crown,' she said. 'In my head I'm the winner and I really don't give a toss.'

1 7

Back To The Future

ANT AND DEC were back in the UK and for one of them, at least, romance was on his mind. Dec had still not met another girlfriend since breaking up with Clare, and it seemed increasingly as if this was because it was still Clare that he wanted. Indeed, shortly after he returned, he was spotted visiting Clare at the De Monfort Hall in Leicester, where she was appearing in the musical *The Little Shop of Horrors*. 'He was really happy with how the reunion went,' said a friend. 'He would love it if they could get back together as a couple over the festive season. Dec wants her back and opened up to her but she isn't as sure.'

The two had, in fact, been very open about their heart-to-heart. Dec sat in the audience watching the show, after which he joined Clare in her dressing room. The two then drove to the nearby Hilton Hotel, where Dec had booked a suite, and chatted for two hours before Clare eventually left. 'She left in a very happy, positive mood, although Dec desperately wanted her to stay,' said a friend. 'He didn't want her to leave. It's clear she is the only woman for him. He misses her so much. It had been a real struggle for him to let her walk away. He was desperate to catch up with Clare again after returning from Australia. She's always in his thoughts.'

Given how strongly Dec clearly felt about Clare, mutual friends were increasingly keen to see the two reunited. 'He and Clare stayed friends and kept talking regularly after they split,' said one. 'Now we are all hoping and praying that they can get back together. Dec and Clare were made for each other and last Christmas was awful – their first apart in eleven years. Fingers crossed that 2005 is going to see them reunited. The fact that he is willing to dash across the country for a few snatched hours with her shows just how much of a bond there still is between them. He can't get her out of his mind.' Whether that reunion will ever really take place, though, is unclear. At the time of writing, the pair remain just friends. And Dec still hasn't found anyone else.

If he was upset, however, at least another clutch of awards awaited the duo at the end of 2004. In December's British Comedy Awards, Ant and Dec won both the Best Entertainment Personality and Best Entertainment Show for *Saturday Night Takeaway*. And the BBC was showing just how important the duo are to ITV in the most backhanded form of compliment – by planning to schedule one of their strongest forthcoming new shows, *Dr Who*, against *Saturday Night Takeaway*. This was to be a challenge to the boys – it was the Time Lord's return to television after fifteen years, starring Chris Eccleston as the Doctor and Billie Piper as his assistant. If that were not enough, the show was to be written by Russell T Davies, who was also the author of the successful TV drama *Queer As Folk*.

And Davies, like everyone else, knew what was going to be at stake. 'We're going to be up against Ant and Dec,' he said. 'So you can't be boring. You can't sit still with it. It's got to be emotional and it's got to be fun at the same time. It's got to move like shit, really – and it does. We're getting there. There are about eighty scenes per episode. It's a massive turnover of material and we're telling good stories.'

Nor was that the only competition on the horizon. On Saturday mornings on the BBC, a new duo were emerging in a show that provoked quite as much outrage as Ant and Dec's had done some years earlier: *Dick And Dom In Da Bugalow*. Even the names of the rising young stars echoed the older two, who were now nearing thirty, as did the controversy they were beginning to stir up. Indeed, the Tory MP for Mid Worcestershire, Peter Luff, was so appalled that he singled it out for criticism in a speech aimed at Culture Secretary Tessa Jowell.

'You can join me in playing, How Low Can You Bungalow? – a test to see your response to grossly embarrassing personal situations, largely of a lavatorial nature;' he fumed, 'Pants Dancers In The Hall Of Fame – photos of children with underwear on their heads; Make

Dick Sick, a game which I think speaks for itself; and finally Bunged Up, in which you play a character in a sewerage system avoiding turtle poos coming from various lavatories. Is that really the stuff of public service broadcasting?'

That was almost exactly the tone that Ant and Dec had also provoked in their days as children's broadcasters but Dick and Dom – actually Richard McCourt and Dominic Wood – were actually keen to play down the comparison. 'Everyone compares us to Ant and Dec and we've always admired them,' said Dick. 'But what we do is very, very different. We don't see ourselves in suits on Saturday night, like Ant and Dec.' He was talking about the Ant and Dec of today, however – not their earlier days when the comparisons were very strong indeed.

If Ant and Dec were worried about the competition now making itself felt from all sides, they certainly weren't showing it. Indeed, the two kicked off the year by signing up to host a Ryder Cup-style golf event for celebrities in August 2005 from the Celtic Manor course in South Wales, which, if it happens, will be the most star studded reality show the world has ever seen. Stars rumoured to be participating include, for starters, Robbie Williams, David Beckham and Hugh Grant. Colin Montgomerie was said to be captain of the European team, and it is his involvement that has attracted so many big names: contestants are to include Catherine Zeta-Jones, Sir Steve Redgrave, Boris Becker, Frankie Dettori and Jodie Kidd. The US team, to be captained by Mark O'Meara, is set to be starrier still:

Michael Dougles, Samuel L Jackson, Cindy Crawford, Kevin Costner and Bill Clinton were all rumoured to be taking part. The project, if it comes off, will be made by Gallowgate Productions and is estimated to be worth £10 million to the company. Everyone involved was, understandably, wildly excited about it: 'Ant and Dec love golf and can't wait,' said a source on the show. 'This could open the floodgates for similar sports shows.'

But even the boys are feeling the march of the years. Both will turn thirty in 2005 and neither seems to be looking forward to it: 'I'm quite scared,' said Dec. Ant looked a little nervous, too, although for a slightly different reason. 'Just because you're turning thirty, it doesn't mean you have to think, "Right! Must get married and have kids right now!"'

So what of the future? The two have certainly proven themselves adaptable to date – from schoolboy actors on a teen drama to pop stars, to children's television presenters, to adult actors, to variety entertainers, to reality television presenters, to producers and movers and shakers behind the scene – and all this before they were thirty. The two are financially secure and need not work ever again, but given their continuing and massive popularity, that seems an unlikely scenario. And above all else, of course, their friendship continues to flourish. 'It's nice to hide behind this persona of the TV presenter, which is an exaggerated version of your real personality,' said Dec. 'Ant still makes me laugh every day. At work you can develop a siege mentality and sometimes think it's us against the world, so we have to trust each other. It's fraud when double acts pretend to be friends on telly but really don't get on.'

Perhaps the person who has most successfully defined their appeal is someone who was close to one of the greatest double acts of them all: Gary Morecombe, son of the great Eric. Ant and Dec have often been compared to Morecombe and Wise, and although they are not comedians in the same vein, their undoubted appeal and popularity does bring the heyday of that late and very much lamented duo to mind. And, according to Gary, they have some very similar qualities to his father and Ernie.

Gary first met Ant and Dec because he was writing a book about his father and wanted to meet the young men who were inviting comparisons with the greatest comedians of 20 years ago. 'I decided I had to meet them if possible and to ask them what they thought about being the new Morecombe and Wise,' he recalled. 'They were remarkably easy to get hold of and invited me to chat in their dressing room. They felt the comparison was undeserved and were a bit embarrassed about it. They were, genuinely, two of the nicest people I've met in the show business world and I've met quite a few.

'Strangely enough, it was when they protested that they could never fill those shoes that I was most convinced that one day they might. Ant said, "Oh no, we're still learning our trade, we're just kids lucky enough to be doing something we love." I thought, Well, yes, it took Dad and Ernie 20 years to reach the peak of what they were capable of. If you went back to those first half-hour shows they did for Lord Grade at ATV, you'd find that they're quite good telly but not the comic genius that the two of them became.

'What really struck me about Ant and Dec was the way they finished each other's sentences – something I had only ever come across before between Dad and Ernie. There was that same sense of being two halves of a whole, with a genuine friendship they couldn't possibly fake. I'd put my money on them lasting that long and being that good – in their own way and with their own style. But they have that same indefinable something that you can't manufacture.'

Another way in which Ant and Dec are unusual in the shark-infested waters of Planet Celebrity, is that it is well nigh impossible to find anyone who has a bad word to say about them. They treat everyone, be it fellow celebrities, fans or programme makers, with exactly the same degree of affability and charm. They would appear to have no ego at all and, more than that, are prepared to go out of their way to make other people happy. One person who can testify to that is Lino Carbosiero, their hairdresser and team mate in Celebrity Soccer Sixes. He works as a stylist at Daniel Galvin in London, where his other clients include Martine McCutcheon, Amanda Holden, Minnie Driver, Lucy Benjamin and Dolph Lundgren.

'You know how people had their dreams come true on *Jim'll Fix It?*' asked Lino. That's what they did for me, because they asked me to play on their team and I'm sure they could have invited so many celebrities to play. I'm sure everybody would have liked to play for the Ant and Dec team. I still dream about my goal, that I caught on the volley. When they told me months before, if I wanted to play they would have me in their team, you know, I always thought, Oh, is it gonna happen?

'But they were true to their word, they said that I was on the team and they could have had anybody they wanted to. It just goes to show how loyal and nice they are. I have worked with a lot of celebrities in my life and I've got to say, Ant and Dec are class. They gave me, honest to God, a dream come true. I was able to score at my home ground, at Chelsea. They truly deserve their success and fame. You will never find anybody like it. I can't think of two nicer people. Genuine, honest, decent people.

'I'm friends with a lot of my clients and, whether they are famous or not, I socialise with them. The difference is, with Ant and Dec we travel playing football and it's a whole different bond. And also the fact that I class them as amazing friends, it's not that they are celebrities. I mean, I would do anything for them. They are just nice, hard-working guys. Good guys, really good guys.'

That is praise indeed, but the boys really do inspire such loyalty in those who know them. And it is this ability to get on with so many people, while working hard and keeping their feet on the ground, that assures them success in the future. Morecombe and Wise, of course, remained on screen until Eric's tragically early death in 1984, and it seems entirely likely that Ant and Dec will do likewise, but should they ever tire of performing, they have increasingly solid experience in production and developing shows to stand them in good stead, too.

Their personal lives are stable, although they may yet develop further. Dec has never found anyone to replace Clare and Ant has not yet got married to Lisa, although recent pictures of a shopping trip to the jewellers suggest it is on the cards. Both Ant and Dec have spoken of their desire – eventually – to marry and have children and so one day, it can be assumed, they will do just that. But in their professional lives, they can virtually name their terms when it comes to anything they do, for they are indisputably two of the biggest stars on television.

And the best may yet be to come. Both have long hankered to do a film and a sitcom; if they find the right material, they may well kick off a whole new chapter in their long and joint career. Incredibly, the duo have now been famous for the best part of two decades and yet to see them is to see two personable young men who have never let it all go to their heads. For Ant and Dec, everything is still to play for.